In her 25 years as an author, food editor, consultant, teacher and publisher, Anneka Manning has worked for an impressive list of leading food publications, including *Australian Gourmet Traveller*, *Australian Good Taste*, *The Australian Women's Weekly* and *The Sydney Morning Herald*. She has also compiled, written and contributed to numerous bestselling books, including *Mastering the Art of Baking* (Murdoch Books).

Anneka writes regularly for a number of print and online publications, as well as having a significant television and radio profile. Through her Sydney-based baking school, BakeClub, Anneka teaches home cooks the tricks of the trade in practical, approachable and inspiring one-off classes and in her unique, six-month Make Me a Baker program. She is also a proud ambassador for Wiltshire, Australia's largest bakeware brand.

Anneka grew up on her parents' sheep and cattle property in southern New South Wales and now shares her life in Sydney with her husband, Paul, and their two children, Brooke and Benjamin. Her friendly and engaging approach to her writing and teaching comes from her vast experience, and she holds a firm belief that baking is something to be valued, and, ultimately, shared.

bakeclub.com.au
annekamanning.com.au
bakeclass.com.au

BAKECLASS

BAKECLASS

ANNEKA MANNING

MURDOCH BOOKS

SYDNEY · LONDON

'Baking is love
made edible.'

Contents

Introduction

My love affair with baking started early.

I grew up on a sheep and cattle property near the small town of Delegate in southern New South Wales, Australia, where my two great passions, horse riding and cooking, were allowed to flourish. Endless hours spent in the saddle, mustering sheep for shearing, cattle for marking, or simply moving a mob from one end of the property to the other were an integral part of the day-to-day running of the farm. My mum, Jocelyn, is a beautiful gardener and sewer (so good that she even made my wedding dress!), but she has never particularly enjoyed being in the kitchen. So she was more than happy for me to cook anything I wanted to, as long as I cleaned up afterwards. And so I did. And, just like horse riding, cooking served a practical purpose, but was also an incredibly pleasurable pastime for me.

Over time my interest in cooking grew, and so did my repertoire as I pored over Mum's cookbooks and, at the ripe old age of seven, began my own collection. I can confidently say I was the only one in my primary school who ordered cookbooks through the Scholastic Book Club! One particular favourite was the fun and easy-to-follow *The Kitchen Wizard* by Deborah Jarvis (costing me all of $1.50, by the way), which introduced me to really cool cooking science, where bicarb soda made toffee foam for honeycomb, and soft clouds of whisked egg whites and sugar were transformed into crisp, sweet meringues.

Even at that time I found myself being drawn to recipes that involved baking. I loved cooking the Country Women's Association's (CWA's) cinnamon tea cake for Sunday afternoon tea (it was Dad's favourite), making scones for the shearers' smoko, and entering cakes in the annual Delegate Show – with great success, I might add. This was just the beginning of a life that was destined to be one long foodie journey: I went on to study Home Economics and since then have enjoyed a 25-year career in food magazines, newspaper supplements and books, with baking always at the forefront. I now run my own baking school, BakeClub, in Sydney, giving hands-on practical and inspiring classes for the home cook.

But I'm very aware that baking frightens some people. I know lots of home cooks who are really talented, yet they're terrified of making pastry. They can easily pick up a new recipe for a whole baked fish or a slow-roasted shoulder of lamb and make it with great success. But they'd never attempt a double-crusted apple pie or a homemade quiche, because they just don't have the confidence to tackle this sort of recipe. Baking is not instinctive to them – it feels to them like a complicated puzzle that they can't decode. And that's usually because they've never had anyone teach them: actually stand beside them and show them the fundamentals. What these home cooks need is someone who is good with puzzles to take them through the process and help them put the pieces together! This was a role once naturally fulfilled by mothers and grandmothers, family members and friends. Sadly, in recent times a lot of this know-how has been lost, and there are fewer people spending time in the kitchen passing on their knowledge and teaching loved ones to bake.

There are many good reasons to learn to bake, not least that exquisite pleasure of sneaking a taste of your own homemade cake or biscuits, still warm from the oven. The physical steps of combining simple, everyday ingredients, often with your bare hands, to produce nourishing food for those you love is incredibly satisfying. The control you have over what ingredients you use is empowering. And the emotional by-products of the whole experience are something else completely: from the endless planning and dreaming about what to bake, to the almost meditative practice of the techniques, and, finally, the sharing of the results. I call this powerful emotional aspect the 'essence' of baking. It's a very individual experience that's hard to describe, but it represents the way the act of baking and sharing can make people feel nurtured, comforted, loved and part of something special. It brings people together, inspires compliments and gratitude, and simply makes people feel good.

There's more to learning how to bake than just following a recipe. The value of having someone show you first-hand

how pastry should feel, what a cake batter should look like or how to use your hands when kneading a dough is inestimable. Then, as your knowledge bank grows, as you gather skills through baking experiences of all kinds, so your confidence and efficiency will grow. Soon, before you know it, you'll be tackling more difficult tasks, more complex recipes, and becoming ever more skilled, efficient and confident. And soon you'll start passing on this knowledge to others. I hope that I can, through these pages, be that person standing by your side, giving you advice and helping you through the process, step by step.

This book is not like other baking books. It follows a unique lesson sequence that will build your skill levels and confidence in a progressive and practical way so that, ultimately, you become the baker you want to be. I've

Before you even touch a spatula or learn a single technique, take the time to think about what's been stopping you from baking more often than you do. There are many valid reasons why some people don't bake. Do any of the following sound familiar?

- I don't have the time
- I don't have the right equipment
- I don't have the ingredients
- I don't know how to bake
- I don't have the confidence
- I don't know how to find a reliable recipe

Let's also think about how you feel about baking. Do any of the following ideas apply to the way you think?

- Baking is just all too difficult
- It's too messy
- It's too time-consuming
- It's too complicated
- It's not worth the effort; it's easier to just buy something ready made

But it doesn't have to be this way. Knowing how to bake, having the skill to approach it without hesitation and being able to share this knowledge with family and friends – to pass it on – is worth so much.

included the ten most commonly used mixing methods, in succession from the most simple to the trickiest, that provide the basis for all baking recipes.

I'll also help you find inspiration to suit your skill level; teach you how to read and follow a recipe; show you how to find good, reliable information about baking; help you set up a basic baker's pantry; explain what essential equipment you will need to get started (don't worry – you probably already have most of this in your kitchen); and show you all the clever tricks I've learnt over the years to make your baking experience all the more enjoyable and successful.

I encourage you to work your way progressively through the steps and follow the lessons in sequence. By doing this, you'll start with the easy stuff, and gradually work towards the more tricky techniques and recipes, learning valuable skills along the way and building a strong foundation for your future baking. A comprehensive glossary, a baking measurement abbreviation guide and a quick-reference weights and measures conversion guide are also included at the back of the book so that you are armed with all the information you will need.

This book is for any home cook who wishes to develop or improve their baking ability, no matter what their current skill level. Consider it as a helpful friend at your side in the kitchen – one you can rely on and ask questions of, who will support, guide and reward you. Use this book as a companion and reference every time you bake; and I hope it will become a book that you come back to time and time again.

Welcome baking into your life with open arms and, I promise, it will reward you in ways you never expected. Baking nurtures conversations, inspires creativity and encourages discovery. This is your invitation to bake.

Annika.

BEFORE
YOU
BAKE

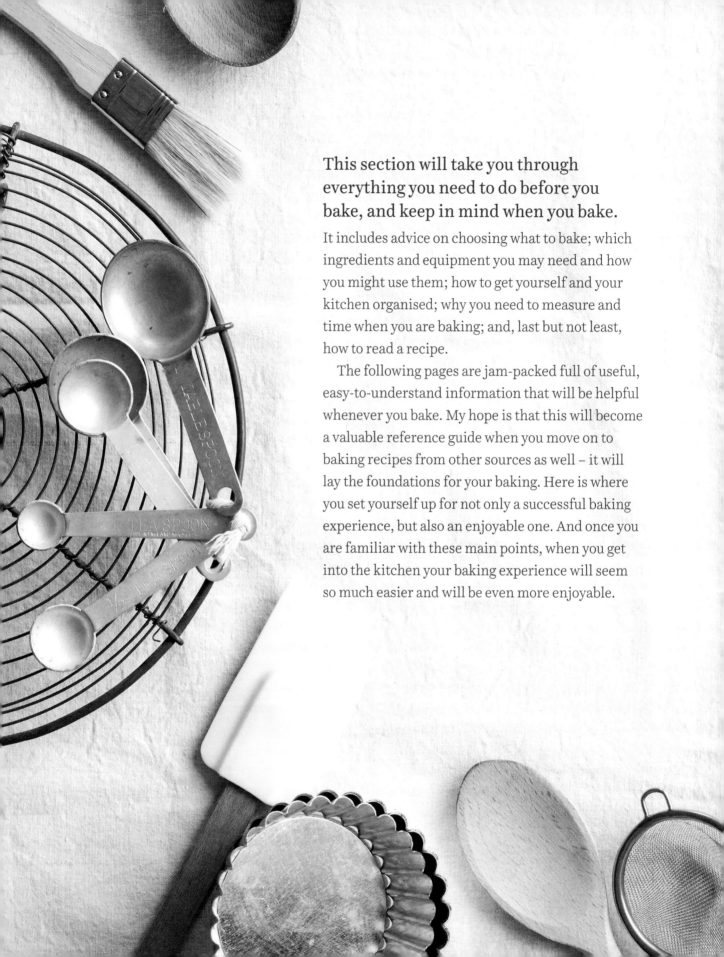

This section will take you through everything you need to do before you bake, and keep in mind when you bake.

It includes advice on choosing what to bake; which ingredients and equipment you may need and how you might use them; how to get yourself and your kitchen organised; why you need to measure and time when you are baking; and, last but not least, how to read a recipe.

The following pages are jam-packed full of useful, easy-to-understand information that will be helpful whenever you bake. My hope is that this will become a valuable reference guide when you move on to baking recipes from other sources as well – it will lay the foundations for your baking. Here is where you set yourself up for not only a successful baking experience, but also an enjoyable one. And once you are familiar with these main points, when you get into the kitchen your baking experience will seem so much easier and will be even more enjoyable.

What to Bake?

Choosing what you are going to bake is the very first decision you need to make. Simple? Yes, but there are a few things you need to keep in mind so you don't go down the rocky baking road that's paved with frustration and disappointment. Before you begin the search for inspiration, information and recipes, think about the following questions.

What kind of baker are you?

The very first thing to consider is your baking skills. Would you call yourself a beginner baker or someone who is confident and experienced? I can't stress enough how important it is to choose a recipe that is appropriate to your baking ability. There is no use attempting a croquembouche if you find making pastry a daunting process to start with.

Going with something you have baked before or that uses a method you have already tried is a good idea if your skills are limited. The idea is to choose something you feel confident with – a recipe that will work to make something you will be proud to share with others. As your experience, know-how and skills grow, so too will your repertoire and, in the not-too-distant future, you will be able to try more difficult and involved recipes.

Choosing a recipe that is well matched to your baking ability will just mean you won't become overwhelmed, frustrated and disheartened, which is especially important if you are just starting on your baking journey. Don't make it hard for yourself and, remember, everyone loves anything that's home-baked. Believe me, something simple done well will trump anything tricky but done not-so-well every time.

What ingredients and utensils do you have?

As well as matching your baking skills, a recipe should suit the utensils and ingredients you have on hand. Think about what you have in your cupboard, pantry, fridge and freezer, and what your local shop or supermarket stocks. Do you need to do some serious searching just to find one special ingredient or utensil that a particular recipe relies on, and are you willing to make the effort to find it?

Remember that good recipes really don't have to be complicated – there are plenty of simple baking recipes that use basic kitchen equipment and easily obtained ingredients to create something absolutely delicious. You will always have greater success if you choose a recipe that is well matched to your supplies and tools.

Where are you looking for a recipe?

Nowadays the number of recipes available to us is staggering. But, believe me, there are a lot of terrible recipes out there that can be confusing, are missing important elements, contain ingredients that aren't balanced proportionally or have an odd combination of flavours. If you don't have a good recipe to start with, the results aren't likely to be spectacular. Quite simply, a bad recipe equals a disappointing result, no matter what your baking ability.

So, how do you tell a good recipe from a bad one? As a simple guide, a good recipe will be easy to follow and never leave you feeling lost. When you read through it, everything should be easy to understand and it should all make sense. If it doesn't, just avoid it.

It's wise to use recipes from reputable sources, such as reliable books, magazines and newspapers. There are many websites and blogs with good recipes, too, but you need to be discerning. Question who wrote the recipe – do you trust their ability? Can you source all the ingredients and utensils? Will you need to convert any measurements?

Also, ask your friends and family where their favourite recipes come from. When you find one you like, make a note of the source so you can easily go back for more.

Why are you baking?

You may be a person who bakes for no good reason other than enjoyment of the process. I can totally relate to this – after a stress-filled day I often find myself gravitating towards the kitchen with no real purpose other than to do something that I find therapeutic, calming and enjoyable. However, this is not the case for everyone. Most of us bake for a reason – for a cake stall, a picnic, a dinner, a gift, an afternoon tea, or simply to entertain the kids for a while during the school holidays.

Have a think about why you are baking and make sure you choose a suitable recipe. Don't choose a sponge to take on a picnic, a brandy-soaked fruitcake for your child's birthday or a batch of scones for a special-occasion dessert.

Also consider who you will be sharing your baking with. Do they have likes and dislikes? Do they have allergies or food intolerances to gluten, wheat or dairy? Do they go mad for a particular shortbread you make? What do you think they would like to eat? Your decision doesn't have to be ruled by these things but if you keep them in mind, the time, effort and love you put into your baking will not go to waste.

When are you going to eat the baked goodie?

Home-baked goodies such as muffins, sponges and scones are at their best almost straight from the oven, so make them the same day you are going to eat them. Most biscuits and many cakes will keep really well in jars or airtight containers for a number of days, or even weeks. Some, such as a dense fruitcake, even improve in flavour and texture after storing for weeks or months. Most recipes will indicate the way to store the baked goodie and for how long (all of them in this book certainly do). Take note of this: there's no point being organised and baking a couple of days ahead if the cake is going to go stale quickly.

How much time do you want or have for baking?

This is a biggie. There have been times I've started a recipe without reading it through fully, only to run out of time before I needed to go out, go to bed or serve it – completely frustrating! So make sure you work out how much time you have (including preparation and cooking time) and keep this in mind when selecting your recipe.

Every one of the recipes in this book has both preparation and baking times included so take note of them and use this information to help plan your baking. If a recipe doesn't have these times, make sure you read it thoroughly before you start and estimate how long it will take you, allowing plenty of time for each task and adding any standing, resting, cooling, chilling and freezing steps.

What do you like to bake?

This is a crucial question to ask when choosing a recipe. Be a little selfish and make sure you choose something you will enjoy making (and eating).

Don't think you have to make pavlova if you simply don't like making meringue mixtures. If you enjoy using a rolling pin, choose cut-out biscuits or a tart. Like anything in life, if you enjoy something you are usually good at it.

Baking Supplies

||||||||||||||||||||||||||||||||||||||||||||||||||||||||||||||||||||||||||||||||||||||||||||||||||||||||||||||||||||||||||||||||||

Understanding the basic ingredients most commonly used in baking is essential to becoming a good baker. Here is what you need to stock your fridge and pantry, and how to use and store these ingredients that form the basis of about 90 per cent of all recipes.

Butter

When it comes to baking, butter is a key ingredient. It adds richness and flavour, and is used to add tenderness (such as the 'tender' crumb of a butter cake) and shortness (as in a shortcrust pastry), as well as colour.

Butter is used at different temperatures and states – well chilled, softened at room temperature or melted – depending on what you need it to do in your baking. For example, butter is best used chilled when making pastry, softened at room temperature when making cakes that use the creaming method (page 116) and melted when making slices that use the measure and mix method (page 40). Later you will see when you start exploring these methods how important it is to have your butter at the consistency stated in the recipe.

TYPES OF BUTTER

You can buy salted, reduced-salt or low-salt, unsalted or cultured (salted and unsalted) butter. Personally, I generally like to use unsalted butter, which is slightly 'sweeter' than salted butter and gives me greater control over the amount of added salt in a recipe. I opt for cultured unsalted butter (also sometimes known as Danish-style butter) for delicate pastries and cakes that I want to benefit from the slightly acidic flavour it imparts.

STORING BUTTER

You need to store butter correctly, as warm temperatures, light and water will all cause butter to deteriorate quickly and become rancid. Have you ever noticed when cutting through a block of butter that it has developed a darker yellow layer around the outside? This, and a slightly sour smell, are signs that the butter has started to go rancid.

To prevent this, always buy butter that has a foil-like wrapping (light can easily penetrate thin, paper-like wrapping and the oxidation process that causes the butter to go rancid may well have started before you even get it home). Keep the butter in its original wrapping in the main part of the fridge; the butter compartment is not cold enough for storing blocks of butter for any length of time. Any leftover butter should be re-wrapped and placed in an airtight container or sealed plastic bag and used soon after to prevent it absorbing other flavours from the fridge – you certainly don't want your chocolate brownies tasting of fish.

Butter will keep for up to eight weeks in the fridge if stored correctly but I would recommend buying it as you need it. Also remember to check the use-by date for optimum freshness. Unopened butter can be frozen in a sealed freezer bag for up to six months. Thaw it in the fridge before using.

HOW TO SOFTEN BUTTER

Recipes that use the measure and beat method (page 66) or the creaming method (page 116), such as my One-bowl Chocolate Cupcakes (page 79) or Melting Moments (page 125), will ask for butter to be at room temperature or softened. This is so the butter is soft enough to be easily and evenly combined with other ingredients. To do this, take the butter out of the fridge at least one hour before you start to bake; I often leave mine out overnight, depending on the temperature. Cutting the butter into small cubes or coarsely grating it will also help it soften more quickly and evenly. Don't ever be tempted to soften butter in the microwave, as you are likely to end up with partially melted butter that isn't suitable for these recipes.

Eggs

From providing structure, texture and richness through to binding, giving flavour and providing a golden glaze for breads and pastries, eggs are important in most baked recipes.

When it comes to freshness, eggs are best used as fresh as possible in baking. Eggs, by nature, are acidic when fresh, and this acidity causes the proteins in the white to be tightly knit. As eggs become older they become more alkaline and the proteins start to pull away from each other, causing the whites to become thinner. Now, when you whisk egg whites you are actually forcing these proteins apart and then recombining them in a new structure around small bubbles of air, hence forming a foam. With fresh eggs, initially it is a little harder to break these tightly knit proteins apart and the whisking will take longer. You may have heard that less-fresh eggs have the ability to whisk to a foam more quickly, which is true, but the foam from fresh eggs will be more stable than from older eggs.

All recipes in this book use 59–60 g (large)/2–2¼ oz eggs. In other recipes always use this weight if the egg size isn't stated.

CHECKING FOR FRESHNESS

Eggs bought from the supermarket will have a use-by date on the carton but if an egg has come from elsewhere, or you want to double check its freshness, you can place it in a small bowl of water and if it lies on its side it is quite fresh; if it stands on its end with the rounded side up it will be two to three weeks old. Be cautious if an egg floats completely as it may be a couple of months old and not suitable to use in your baking. The ultimate test is to break a suspect egg into a cup – believe me, you will know by the smell if it's too old to use.

Baker's tip

Adding eggs to a mixture
When using eggs in baking always break each one into a small bowl or ramekin before adding to a mixture so that if there's a problem with a single egg, the whole mixture isn't ruined. It's also easier to remove any broken eggshell this way.

STORING EGGS

Always store your eggs in the fridge in the carton they came in with the rounded end down. This will not only help prevent moisture loss but will also stop the eggs from absorbing other flavours from the fridge through their porous shells.

For baking, eggs are best used at room temperature, when they are easier to incorporate into mixtures. If whisking, you can incorporate greater quantities of air if the eggs aren't chilled. So take the eggs from the fridge at least one hour before you start baking. If you forget or don't have time just pop them in a bowl of warm (not hot) water for 5–10 minutes to bring them to room temperature quickly.

Baker's tip

Separating eggs
I like to use the shell to separate eggs, as it cuts through the egg white easily. When separating more than one egg, let the white fall into a clean cup or bowl each time so if any yolk breaks in you don't contaminate all of the whites.

1 First tap the egg at its broadest point on the edge of a bowl or bench top to crack it.
2 Use your thumbs to gently but firmly break the egg open, allowing the excess egg white to fall over the edge of the shell and into the bowl.
3 Use the two halves of the eggshell to tip the yolk from one to the other, separating the rest of the white. If some of the yolk breaks and falls into the white, simply remove it with the eggshell.

Milk and buttermilk

Often used in baked recipes to help bind and moisten the dry ingredients, milk also adds flavour and a little richness. Unless a recipe specifies, use full-cream (whole) milk and check the use-by date.

Buttermilk is a cultured milk made by adding a souring agent to regular milk. It is a fabulous addition to cakes, muffins and other quick breads when you want a slightly acidic flavour. It is often used in recipes that also include bicarbonate of soda (baking soda), as the acidic nature of the buttermilk reacts with the alkaline properties of the bicarbonate of soda to produce lots of air bubbles, which helps the mixture rise during baking and gives it a light texture.

If you don't have buttermilk you can make your own – add 3 teaspoons lemon juice to every 1 cup (250 ml/9 fl oz) milk.

Cream and sour cream

Cream is used in some baking recipes to add richness while sour cream adds both richness and a subtle sour flavour. Because of their fat content they also give a more tender crumb to cakes and quick breads.

TYPES OF CREAM

Buying cream for a recipe can be confusing because of the various types available, so I will explain the terminology.

The richness of a cream and its ability to be whisked is basically a reflection of its fat content – the higher the fat content, the easier it is to whisk or 'whip' and the thicker it will become once whisked.

● Double cream, also known as thick or heavy cream, has around 48 per cent or more butterfat and is the thickest of all creams.

● Pouring cream, also known as thin or single cream, and often labelled as pure cream, is generally sold in cardboard cartons and has a 35–40 per cent butterfat content.

● Normal sour cream has the same butterfat content as pouring cream.

● Thickened cream, also called whipping cream, is often sold in plastic containers and is simply pouring cream with a thickening agent, such as gelatine, vegetable gum or other modifying agents, added to thicken it slightly and make it more stable and easier to whisk – it is therefore a good choice when you need to whisk cream.

● Reduced-fat or 'lite' cream and sour cream contain 18 per cent butterfat and, because of their low fat content, won't thicken when whisked – so don't bother trying!

STORING CREAM AND SOUR CREAM

Once a carton is opened, transfer any remaining cream or sour cream to a sealed container so it doesn't absorb any other flavours from the fridge. And always check the use-by date.

Sugar

As well as being added in recipes for sweetness, sugar also adds moisture and tenderness to your baking.

TYPES OF SUGAR

● Caster (superfine) sugar is generally the most versatile and universally used as its small granules dissolve more readily than regular granulated sugar when combined with other ingredients, giving cakes and biscuits a more even texture.

● Brown sugar, or light brown sugar, which is basically fine white sugar with added molasses, will add a slight caramel flavour to your baking, as well as a little moisture. You can also buy dark brown sugar, which has a higher molasses content and a richer flavour. If you want to give a subtle caramel flavour, just substitute brown sugar in place of white sugar in weight (not by cup measure).

● Icing (confectioners') sugar is available as both pure icing sugar and icing sugar mixture, the only difference being that icing sugar mixture has a little cornflour (cornstarch) added to prevent it from forming lumps if it gets moist. Pure icing sugar is the best choice if you are making icing such as royal icing, which you will want to set hard.

● Honey and golden syrup (light treacle) are liquid forms of sugar and impart their own unique flavour. I like to measure them in grams instead of millilitres as I find I get a more accurate measurement that way.

STORING SUGAR

Keep all types of sugar, as well as honey and golden syrup, in sealed containers in a cool, dry place.

Baker's tip

Replacing sugar with honey or golden syrup
If you want to replace sugar (either brown or white) with honey or golden syrup (light treacle) in a recipe, I recommend you use the same amount in weight but also reduce the amount of liquid ingredient (such as milk or water) by 1 tablespoon for every 110 g (3¾ oz) sugar to account for both the intense sweetness and the higher moisture level of these sweeteners.

Flour and cornflour

The main purpose of using flour in baking is to provide structure. Flour with a high protein content, such as wheat flour, is often used because of its ability to develop gluten strands that form the framework for so many baked products, especially breads (more on this in the kneading method, page 236).

The most accurate way of measuring flour is by weight, but you can also measure it by volume in cups (see page 32 for tips on this).

TYPES OF FLOUR

Many different flours are used in baking, including white (wheat), wholemeal, semolina, rye and spelt.

For a start it is good to have both plain (all-purpose) and self-raising white flour in your pantry. If you only have plain flour, you can make it into self-raising flour by adding 2 teaspoons baking powder to every 150 g (5½ oz/1 cup) plain flour, and then sifting this mixture a few times until it is evenly combined.

Cornflour (cornstarch) is simply another type of flour and, like arrowroot and rice flour, it is used in recipes, often alongside wheat flour, to add lightness, such as in a sponge cake.

All flours should be kept in sealed airtight containers in a cool, dry place away from light for up to about six months. Wholemeal flours and those made from the whole grain can go rancid more quickly and are best stored in an airtight container in the fridge or freezer.

> ## Baker's tip
>
> **Distinguishing plain from self-raising flour**
> If you ever get your plain (all-purpose) and self-raising flours mixed up (as sometimes happens to me) there is an easy way to tell the difference. Simply put a little of each on your tongue, one type at a time. The one that tingles and fizzes slightly is the self-raising flour, thanks to the baking powder it contains.

Cocoa powder

Cocoa powder is a bitter, fine-textured powder that is made by grinding cocoa solids, which are what is left when most of the fat component (cocoa butter) is removed from cocoa liquor (a product of cocoa beans). It is also referred to as unsweetened cocoa powder. It adds an intense, rich flavour to baked products and is a must in your pantry if you love anything chocolatey. Dutch cocoa is considered the best-quality cocoa. It is treated with an alkali that gives it a more intense flavour. Always sift cocoa powder to remove any lumps before using.

STORING COCOA POWDER

Store it as you would flour, in a sealed airtight container in a cool, dark place.

Baking powder and bicarbonate of soda

Both baking powder and bicarbonate of soda (sometimes called sodium bicarbonate and called baking soda in the US) are known as chemical leavening or raising agents (yeast is also a raising agent but it is a natural one) and are the most common type used in baking to aerate mixtures.

Bicarbonate of soda is activated when it comes into contact with an acidic ingredient, such as buttermilk, sour cream, yoghurt, golden syrup (light treacle) or molasses. The reaction is immediate and obvious – air bubbles will start to

form and the mixture will become foamy (something that always amazed me as a child). It is important to get these mixtures into the oven quickly to make the most of this leavening ability.

Most baking powders are a mixture of bicarbonate of soda, a little moisture absorber such as rice flour or cornflour (cornstarch) to prevent it being activated, and a combination of acids that are activated at different stages – one, such as cream of tartar, at room temperature when liquid is added and another, such as sodium phosphate, when the mixture is exposed to heat in the oven. This composition is often referred to as 'double-acting' as it triggers the leavening process at two stages.

Baking powder is the simple difference between self-raising flour and plain (all-purpose) flour (to make your own self-raising flour, see page 19) and is used when making cakes and other baked products that require a light texture. It also comes in handy when you want to add extra lightness to flourless cakes, like those based on ground nuts, where it can be added on its own.

Always use a dry spoon when measuring either bicarbonate of soda or baking powder to avoid activating them prematurely.

Oil

Oils are often used in quick-mix and one-bowl cakes that use the measure and mix method (page 40), where the recipe doesn't rely on air being incorporated into the mixture through beating or whisking. The texture of these cakes is often heavier but they are also moister.

Oil-based recipes quite often have longer keeping times than those based on butter. My favourite oils to use when baking are the lighter-flavoured ones such as light olive oil, sunflower oil, peanut oil and canola oil.

Keep oils sealed in their bottles in a cool, dark place.

Vanilla extract and essence

Both vanilla extract and essence are liquids derived from vanilla beans that can be added easily to flavour mixtures. They are made by soaking vanilla beans in alcohol, extracting both the flavour and fragrance, and then distilling some of the alcohol to leave the more intense vanilla flavour. To this a little sugar (such as cane sugar, corn syrup or glucose) and water is often added to give you the final product that

can be called vanilla extract or essence, depending on the preference of the manufacturer.

Quality and intensity of flavour does vary between brands, so find the one you like and stick with it. The word 'natural' is the key here when buying. Be wary of 'imitation' essences or extracts, which are simply a chemical combination that also contains artificial vanillin – that is, not real vanilla.

Take a quick look at the ingredient list on the label and it will soon tell you if it is the real thing – vanilla beans, alcohol, sugar and water are all normal ingredients in a natural vanilla extract or essence. The imitation ones don't have the quality or intensity of flavour the natural ones do.

Keep liquid vanilla sealed in its bottle in a cool, dark place and check the use-by date.

Vanilla beans

These are a joy to use in your baking but remember that good vanilla beans are expensive and best used where the intense flavour from the little black seeds can be appreciated (such as in meringue mixtures and whipped cream to sandwich a sponge or to fill a pavlova).

The freshness of a vanilla bean is evident by how flexible it is – it should bend like a piece of licorice, so one that snaps won't be much use to you – and its fragrance should be immediate and intense.

Keep vanilla beans in an airtight container in a cool, dry, dark place to retain their freshness for up to 18 months.

Baker's tip

DIY vanilla sugar
Don't throw out your vanilla bean pod once you have scraped out all the seeds because there is still a lot of flavour contained within the pod. Instead, put it into a jar of sugar where over time it will give a subtle vanilla flavour that will likewise subtly flavour your baking.

Salt

Although not essential in all baking recipes as far as texture is concerned, a little salt will greatly enhance the flavour of a baked product, whether sweet or savoury.

As I mentioned previously, I generally like to use unsalted butter in my baking so I can control the amount of salt in a recipe. As a guide, I usually add about half a teaspoon of granulated salt to a recipe using 250 g (9 oz) unsalted butter.

Some recipes will ask you to add a pinch or even a teaspoon of salt (or sometimes more), for example if you are making pizza dough.

Yeast

Unlike baking powder and bicarbonate of soda (baking soda), yeast is a natural raising agent. While baking powder and bicarbonate of soda rely on a chemical reaction to create carbon dioxide to make baked goods rise, yeast – because it is a living organism – produces carbon dioxide by 'feeding' on the other ingredients in the mixture.

TYPES OF YEAST

Dried yeast, which comes as dehydrated granules in sachets, can be bought from the supermarket in the baking section. Fresh yeast, which comes in compressed blocks and is available in some health food stores, delicatessens and good bakeries, needs to be 'activated' by dissolving it in lukewarm water and allowing it to stand until it becomes frothy. It is then mixed with the dry ingredients. Dried yeast is the no-fuss option that can be added directly to the other ingredients without being activated first.

STORING YEAST

Store dried yeast in its sealed sachets in a cool, dry place away from sunlight. If buying dried yeast in a container or jar, store it in the fridge once opened and check the use-by date.

Fresh yeast needs to be kept in an airtight container in the fridge and is best used soon after you have bought it.

Baker's tip

Swapping dried and fresh yeast
Dried and fresh yeast are interchangeable in recipes. Just remember you will need to use twice as much fresh yeast (by weight) as dried.

Baking Tools

Having a carefully selected collection of utensils and equipment will do a lot for your baking confidence and success. Here are the essential basics to get you started on your baking journey.

Gathering the essential utensils and equipment

Except for an oven, which you most likely already have, you will be able to pick up most of these items at a supermarket or kitchenware store. Remember, you will get what you pay for and quality does vary enormously so choose carefully and seek advice from a trusted baker if you are unsure. As your baking repertoire evolves you will probably want to expand your equipment collection.

Below I have outlined what to look for when buying baking equipment, what tasks each item is most suitable for and any special care instructions.

THE OVEN

Ovens, a key requirement for baking, can vary enormously in accuracy and usability. On top of this, home cooks quite often don't know how to get the most from their oven when baking – what setting to use, which rack to place the food on, that kind of thing. And that is why it is so important to get those instruction books out and get to know your oven.

Meanwhile, this information will help with essential bits.

Oven temperature and hot spots

Just like children, no oven is exactly the same (and they sometimes misbehave!), so it is important to get to know yours so you can trust your own judgement when using it.

The first step is to buy a good-quality oven thermometer from a kitchenware store. Place it in the oven and preheat to a particular temperature, say 180°C (350°F), using the oven dial and take note of the temperature on the thermometer against that indicated on your dial. This will generally show you whether the oven temperature dial is accurate or not. If it's not, you need to adjust the setting for recipes as required. For example, if your oven runs 10°C (50°F) hotter than indicated on the dial, you should preheat your oven to 10°C (50°F) lower every time you use it.

You can also use your thermometer to check for hot spots in your oven, which sometimes cause baked products to rise and brown unevenly – yes, this could well be why your cakes are always lopsided and your biscuits are never evenly coloured! Each time you preheat your oven (to the same temperature), move the thermometer to a different position and see if the temperature varies. This way you can see if your oven has hot spots, which you can get fixed, or you can turn your tins or trays around at least once during the baking time to help cook and brown your cakes or biscuits evenly.

Oven settings

Most ovens are multifunctional and have different settings for a number of cooking methods. The recipes in this book have been tested in a standard domestic oven using a conventional setting. This is the most basic of settings and means that both the top and bottom elements heat the oven with no fan. If using this setting, remember that most of the heat will be at the bottom and top of the oven. Therefore, when you are cooking a couple of trays of biscuits or multiple layers of a cake at the same time on different racks, you will need to swap them around about halfway so they cook evenly and in the same amount of time.

Two other settings you may like to use for your baking are fan-forced and fan-assisted. Both are suitable for all types of baking except recipes that require long, slow cooking, such as a rich fruitcake.

When you use the fan-forced setting, the fan in the back wall of the oven evenly distributes the heat from the element that surrounds it. This means that, if your oven does it the way it should, there is no need to swap or move trays of biscuits or cake layers around during the cooking process to ensure even cooking and browning.

The fan-assisted (sometimes called convection) setting works in a similar way to the fan-forced but it is the top and bottom elements in the oven, not the one at the back around the fan, that heat the oven. Again, it is the fan that distributes the heat around the oven. The benefit of this setting is that the food gets direct heat from above and below it (to crisp and brown), plus circulating air (to cook the food evenly). It is a good setting to use when baking at a reasonably high temperature (180°C/350°F and above) for a reasonably short period of time, such as is required when baking pies, pastries, biscuits and scones.

If you are using either the fan-forced or fan-assisted settings you will need to make minor adjustments to the temperature and/or cooking time (keeping in mind that the temperature isn't actually higher on fan-forced or fan-assisted settings, it's just that the heat is more intense and therefore bakes more quickly). As a rule of thumb, I usually start with dropping the temperature by 20°C/70°F (for example, if the recipe specifies to preheat the oven to 180°C/350°F you will need to set the temperature to 160°C/315°F fan-forced) to allow for the more intense heat of these settings. I then bake for the recommended time, checking the item 5 minutes before the end of cooking. Make sure you note these adjustments on your recipe for next time.

Remember, as I've said before, ovens do differ and it is worthwhile going through the instruction book or getting in contact with the manufacturer for more specific guidelines if you are unsure or are having trouble understanding which setting is best to use for specific recipes. Also, many manufacturers have fantastic support for their customers, including pre- and post-purchase advice and at-home services, so make sure you look into what is available and take advantage of it, especially if your oven is misbehaving.

MEASURING TOOLS

More than in any other type of cooking, the precise measurement of ingredients is absolutely essential in baking. So spend that little extra time making sure you have accurate measuring equipment to suit the various cooking tasks and your baking life will be, well, easy as pie!

Scales

I love my scales (I know, it's sad, really). I bought my first set of electronic scales about 20 years ago and although they were expensive at the time, they were invaluable. Nowadays you can pick up a good set of electronic scales for a reasonable price, and my advice would be to buy a set before anything else because they will make baking so much easier.

Electronic scales have a number of features that will save you time in the kitchen, including the ability to 'zero' the reading (the tare weight) so you can measure a number of ingredients, one after another, into the same bowl – brilliant for one-bowl mixes, not to mention saving on washing up!

Whenever I demonstrate this feature in my face-to-face BakeClasses, my students are usually so impressed by this revelation they go out straight from the lesson and buy a set. Most electronic scales can also switch between metric and imperial measures.

Measuring cups

These are used for measuring dry ingredients and 'soft' non-liquid ingredients. They are most commonly plastic or metal and are usually available in a set that includes 1 cup, ¾ cup, ½ cup, ⅓ cup and ¼ cup.

Measuring spoons

These are readily available from most supermarkets and kitchenware stores and are used to measure small amounts of both dry and liquid ingredients. They usually come in a set of four that includes 1 tablespoon, 1 teaspoon, ½ teaspoon and ¼ teaspoon.

Don't be tempted to use your everyday serving tablespoons and teaspoons – they don't hold the same amount and this could affect your baking results. Standard measuring spoons are very cheap (especially if you buy them from the supermarket) and will probably prove to be the most valuable piece of baking equipment you own.

A word of warning, though – many kitchen utensils are imported from overseas countries that don't share our standard units of measurement. For example, in Australia the standard measuring tablespoon holds 4 teaspoons or 20 ml, while in the UK and the US, 1 tablespoon holds 3 teaspoons or 15 ml. This won't make a big difference when you are measuring ingredients such as flour or sugar, but if you are measuring a concentrated ingredient such as baking powder or yeast, it can cause real imbalances in your baking.

Baker's tip

Standard spoon measurements
All the recipes in this book use the Australian standard tablespoon of 4 teaspoons or 20 ml.

Take a look at your measuring tablespoon now – does it hold 15 ml or 20 ml? You can keep this in the back of your mind, along with where a recipe was first published, whenever you are measuring ingredients and make adjustments where needed; or you can simply go out and buy the alternative tablespoon measure and make sure you match the tablespoon size with the recipe origin.

Measuring jug

A clear plastic or glass jug is the best to use, and its measurement markings should be easy to read. I prefer a measuring jug that is not too large – with anything over 2 cups (500 ml/17 fl oz) it will be hard to measure smaller quantities accurately. And make sure you get one that is marked with metric and imperial measures.

You spend a lot of your baking time mixing, so choose mixing apparatus and tools wisely.

Electric mixer

An electric mixer is an indispensable appliance for the home baker as it allows you to beat, whisk and mix with great speed and efficiency. You can opt for hand-held beaters or stand mixers – or get both.

● Hand-held electric mixers with detachable beaters also sometimes come with a whisk attachment and work at a number of different speeds. They are small, convenient to use and inexpensive. They are suitable for mixing, beating and whisking all mixtures except bread dough, which they don't have the power to handle. Hand-held electric mixers are perfect to use when whisking a mixture such as eggs and sugar over a saucepan of simmering water, and are a great choice if you are a beginner and don't want to spend too much money on equipment to start with.

• Stand mixers are mounted on a stand and don't need to be held while in use. They are larger and more efficient than a hand-held mixer, and can deal with larger quantities and thicker, firmer mixtures thanks to their powerful motor.

They are more expensive than hand-held mixers but will generally last a lot longer (often a lifetime if you buy a good-quality one and look after it). They usually come with a range of attachments including a paddle (used for beating and creaming mixtures), a whisk and a dough hook to knead bread dough, and can be used on a range of speeds. If you do a lot of baking and you don't already own one, this would be the appliance to put at the top of your shopping list. I would also recommend that you buy the best-quality mixer you can afford.

Food processor

A food processor is not an essential appliance when baking but it will make the mixing step easier and more efficient (as you will experience when you get to the mixing in a food processor method, page 96). From making pastry and mixing cake batters to chopping nuts and puréeing fruit, a food processor basically allows you to take shortcuts.

When buying one, make sure it has a reasonable-sized bowl and is easy to clean. Mini food processors are also a good investment, especially if you are chopping nuts often.

Mixing bowls

Stainless steel, glass and ceramic bowls are the best options. I never use plastic bowls when baking as they can trap fat and grease that will stop egg whites from foaming when they are whisked and can be easily tainted by smells.

Make sure you have enough bowls of varying sizes so you aren't washing up constantly. In my home kitchen I have three each of four different-sized stainless steel bowls, plus a number of ceramic and glass ones.

Mixing spoons

Keep a couple of sturdy wooden spoons on hand for vigorous mixing and stirring. I also have several large metal spoons, which I use for their clean 'slicing' edge, and a couple of flexible spatulas, to gently combine mixtures and to fold in whisked egg whites so that the incorporated air isn't lost. Another of my favourite baking tools is a spoon spatula – basically a rubber or silicone spatula with a shallow bowl like a spoon – which makes light work of folding mixtures, transferring them to cake tins and then scraping the bowl.

Balloon whisk

This handy tool is perfect for whisking, especially egg whites and cream, mixing liquid ingredients and gently combining and removing lumps from mixtures. When buying a balloon whisk make sure the handle sits comfortably in your hand. Remember the more wires it has, the more efficient it will be at whisking and therefore the quicker your mixture will reach the desired consistency.

BAKEWARE

Along with your oven, these are the real tools of the baking trade so it's worth investing in a few good-quality basic items. In time, as your baking expertise increases, your collection will grow – and require a stocktake every now and then to control it!

Cake tins and baking trays

Every baker needs a basic selection of cake tins and baking trays – and a ruler to measure them. It is important to use the size and shape of tin or tray as specified in a recipe or the final cooking time, texture and look of your baked goodies may be affected.

Cake tins come in numerous shapes and sizes, which do vary slightly between brands. The materials they are made from and their finishes will also vary and, again, you get what you pay for so buy the best quality you can afford.

Heavy tins and those coated with a dark non-stick finish will absorb heat and create a more golden, slightly thicker crust than lighter bakeware that has an uncoated finish.

For the most uniform look to your baked products, buy round and square tins with straight sides that join at right angles at the base.

Choose flat trays with a slight lip to prevent food from sliding off, and make sure they are reasonably heavy so they don't buckle. Also, most importantly, make sure they fit in your oven!

Baker's tip

Care of your bakeware
Clean all cake tins and baking trays in hot, soapy water, then rinse well and place in a low oven (about 100°C/200°F) to dry completely before storing.

Baker's tip

What size?

It's a good idea to measure all your bakeware – in centimetres/inches across the middle of the base for cake and tart (flan) tins and pie dishes, and in cups or litres/fl oz for ovenproof dishes and ramekins. Then use a permanent marker to note the size on the base so you can see the correct measurement at a glance the next time you go to use them.

To get you started I would recommend the following basic cake tins (all measured across the base) and baking trays:

- 22 cm (8½ in) round tin (deep)
- 20 cm (8 in) square tin (deep)
- 16 cm x 26 cm (6¼ in x 10½ in) slice tin (shallow)
- 22 cm (8½ in) spring-form tin
- 9 cm x 19 cm (3½ in x 7½ in) loaf (bar) tin
- 12-hole 80 ml (2½ fl oz/⅓ cup) muffin tin (standard)
- 2 x large oven trays

Tart tins and pie dishes

I prefer to use metal tart (flan) tins and pie dishes rather than ceramic or glass if I'm lining them with pastry, because the metal will conduct the heat more efficiently and minimise the chance of soggy pastry. Look for tart tins with removable bases – where the base is loose and can be removed easily. I have found that non-stick tins with a dark coating aren't great for baking tart shells as the pastry has nothing to 'grab' hold of when baking and will tend to slip down the sides of the tin, causing it to shrink dramatically. It is best to just stick to the traditional uncoated metal tins.

Tart tins and pie dishes come in a range of sizes, depths and finishes to suit different kinds of recipes, so it's important to check the recipe and use the right tin or dish for the job. Metal pie dishes and tart tins should be cleaned and dried the same way as cake tins and oven trays (see Baker's tip at left).

Ovenproof dishes and individual ramekins

These are mainly used for puddings and baked desserts such as fruit crumbles, soufflés and self-saucing puddings, and can be made of ovenproof glass or ceramic. Their size is usually measured by volume in recipes.

Cake tester

Basically this is just a thin skewer of metal that can be bought at the supermarket or a kitchenware store. If you have a thin bamboo skewer, it will work just as well. You stick it into the centre of a cake (or muffin or cupcake or slice) to check if it is cooked – the skewer will come out clean if it is. If wet batter is sticking to it then you need to cook it for longer.

Sometimes, however, particularly for brownies or flourless chocolate cakes, the recipe will specify that 'crumbs cling to a skewer when inserted'. This is what you will be looking for when testing and this will ensure that the brownie or cake ends up with a 'fudgy' texture.

Pastry brush

Use it for brushing egg wash, milk, glazes and sugar syrups over dough, tarts and cakes. It is also handy for greasing cake tins and baking trays with melted butter and oil.

Don't use the natural or nylon-bristled brushes in boiling liquids or hot fat (use a silicone brush instead), and avoid really cheap pastry brushes that can lose their bristles easily.

To care for your pastry brush, wash it by hand in hot soapy water, rinse it well and then let it air-dry thoroughly before storing, so it won't hold any grease, odours or moisture.

Ruler

You'll need a ruler handy to make sure you have the right-sized equipment. Cake tins, biscuit cutters and piping nozzles are just some of the things you will need to check the size of. Remember, what you may think is a 20 cm (8 in) round cake tin may in fact be a 24 cm (9½ in) one – a little detail that could mean the difference between success and failure of your cake.

It is also handy to have a ruler when you are rolling out biscuit dough or pastry so you can tell when you have reached the right thickness. A clear plastic one is the best to have.

Rolling pin

If you are going to make pastry or biscuits that involve rolling and cutting out, a good rolling pin is essential. I like to use a rolling pin made of wood that is completely straight and doesn't have handles cut into the ends, is about 45 cm (18 in) long, and is reasonably wide (a diameter of roughly 5 cm/2 in). The wood grain has the natural ability to hold a fine layer of flour so the rolling pin doesn't stick to the pastry or dough.

Don't ever immerse a wooden rolling pin in water to clean it; simply wipe it with a damp cloth and make sure you air-dry it completely before putting it away.

Sieve

Although they are available in both metal and plastic, I would recommend a metal sieve as it will last longer and is easier to clean. You will need it for sifting ingredients such as icing (confectioners') sugar, cocoa powder and cornflour (cornstarch) to remove lumps. A small one is also good to have for dusting cakes, meringues and biscuits with icing sugar or cocoa. Make sure it is thoroughly clean and dry before storing.

Timer

Another extremely handy tool for your kitchen, even if your oven has an inbuilt one already. Mainly because I get distracted easily by other things, and even with my experience, I always like to use a timer. It's a small price to pay to prevent overcooking something, which can be incredibly disappointing. I would recommend a digital timer for accuracy.

Grater and zester

Whatever the grating job, a box grater with a number of perforation sizes will usually cover them all. However I also love my rasp-like Microplane for finely grating citrus zest, nutmeg and parmesan cheese.

Knives

Another kitchen tool worth investing in, as good-quality ones will give better results and last longer. I would suggest having a minimum of three knives: a cook's knife for slicing, chopping and general preparation; a bread or serrated knife for cutting bread and dense cakes; and a small paring knife for preparing fruit, removing cores and thinly slicing.

Always wash your knives by hand in hot soapy water and dry thoroughly before storing.

Baking paper

Always have a roll of baking paper in your cupboard to line cake tins and baking trays, as foil or greaseproof paper just don't do the same job.

Reusable non-stick baking mats, which you can buy from kitchenware stores, are also a good investment if you bake a lot of biscuits. These mats can also be cut to size to line specific cake tins. They should be washed in hot soapy water, rinsed well and air-dried thoroughly before storing.

Airtight containers

Most baked products need to be kept in an airtight container of some sort to retain their freshness. Have a selection of well-sealing airtight containers, cake tins and biscuit jars in which to keep your baked goodies.

Baking weights

Ceramic or metal baking or pastry weights are handy but not necessary for blind baking pastry because you can use dried beans or uncooked rice instead. Remember that the metal and ceramic varieties will be very hot when you remove them from the pastry case after baking, so handle with care.

Oven thermometer

As mentioned earlier, this allows you to keep an eye on the accuracy of your oven temperature, and to adjust it if needed. Oven thermometers also help you check for hot spots, so you can decide if something needs to be turned or moved during baking to help it cook and brown evenly.

Palette knife

Handy to use for icing cakes, cupcakes and biscuits but a thin-bladed butter knife (without a serrated edge) can be used instead.

Biscuit cutters

A small selection of these is good for cut-out biscuits. Round cutters are also good for making scones (although you can use a knife to cut these out instead) and small, individual tarts (flans) and pies.

Scissors

Use these for cutting out baking paper when lining cake tins and cutting dried fruit into smaller pieces.

Getting Organised

These four steps are the golden rules of preparation for baking. Follow them each time before you bake and you will be on the most efficient path to baking success.

Step 1: Read through your recipe

If you haven't done so already, now is the time to spend a few minutes reading through your recipe. As you do, take note of the following things.

CHECK THE INGREDIENTS AND EQUIPMENT YOU'RE GOING TO NEED

There is nothing more frustrating than getting halfway through a recipe and realising you don't have a particular ingredient or not enough of it, especially when it's eggs or butter, which are essential and for which there is no substitute.

Get all your equipment and ingredients out onto the bench top so they are in easy reach when you start. Make a habit of doing this every time you cook – it will help you to be more efficient because you won't be stopping every couple of minutes to get another thing out of the cupboard.

ARE THERE ANY SPECIAL DIVERSIONS?

Is there any extra process or step involved that is going to add to the overall time it will take you to make and bake your recipe? This could include standing or chilling times (such as proving times when making bread or when a biscuit dough needs to be chilled before shaping and baking) and cooling times (such as if melted chocolate needs to be cooled to room temperature before it is mixed with the other ingredients, or if a cake or slice needs to be cooled before icing it).

DO THE BUTTER OR EGGS NEED TO BE AT ROOM TEMPERATURE?

If so, take them out of the fridge now so they have a chance to reach the desired temperature or consistency. I often take the butter and eggs out of the fridge the night before, depending on the weather. But cutting the butter into small cubes or coarsely grating it will help soften it more quickly and popping your eggs in a bowl of warm (not hot) water will help bring them to room temperature faster.

CHECK THE MIXING METHODS AND TECHNIQUES TO BE USED

In the Lessons & Recipes section (page 38) you will learn about the 10 basic mixing methods most commonly used in baking. In the future, you'll be able to make a mental note of what method will be involved. If you are unsure of any particular terms in the recipe, refer to the Glossary (page 266).

Step 2: Get the racks in the right position

Rearranging the racks in your oven and making sure they are at the right level before you preheat it is always a good idea.

Aim to have whatever you are baking directly in the middle of the oven, which will mean placing the rack in the centre for biscuits but possibly the next level down for cakes and other recipes that have some height.

If you are using multiple racks, say for when you are baking a couple of trays of biscuits at the same time, put one rack towards the top of the oven and place the other towards the bottom, allowing plenty of room both above and below them, as well as in between, for the heat to circulate easily.

Step 3: Preheat your oven

You must always preheat your oven, no matter what setting you are using. Make it the first thing you do, even before getting out your ingredients, as the average oven will take at least 10–20 minutes to preheat properly. If you don't preheat your oven, the temperature won't be hot enough and the end result may be a heavy, undercooked mess – a great reason to turn on your oven as early as possible.

Once the temperature is reached, the oven will let you know, usually by turning off its thermostat light. It's ideal to let the oven settle into this temperature for 10 minutes or so before you place your batter or dough in to cook. This is because the oven (depending on the brand) often runs through cycles of slightly higher and slightly lower temperatures, with the indicated temperature as the average.

Step 4: Prepare your tins or trays

Different recipes will require you to grease and line your tins in different ways, depending on the ingredients and cooking time. Always follow the instructions in the recipe to prevent any unfortunate sticking incidents – it is so disappointing to have half your cake left in the tin when you go to turn it out. These are the basic methods.

TO GREASE

Melt a little butter and use a pastry brush to grease the cake tin or tray evenly, and not too thickly. You can also use oil, if the recipe uses it, or alternatively spray it with an oil spray for an ultra convenient greasing.

TO DUST WITH FLOUR

This method is used generally with tins you can't line, such as fluted or ring tins. The flour adds a thin barrier between the mixture and the tin to help stop it sticking.

Grease the tin as described and then sprinkle with a little plain (all-purpose) flour. Tap the tin on the side, turning it as you go, so the flour coats it evenly. Tap out any excess flour. This will give a cake a nice crust if done with restraint. Too much butter or flour when using this method will leave a patchy coating on the crust of your cake.

TO LINE YOUR TINS

Baking paper is best for lining cake tins and baking trays. Reusable non-stick baking mats are also a good option for lining trays. The lining technique will vary slightly according to the shape of the tin or tray.

Square tins

Grease the cake tin as described. Cut two strips of baking paper as wide as the tin and about twice as long. Place one strip over the base, run it up two opposite sides to line and press it into place. Brush a little more melted butter or oil over the paper on the base and then smooth the remaining strip over the base again and up the unlined sides.

Round tins

Grease the cake tin as described. If the recipe requires only the base and not the side to be lined, place the tin on a single piece of baking paper and draw around it. Cut out and place the circle over the base of the tin.

If the recipe requires the side to be lined as well, grease the cake tin as above. Place the tin on a double piece of baking paper and draw around it. Cut out and place one of the paper circles over the base of the tin.

Cut a strip of baking paper a few centimetres (about an inch) longer than the circumference of the tin and a few centimetres (about an inch) wider than the depth of it. Fold over about 2 cm (¾ in) of the paper to form a cuff along one of the long sides. Use scissors to cut slits on the diagonal in the cuff down to the folded line, about every 1 cm (½ in) or so.

Place the paper strip around the inside of the tin with the folded line sitting where the side meets the base and the cut collar sitting on the base of the tin, and smooth it into place. Place the remaining paper circle over the base of the tin to cover the pleats and to hold the strip of paper in place.

Slice and loaf (bar) tins

Generally, these only need one strip of paper to line them. Grease the cake tin as described. Cut a strip of baking paper as long as the tin and about three times as wide. Place the paper strip over the base, run it up two opposite long sides and smooth into place.

Spring-form tins

I don't fuss around when lining spring-form cake tins. I simply tear off a square of baking paper about 8 cm (3¼ in) larger than the tin. Release the outside of the tin and turn the base upside-down (this will create a base without a lip, which makes removing the cake or cheesecake from the tin much easier). Place the paper over the base of the tin and then clamp the side of the tin around the base, to hold the paper in place. The paper will stick out the sides but this won't matter and the extra paper hanging out will actually give you something to help lift the cake off the base once it is cooked.

Baking trays

Grease as for cake tins; it isn't actually necessary when lining a tray but will help keep the paper in place. Cut out a piece of baking paper the size of the tray and smooth it over.

Baker's tip

No need to grease pie tins
When cooking pies and tarts (flans), you don't need to grease the tins because the high butter content in the pastry helps prevent it from sticking.

Measure Up

Baking is a science and success often depends on accuracy. So it makes sense to always measure and always time. But don't worry, this doesn't need to be complicated or time-consuming.

The importance of measuring and timing

You might get away with a dash of this and a handful of that, and a few minutes here and there when you cook soups, stir-fries and roasts, but baking is all the more challenging and satisfying because of the simple but special care you need to take in measuring and timing.

MEASURING INGREDIENTS

Electronic scales (see page 24) are the most accurate and convenient way to measure dry ingredients, such as flour and sugar, and also what I call 'soft' ingredients, such as sour cream, jam and yoghurt.

If you don't have scales on hand, cup measurements can give you equally good results if you follow this simple sequence every time you measure.

1. Use a tablespoon to spoon an ingredient into a cup measure without packing it down but making sure there are no air pockets.
2. Use the straight edge of a knife to level the surface in line with the top of the measuring cup.
3. Don't tap the cup on the bench top or force the ingredient into the cup.

In this book all measures equal to and above ¼ cup have equivalent gram and ounce measures, so you can choose which way you would like to measure.

Liquid ingredients are best measured in a clear measuring jug (see page 25) so the level of the liquid is easy to read against the markings. Sit the jug on a flat surface and check the quantity at eye level.

One exception is thick liquids such as honey and golden syrup (light treacle), which I like to weigh because it is more convenient and tends to be more accurate. That is why these have a weight measurement in the recipes in this book.

For both dry and liquid ingredients, any measurements below ¼ cup are best measured in standard spoon measures (see page 24). For dry ingredients, always level with the back of a knife in the same way as you would if measuring in a cup, and bring the spoon to eye level when measuring liquids to make sure it is level.

Be mindful that recipes published in Australia and in New Zealand use 4 teaspoon (20 ml) tablespoons, while in the UK and US 3 teaspoon (15 ml) tablespoons are used. This is not a big issue with ingredients such as flour or sugar, but for baking powder or yeast exact and correct measurement is essential, so be mindful of what size your tablespoon measure is and adjust the recipe as required. (See more about this on page 24.)

MEASURING TINS

As I've mentioned, a ruler is very handy to have in the kitchen. I recommend you never guess at the size of a cake or tart (flan) tin and always measure it – across the base and through the centre is the best. All the tin sizes mentioned in this book have been measured in this way.

I cannot stress enough the necessity for always measuring tins. I have come across many spring-form tins that have the incorrect size written on their base, that were actually 2 cm (¾ in) smaller than the measurement given. So never think someone else has done the work for you and always measure the tin yourself. To save doing it every time, you can use a permanent marker to note the size of your tins on the base after measuring them yourself.

Baker's tip

Not all ingredients are equal
Remember that, generally, no two ingredients weigh the same. For example a cup of plain (all-purpose) or self-raising flour (150 g/5½ oz) doesn't weigh the same as a cup of unsweetened cocoa powder (105 g/3½ oz), nor the same as a cup of caster (superfine) sugar (220 g/7¾ oz). So don't ever guess the weight of an ingredient by comparing its volume with another.

ALWAYS USE A TIMER

Even though I have baked thousands of recipes over the
years, I still use a timer, and not just when I'm recipe testing.
You think you are going to keep your eye on the clock but
inevitably you get caught up with doing the next thing –
making a phone call, watering the garden or helping the
kids with their homework – and before you know it, the
time, effort and love you have just poured into that flourless
chocolate and hazelnut cake is now wasted. Rather than
end up with a dry, overcooked and slightly charred disc
you would hate to serve up to anyone, pop on the timer.

I would recommend having a portable digital timer that
is accurate and easy to set – unlike your inbuilt oven timer,
you will be able to take it with you even if you want to squeeze
in a little gardening while your cake is cooking.

And just a little word about times in recipes – these are
just estimations. They are what worked for the person who
wrote and tested the recipe. But, as I said earlier, every oven
is different and you may find that your oven takes a little less
time or even a little longer. Quite often recipes give you a
range, such as 40–45 minutes, for this very reason.

Recipes will often – mine always do – give you a little
visual hint about what to look for when your baked item is
ready to be taken from the oven. Phrases like 'until a skewer
inserted in the centre of the muffin comes out clean', 'until
the cake is lightly golden brown and has shrunk away from
the sides of the tin slightly' or 'until the scone is golden on
top and sounds hollow when tapped on the base with your
fingertips' are all cues to help you work out what the best
timing in your oven is.

When judging if something is cooked, use these cues along
with your logic and also your sense of smell – over time you
will get to know when something is ready just by the aroma
that fills your kitchen.

How to Read a Recipe

I don't entirely agree with the saying that goes, 'If you can read, you can read a recipe.' There are many elements that make up a recipe and, even with a well-written one, you will need to understand the ways it can be structured and the terms that may be used.

Understanding the structure and language

Just over 25 years ago I was taught how to write a recipe at college. Since then, through my writing and experience in cooking from many hundreds of recipes for both work and pleasure, I have refined how I write recipes in the hope that they are clear, informative and concise, yet friendly.

I always aim for a recipe to be simply written, no matter how complicated the technique – I strongly believe a good recipe should never leave you lost in your own kitchen.

A recipe is simply the description of a process, a guide to a procedure. A well-written one should give you all the information you need to make something successfully – it should leave nothing unclear or in doubt.

Using one of my favourite cookie recipes (pictured opposite, and featured on page 126) as an example, I'm going to show you what you should be looking out for when reading a recipe, and how to get the most out of it.

THE PRELIMS

Recipe title

The recipe title should tell you a little about what you can expect at the end of your baking. It is usually a combination of words that will include some, or all, of the following:

1. A name, such as cake, bread or, in this case, cookies.
2. An ingredient (usually the main ones), such as banana, sultana, cinnamon or, in this case, chocolate and walnuts.
3. A texture description, such as sponge, chewy, crisp or, in this case, chunk (which refers to the chocolate) and fudge.
4. An overall experience description, such as luscious, indulgent or heavenly.

A good recipe title will always be a clear representation of the end result and won't leave you disappointed at the end of your baking experience because it wasn't what you expected. However, it won't include everything about the recipe – this would just mean a ridiculously long (and boring) title.

'Makes' or 'Serves' information

This tells you how much the recipe will make or how many people it will serve. It's a good thing to check when you are choosing a recipe that it is going to make a suitable quantity. It is also a good guide when making biscuits as to how big they should be – make them too big and you won't get as many, too small and you'll end up with an extra batch to bake.

Preparation and baking or cooking times

In this book, the preparation time is the estimated time it will take you to prepare the mixture (including the gathering of ingredients and equipment, any measuring and chopping, and any pre-cooking on the stovetop you need to do) up to the point that it is ready to put into the oven.

The baking (or cooking) time is the total time your mixture will be in the oven. In other recipes, what is included in these times may vary. For example, some include the time that it takes to melt chocolate or toast nuts (anything that requires heat) in the cooking time, not the preparation time. Some recipes don't state preparation or cooking times at all. I like to include them to give you a better understanding of the time it will take to complete different stages of the recipe.

I also include what I call 'diversions' – standing, soaking, cooling, chilling or freezing times. These are additional periods of time that need to be factored in, but are actually 'down times' when you aren't required to do anything.

In the recipe opposite there is an additional 20 minutes cooling and 1 hour of chilling time given. I like to note these so you know how long it is going to take to complete a recipe, even if some of that time you don't need to be doing anything.

When it comes to the baking time, this is usually noted as the total time. However if, like in this recipe, you need to cook it in a number of batches, I find it more useful to give the time it takes to bake one batch (and state this). This is because the number of batches you can cook at once often depends on the size of your baking tray and oven.

THE INGREDIENTS LIST

Logical ordering

Ingredients in a well-written recipe will be listed in order of use, allowing you to keep track of what has been added.

Preparation instructions for an ingredient are often listed in the ingredients list if it is logical to do this before you actually start making the recipe (see below).

Preparation instructions

You will notice words like sifted, chopped, lightly whisked, at room temperature and melted attached to certain ingredients. Do these things before you get into following the actual 'method' of the recipe.

Take note if there is a particular way of preparing an ingredient. For example, if something is to be chopped, you need to know if it is to be finely chopped, coarsely chopped or just chopped (which means that it is chopped into medium-sized pieces).

In this recipe the chocolate needs to be coarsely chopped as you want chunks of chocolate in the cookies. It also helps when melting some of the chocolate if it is coarsely chopped and not left in large pieces.

Measurement options

Sometimes in a recipe you are given weight measurements in metric and imperial, along with cup measurements if there is an equivalent. This is giving you an option for the way you measure, so choose a method and stick with it for the whole recipe for consistency. Again, take note of any 'special' instructions linked with the quantity and the measuring of it. For example, in this recipe you need '110 g (3¾ oz/½ cup, firmly packed) brown sugar' so if you choose to measure in cups, you will need to 'firmly pack' the sugar, because if you 'lightly' pack it you will end up with only 100 g (3½ oz).

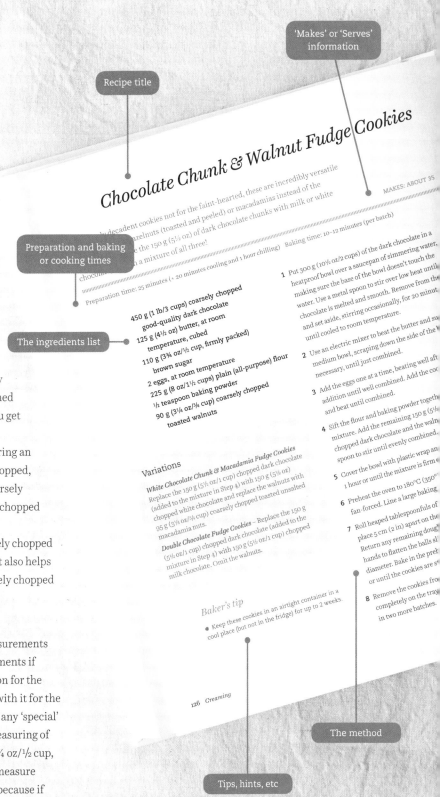

Recipe title

'Makes' or 'Serves' information

Preparation and baking or cooking times

The ingredients list

Tips, hints, etc

The method

Chocolate Chunk & Walnut Fudge Cookies

MAKES: ABOUT 35

... decadent cookies not for the faint-hearted, these are incredibly versatile ... hazelnuts (toasted and peeled) or macadamias instead of the ... the 150 g (5½ oz) of dark chocolate chunks with milk or white ... a mixture of all three!

Preparation time: 25 minutes (+ 20 minutes cooling and 1 hour chilling) Baking time: 10–12 minutes (per batch)

450 g (1 lb/3 cups) coarsely chopped good-quality dark chocolate
125 g (4½ oz) butter, at room temperature, cubed
110 g (3¾ oz/½ cup, firmly packed) brown sugar
2 eggs, at room temperature
225 g (8 oz/1½ cups) plain (all-purpose) flour
½ teaspoon baking powder
90 g (3¼ oz/¾ cup) coarsely chopped toasted walnuts

1 Put 300 g (10½ oz/2 cups) of the dark chocolate in a heatproof bowl over a saucepan of simmering water, making sure the base of the bowl doesn't touch the water. Use a metal spoon to stir over low heat until chocolate is melted and smooth. Remove from the ... and set aside, stirring occasionally, for 20 minut... until cooled to room temperature.

2 Use an electric mixer to beat the butter and su... medium bowl, scraping down the side of the ... necessary, until just combined.

3 Add the eggs one at a time, beating well aft... addition until well combined. Add the coc... and beat until combined.

4 Sift the flour and baking powder togeth... mixture. Add the remaining 150 g (5½... chopped dark chocolate and the waln... spoon to stir until evenly combined.

5 Cover the bowl with plastic wrap an... 1 hour or until the mixture is firm e...

6 Preheat the oven to 180°C (350°... fan-forced. Line a large baking...

7 Roll heaped tablespoonfuls of... place 5 cm (2 in) apart on the... Return any remaining doug... hands to flatten the balls sl... diameter. Bake in the preh... or until the cookies are s...

8 Remove the cookies fro... completely on the tray... in two more batches.

Variations

White Chocolate Chunk & Macadamia Fudge Cookies
Replace the 150 g (5½ oz/1 cup) chopped dark chocolate (added to the mixture in Step 4) with 150 g (5½ oz) chopped white chocolate and replace the walnuts with 95 g (3¼ oz/¾ cup) coarsely chopped toasted unsalted macadamia nuts.

Double Chocolate Fudge Cookies – Replace the 150 g (5½ oz/1 cup) chopped dark chocolate (added to the mixture in Step 4) with 150 g (5½ oz/1 cup) chopped milk chocolate. Omit the walnuts.

Baker's tip
● Keep these cookies in an airtight container in a cool place (but not in the fridge) for up to 2 weeks.

126 *Creaming*

Now 10 g (¼ oz) is not a big difference when it comes to sugar and it certainly won't greatly affect the outcome of this particular recipe, but keep in mind the greater the quantity of an ingredient needed the larger the discrepancy and the more likely it will be to affect the outcome.

You will need to keep in mind the relationship between the preparation instructions and the amount required in cups. For instance, in our cookie recipe '¾ cup coarsely chopped toasted walnuts' is needed. This means the toasted walnuts need to be chopped before measuring with a cup measure. If, however, the recipe said '¾ cup walnuts, coarsely chopped' then you would measure the walnuts before chopping. The overall difference in quantity may not be big in some cases, like this one, but it can be, so this needs to be kept in mind.

Ingredient preferences

Also note whether a particular variety of an ingredient is needed to give you the best results. For example, a recipe may call for unsalted butter, navel oranges, dried dates or desiccated coconut. In this recipe, good-quality chocolate is specified. This means that you will get the best outcome if you use good-quality chocolate – not inexpensive compound chocolate. Obviously the choice is yours and these specifics are here to guide you to the best results possible.

THE METHOD

This is where you find out how all your ingredients are combined and baked. A well-written recipe will divide the method into logical steps that signify different stages in the recipe. It is important to follow this sequence when making the recipe.

Follow the sequence

Preheating your oven and preparing any tins or trays is often the first thing a recipe will ask you to do. However, in this cookie recipe you need to first make the mixture. The reason for this is that the mixture needs to be chilled for 1 hour before you cook it. There is no need to preheat the oven for such a long time – it can just be turned on while the mixture is chilling.

The method will tell you how to combine the ingredients (the technique to use) and the equipment and utensils you will need. For example, in this recipe you need to 'Use an electric mixer to beat the butter and sugar in a medium bowl, scraping down the side of the bowl when necessary'. It will also tell you what to look out for once this step is finished – in this case, 'until just combined'.

Adding some now, some later

Also take note if you need to use only part of the total amount of an ingredient at different stages of the recipe. Part of the dark chocolate (300 g/10½ oz of it) in this recipe is melted and the remaining 150 g (5½ oz) is stirred through in chunks later on. It is extremely frustrating to get halfway through a recipe and realise you have already used the total amount of an ingredient when you need to add a portion of it later.

A suggested range

Often baking times will be given as a range in recipes to accommodate for variations between ovens. In this recipe it is 10–12 minutes for each batch. I recommend always setting your timer for the lowest time. Check to see if your cookies are ready at 10 minutes and put them back in the oven if a little more time is needed.

If the baking time is different because of your oven, make sure you note it on the recipe for next time.

What to look for

Along with the time, a good recipe will always give you an indication of what you need to look for once a process is completed. In this case the cookies 'are still slightly soft to the touch', in muffin recipes you are often asked to cook them until 'a skewer inserted in the centre comes out clean' and with scones 'until they are lightly golden and sound hollow when tapped on the base'.

Use these descriptions to help judge whether something is cooked or not.

Follow the cooling advice

There are a number of ways to cool things you have baked, all suited to different types of recipes. For example, a butter cake is best left in the tin for a few minutes to cool a little before being turned out onto a wire rack – this will give the cake time to 'settle' so it is less likely to fall apart when it is turned out, but the crust may go soggy if the cake is left in the tin for too long or even cooled in the tin.

Always follow what is recommended in the recipe for the best results.

Don't guess, look it up

And remember, always refer to the glossary on page 266 if you are unfamiliar with any words or terms used in the method.

TIPS AND HINTS

Most, but not all recipes, will finish with helpful hints and tips related to ingredients, shortcuts, storage and the like. Always check them out as they can be very useful bits of information that will allow you to make the most of the recipe.

More than a bunch of words

Good recipes are far more than well-written words – they are a thoughtful combination of ingredients and techniques. In a great recipe, the unique flavours and textures of individual ingredients are brought together in a way that results in balance and harmony, to create something utterly delicious that is pleasurable and memorable. Without this balance, even if the recipe is clear, concise and easy to follow, the results won't be good, no matter what you do. As you become a confident baker, your instinct for recognising a well-thought-out, well-written and well-balanced recipe will develop as well.

LESSONS & RECIPES

Lesson 1

||||||||||||||||||||||||||||||||||||||||||||||||||||||

The Measure
& Mix Method

It doesn't get any simpler than this! The measure and mix method is the perfect starting point if you are new to baking or just want to rebuild your baking skills from the ground up.

This method is based on adding the wet ingredients to the dry ingredients (or dry to wet, depending on the recipe) and then mixing the two together. Yep, it's that simple.

The wet ingredients might include eggs, milk, melted butter or oil, melted chocolate, natural vanilla extract or essence, honey and water – basically any ingredient you can pour. They are combined before being added to the combined dry ingredients. The dry ingredients might include flour, sugar, coconut, rolled (porridge) oats, nuts, ground spices and chunks of chocolate.

The best thing about recipes using this method is they only require very basic equipment – a wooden spoon, spatula or whisk and a mixing bowl is usually all that is needed.

Step by step

1 Combine all the dry ingredients, such as flour and sugar, in a mixing bowl with a wooden spoon, spatula or whisk (as directed in the recipe).

2 Combine all the wet ingredients, such as eggs and milk, in a separate bowl or jug. Alternatively, as with the Pecan & Cinnamon Oat Biscuits (page 44), the recipe may ask you to melt the butter with other liquids (the honey and the water, in this case) in a saucepan.

3 Pour the wet ingredients into the dry ingredients.

4 Mix until just evenly combined.

5 Your mixture is now ready to shape and bake.

Keep in mind ...

- Use a larger bowl than you think you will need to make mixing easier.
- Make sure heated or melted ingredients are not too hot when added to the dry ingredients – lukewarm is best.
- Don't overmix when combining the dry and wet mixtures.

Now get baking!

Try this method with the recipes that follow.

Pecan & Cinnamon Oat Biscuits

These biscuits are reminiscent of the ANZAC biscuits that were sent in food parcels to Australian and New Zealand troops stationed in Europe during World War I. Using basic ingredients and basic equipment, they are quick to make, long lasting and totally moreish, and are loved as much now as they were back then.

MAKES: ABOUT 28

Preparation time: 20 minutes   Baking time: 12–15 minutes

150 g (5½ oz/1 cup) plain (all-purpose) flour
150 g (5½ oz/1½ cups) rolled (porridge) oats
90 g (3¼ oz/1 cup) desiccated coconut
165 g (5¾ oz/¾ cup) caster (superfine) sugar
100 g (3½ oz/1 cup) pecans, chopped
1 teaspoon ground cinnamon
150 g (5½ oz) butter, cubed
115 g (4 oz/⅓ cup) honey
  (see Baker's tips)
1 tablespoon water
1 teaspoon bicarbonate of soda
  (baking soda)

1 Preheat the oven to 180°C (350°F) or 160°C (315°F) fan-forced. Line two large baking trays with baking paper.

2 Put the flour, rolled oats, coconut, sugar, pecans and cinnamon in a medium bowl and stir to combine.

3 Put the butter, honey and water in a small saucepan and heat over medium heat, stirring occasionally with a wooden spoon, until the butter melts. Remove from the heat, add the bicarbonate of soda and stir to combine; the mixture will foam up. Add to the dry ingredients and stir with the wooden spoon until well combined.

4 Roll tablespoonfuls of the mixture into balls and place about 7 cm (2¾ in) apart on the lined trays. Use your fingers to flatten the balls until they are about 1 cm (½ in) thick and about 5 cm (2 in) in diameter.

5 Bake for 12–15 minutes, swapping the trays after 6 minutes, or until golden and cooked through. Remove the biscuits from the oven and cool on the trays.

Variations

Macadamia & Oat Biscuits – Replace the desiccated coconut with 65 g (2¼ oz/1 cup) shredded coconut and add 70 g (2½ oz/½ cup) chopped macadamia nuts to the flour mixture in Step 2.

Oat & Raisin Biscuits – Replace the pecans with 85 g (3 oz/½ cup) seedless raisins.

Cinnamon Oat Slice – Grease a 20 cm x 30 cm (8 in x 12 in) shallow slice tin and line the base and two long sides with one piece of baking paper, allowing it to overhang the sides. Omit the pecans. Press the biscuit mixture evenly and firmly into the prepared tin and bake at 180°C (350°F) or 160°C (315°F) fan-forced for 20–25 minutes or until deep golden and firm to touch. Cool in the tin. Use the paper handles to lift out onto a board, and cut into pieces.

Baker's tips

● The honey can be replaced with 115 g (4 oz/⅓ cup) golden syrup (light treacle) for a delicious caramel flavour.

● These biscuits will keep in an airtight container at room temperature for up to 2 weeks (though mine are usually gobbled up in just a few days).

Caramel Pecan Cake

This is a great stand-by recipe that's perfect to whip up at a moment's notice. It's particularly good for cake stalls and picnics, but the best thing about this cake is all you need for the mixing is a saucepan and a wooden spoon!

SERVES: 8

Preparation time: 15 minutes (+ cooling time)   Baking time: 35 minutes

165 g (5¾ oz/¾ cup, firmly packed) brown sugar
80 g (2¾ oz) butter, cubed
125 ml (4 fl oz/½ cup) milk
1 egg, at room temperature, lightly whisked
90 g (3¼ oz/¾ cup) coarsely chopped pecans
150 g (5½ oz/1 cup) self-raising flour
25 g (1 oz/¼ cup) toasted whole pecans, to decorate
1 tablespoon golden syrup (light treacle), to drizzle

Caramel icing
185 g (6½ oz/1½ cups) icing (confectioners') sugar
2 tablespoons golden syrup (light treacle)
3 teaspoons water

1   Preheat the oven to 170°C (325°F) or 150°C (300°F) fan-forced. Grease a 9 cm x 19 cm (3½ in x 7½ in, base measurement) loaf (bar) tin and line the base and long sides with one piece of baking paper, allowing it to overhang the sides.

2   Place the sugar, butter and milk in a medium saucepan over medium heat. Stir until the butter just melts (be careful not to let the mixture get too hot). Remove from the heat.

3   Use a wooden spoon or balloon whisk to stir in the egg and pecans. Add the flour and stir until just combined.

4   Pour the mixture into the prepared tin and smooth the surface with the back of a spoon. Bake for 35 minutes or until a skewer inserted in the centre comes out clean. Leave to stand for 5 minutes before turning out onto a wire rack to cool completely.

5   To make the Caramel icing, sift the icing sugar into a medium bowl. Mix the golden syrup and water in a small bowl until combined. Add to the icing sugar and use a wooden spoon to stir until smooth and well combined. Cover and set aside until needed.

6   Spread the top of the cooled cake with the icing, allowing it to drizzle down the sides. Decorate with the whole pecans and drizzle with the golden syrup. Serve cut into slices.

Baker's tips

● This cake will keep in an airtight container in a cool place (but not in the fridge) for up to 2 days.

● To freeze, wrap the un-iced cake well in plastic wrap and seal in an airtight container or freezer bag. Label and date and freeze for up to 3 months. Thaw at room temperature.

Mini Baked Jam Doughnuts

Everyone loves a jam doughnut and these, which are baked rather than fried, are a clever take on the traditional idea. To make them you'll need an old-fashioned 12-hole patty pan tin with the rounded bases, which can be found in most supermarkets and kitchenware stores.

MAKES: 12

Preparation time: 10 minutes (+ 3 minutes standing time)   Baking time: 10–12 minutes

Melted butter, extra, to grease
150 g (5½ oz/1 cup) plain (all-purpose) flour
1½ teaspoons baking powder
75 g (2½ oz/⅓ cup) caster (superfine) sugar
1 egg, at room temperature
80 ml (2½ fl oz/⅓ cup) milk
50 g (1¾ oz) butter, melted
1 teaspoon natural vanilla extract or essence
1 tablespoon strawberry or raspberry jam

Cinnamon sugar coating
110 g (3¾ oz/½ cup) caster (superfine) sugar
1 teaspoon ground cinnamon
60 g (2¼ oz) butter, melted

Baker's tip

● These doughnuts are best eaten warm or on the day they are baked.

1 Preheat the oven to 190°C (375°F) or 170°C (325°F) fan-forced. Grease a 12-hole round-based patty pan tin with a little melted butter.

2 Sift together the flour and baking powder into a medium bowl. Stir in the sugar.

3 Place the egg, milk, melted butter and vanilla in a jug and use a fork to whisk until well combined. Add to the dry ingredients and use a balloon whisk to stir until just combined.

4 Divide two-thirds of the mixture evenly among the greased patty pan holes. Use the back of a teaspoon to spread the mixture into the holes and make a slight indent in the mixture. Divide the jam among the indents and then top with the remaining doughnut mixture to cover the jam.

5 Bake in the preheated oven for 10–12 minutes or until golden and cooked through. Leave the doughnuts to stand in the tin for a few minutes to cool slightly.

6 For the Cinnamon sugar coating, combine the sugar and cinnamon in a bowl. Using a pastry brush, liberally brush a warm doughnut all over with the melted butter. Add the doughnut to the bowl with the cinnamon sugar and toss to coat. Transfer to a serving plate and repeat with the remaining warm doughnuts, butter and cinnamon sugar. Serve warm or at room temperature.

Chocolate Self-saucing Pudding

It has always fascinated me how a sprinkling of cocoa and sugar followed by some boiling water poured over a pudding batter can magically form a deliciously rich chocolate sauce underneath the pudding when baked. No easy way of explaining – just watch in awe and enjoy!

SERVES: 6

Preparation time: 15 minutes (+ 5 minutes standing time)   Baking time: 30–35 minutes

Melted butter, extra, to grease
150 g (5½ oz/1 cup) self-raising flour
30 g (1 oz/¼ cup) unsweetened
    cocoa powder
100 g (3½ oz/½ cup, lightly packed)
    brown sugar
125 ml (4 fl oz/½ cup) milk
60 g (2¼ oz) butter, melted
1 egg, at room temperature
Icing (confectioners') sugar,
    to sprinkle (optional)
Ice cream or cream, to serve

Chocolate sauce
100 g (3½ oz/½ cup, lightly packed)
    brown sugar
30 g (1 oz/¼ cup) unsweetened cocoa
    powder, sifted
310 ml (10¾ fl oz/1¼ cups) boiling water

1 Preheat the oven to 170°C (325°F) or 150°C (300°F) fan-forced. Brush a 1.5-litre (52 fl oz/6 cup) capacity ovenproof dish with the extra melted butter to grease. Place the dish on a baking tray lined with baking paper.

2 Sift together the flour and cocoa powder into a medium bowl. Add the sugar and stir to combine evenly.

3 Put the milk, melted butter and egg in a separate medium bowl and use a fork to whisk until well combined. Add to the flour mixture and use a wooden spoon to mix until smooth and well combined. Pour the batter into the greased dish and use the back of a metal spoon to smooth the surface.

4 To make the Chocolate sauce, combine the sugar and cocoa powder. Sprinkle evenly over the surface of the batter in the dish. Gradually and carefully pour the boiling water evenly over the sugar and cocoa.

5 Bake in the preheated oven for 30–35 minutes or until a cake-like topping forms over the top of a chocolate sauce. If you insert a skewer halfway down in the centre of the pudding it will come out clean when ready.

6 Remove the pudding from the oven and leave to stand for 5 minutes to settle before sprinkling with icing sugar, if desired. Serve with ice cream or cream.

Variations

Double Chocolate Self-saucing Pudding – Add 100 g (3½ oz) chopped dark or milk chocolate with the sugar.

Chocolate & Hazelnut Self-saucing Pudding – Add 60 g (2¼ oz/½ cup) coarsely chopped toasted and skinned hazelnuts with the sugar.

Individual Chocolate Self-saucing Puddings – Bake the mixture in six 185 ml (6 fl oz/¾ cup) ovenproof dishes or ramekins or 250 ml (9 fl oz/1 cup) recycled jam jars. Bake at 170°C (325°F) or 150°C (300°F) fan-forced for 20–25 minutes.

Raspberry & Almond Friands

These small French tea cakes were first created in the late 19th century and are traditionally baked in oval or rectangular tins. Delicate yet dense with almond, they are the ultimate treat to enjoy with a cuppa.

MAKES: 12

Preparation time: 25 minutes (+ cooling time)   Baking time: 20 minutes

Melted butter, extra, to grease
6 egg whites, at room temperature
185 g (6½ oz) butter, melted and cooled
185 g (6½ oz/1½ cups) icing (confectioners') sugar
125 g (4½ oz/1¼ cups) almond meal
100 g (3½ oz/⅔ cup) plain (all-purpose) flour
Pinch of salt
200 g (7 oz) fresh or frozen raspberries (see Baker's tips)
35 g (1¼ oz/⅓ cup) flaked almonds, to sprinkle
Icing (confectioners') sugar, to dust

1 Preheat the oven to 200°C (400°F) or 180°C (350°F) fan-forced. Lightly brush a 12-hole friand tin or 80 ml (2½ fl oz/⅓ cup) capacity muffin tin with melted butter to grease.

2 Use a balloon whisk to whisk the egg whites in a medium bowl until frothy. Use a spatula or wooden spoon to stir in the cooled butter, icing sugar, almond meal, flour and salt until just combined. Quickly and gently stir through the raspberries.

3 Divide the mixture evenly among the greased holes and scatter over the flaked almonds.

4 Bake in the preheated oven for 20 minutes or until a skewer inserted in the centre of a friand comes out clean. Leave to cool in the tin for 5 minutes, then turn out onto a wire rack to cool. Serve dusted with icing sugar.

Variations

Hazelnut & Chocolate Friands – Replace the almond meal with hazelnut meal and replace the raspberries with 150 g (5½ oz/1 cup) chopped good-quality dark chocolate.

Blackberry & Orange Friands – Add 1 tablespoon finely grated orange zest to the egg whites with the almond meal and replace the raspberries with blackberries.

Blueberry & Lemon Friands – Add 1 tablespoon finely grated lemon zest to the egg whites with the almond meal and replace the raspberries with blueberries.

Baker's tips

● Use frozen raspberries straight from the freezer for this recipe – don't thaw them or they will streak the mixture with their red juice.

● These friands will keep in an airtight container at room temperature for up to 3 days.

White Chocolate Butterfly Cakes

Based on a cake I have made for years as a wedding cake for friends, this recipe is incredibly simple but still has a wonderful celebratory feel. It also makes truly divine individual cakes like these sweet butterfly cakes.

MAKES: 12

Preparation time: 20 minutes (+ cooling time)   Baking time: 25–30 minutes

Melted butter, to grease (optional)
200 g (7 oz) good-quality white
    chocolate, chopped
150 g (5½ oz) unsalted butter, cubed
185 ml (6 fl oz/¾ cup) water
220 g (7¾ oz/1 cup) caster (superfine) sugar
2 eggs, at room temperature, lightly whisked
1½ teaspoons natural vanilla extract
    or essence
225 g (8 oz/1½ cups) plain (all-purpose) flour
50 g (1¾ oz/½ cup) almond meal
1½ teaspoons baking powder
125 ml (4 fl oz/½ cup) thick (double) cream
165 g (5¾ oz/½ cup) raspberry or
    blackberry jam
Icing (confectioners') sugar, to dust

Baker's tips

● The unfilled cakes will keep in an airtight container at room temperature for up to 2 days. Alternatively they will freeze well sealed in a freezer bag or airtight container for up to 1 month. Thaw at room temperature.

● These cakes are best eaten the day they are filled.

1 Preheat the oven to 180°C (350°F) or 160°C (315°F) fan-forced. Grease a 12-hole 80 ml (2½ fl oz/⅓ cup) capacity muffin tray with melted butter or line with paper cases.

2 Put the chocolate, butter and water in a medium saucepan and stir over medium heat until the chocolate and butter have melted and the mixture is smooth. Remove from the heat and set aside until cooled to room temperature.

3 Add the sugar, eggs and vanilla to the chocolate mixture and use a balloon whisk to stir until well combined.

4 In a medium bowl, use a clean whisk or fork to whisk together the flour, almond meal and baking powder, combining the ingredients evenly and breaking up any lumps of almond meal. Add to the chocolate mixture and stir with the whisk until just combined.

5 Divide the mixture evenly among the muffin holes and lightly tap the tin on the bench top to remove any large air bubbles. Bake in the preheated oven for 25–30 minutes or until a skewer inserted in the centre of a cake comes out clean. Leave the cakes to stand in the tin for 5 minutes before turning out onto a wire rack to cool completely.

6 When cool, cut a shallow cone-shaped piece out of the top of a cake, leaving about a 1 cm (½ in) border. Cut the piece of cake in half. Spoon a little cream and then some jam into the hole to fill. Arrange the two pieces of cake in the jam to form wings. Repeat with the remaining cakes, cream and jam. Dust with icing sugar to serve.

Spiced Gingerbread with Lemon Glaze

The combination of warm ginger and tangy lemon may seem like an unlikely partnership but believe me, it is one to try. The glaze on this cake is quite thin and is more like a syrup that will soak through the gingerbread, adding extra moisture and flavour as it does. Serve this cake for morning or afternoon tea, or warm as a dessert with cream or ice cream.

SERVES: 12

Preparation time: 20 minutes   Baking time: 25 minutes

Melted butter, to grease
260 g (9¼ oz/1¾ cups) plain
    (all-purpose) flour
1½ teaspoons ground ginger
1 teaspoon mixed spice
110 g (3¾ oz/½ cup, firmly packed)
    brown sugar
125 g (4½ oz) butter, cubed
175 g (6 oz/½ cup) golden syrup
    (light treacle)
125 ml (4 fl oz/½ cup) water
1¼ teaspoons bicarbonate of soda
    (baking soda)
1 egg, at room temperature
Lemon rind strips (see Baker's tips),
    to decorate (optional)

Lemon glaze
125 g (4½ oz/1 cup) icing (confectioners')
    sugar mixture, sifted
2 tablespoons freshly squeezed lemon juice

Baker's tips

● To make the lemon rind strips, use a vegetable peeler to remove the rind from a lemon. Use a small sharp knife to remove any white pith from the rind and then cut the rind into very fine strips.

● This gingerbread will keep in an airtight container at room temperature for up to 4 days.

1 Preheat the oven to 180°C (350°F) or 160°C (315°F) fan-forced. Grease a 16 cm x 26 cm (6¼ in x 10½ in, base measurement) slice tin with melted butter and line the base and two long sides with one piece of baking paper, allowing it to overhang the sides.

2 Sift together the flour and spices in a medium bowl. Stir in the sugar, breaking up any lumps with the back of a wooden spoon. Make a well in the centre.

3 Combine the butter, golden syrup and water in a small saucepan and heat over medium heat, stirring occasionally, until the butter melts and the mixture is heated through. Stir in the bicarbonate of soda and allow the mixture to foam. Add to the dry ingredients with the egg and stir with the wooden spoon until just combined.

4 Pour the mixture into the prepared tin and smooth the surface with the back of a spoon. Bake in the preheated oven for 25 minutes or until a skewer inserted in the centre of the cake comes out clean.

5 Meanwhile, to make the Lemon glaze, combine the icing sugar and lemon juice in a medium bowl and mix until smooth. Cover and set aside.

6 Remove the gingerbread from the oven and place the tin on a wire rack. Spoon the Lemon glaze over the warm cake, spreading it evenly as you go. Scatter over the lemon rind strips, if using. Set aside to cool in the tin. Use the paper handles to lift the cake from the tin and place on a cutting board. Cut into portions to serve.

Zucchini & Pistachio Loaf

Whether you call this a loaf or bread, it's something I enjoy eating immensely. Not too sweet and slightly nutty, you'll find it's quintessentially simple, old-fashioned and comforting, with the pistachios and orange adding a contemporary edge.

SERVES: 12

Preparation time: 20 minutes (+ cooling time)   Baking time: 50–55 minutes

2 eggs

220 g (7¾ oz/1 cup) raw sugar

170 ml (5½ fl oz/⅔ cup) sunflower or light olive oil

Finely grated zest of 1 orange

300 g (10½ oz/2¼ cups) coarsely grated zucchini (courgette)

75 g (2½ oz) unsalted pistachio kernels, coarsely chopped

150 g (5½ oz/1 cup) plain (all-purpose) flour

150 g (5½ oz/1 cup) wholemeal plain (all-purpose) flour

2 teaspoons baking powder

1 teaspoon ground cinnamon

Butter, to serve (optional)

1 Preheat the oven to 170°C (325°F) or 150°C (300°F) fan-forced. Grease a 12.5 cm x 24.5 cm (5 in x 9½ in, base measurement) 2 litre (70 fl oz/8 cup) capacity loaf (bar) tin and line the base and two long sides with one piece of baking paper.

2 Put the eggs, sugar, sunflower oil and zest in a large bowl and use a balloon whisk to combine well. Stir in the zucchini and pistachios.

3 Sift together the flours, baking powder and cinnamon, returning any husks left in the sieve to the bowl. Add to the zucchini mixture and stir with a large metal spoon or spatula until just combined.

4 Spoon into the prepared tin and use the back of a spoon to smooth the surface. Bake in the preheated oven for 50–55 minutes or until a skewer inserted in the centre comes out clean.

5 Leave to stand in the tin for 5 minutes before turning out onto a wire rack to cool. Serve plain or spread with butter.

Baker's tips

● This loaf is also wonderful toasted.

● It will keep at room temperature in an airtight container for up to 2 days.

● To freeze, wrap whole or individual slices in plastic wrap, seal in an airtight container or freezer bag and freeze for up to 3 months. Thaw at room temperature.

Easy Chocolate Coconut Slice

This is a fail-safe recipe everyone loves. It is perfect to make for cake stalls and picnics, or just to have as a staple in your cake tin.

MAKES: ABOUT 24 PIECES

Preparation time: 20 minutes (+ cooling and 30 minutes standing time)   Baking time: 30–35 minutes

Melted butter, extra, to grease
300 g (10½ oz/2 cups) plain
   (all-purpose) flour
55 g (2 oz/½ cup) unsweetened
   cocoa powder
245 g (9 oz/1¼ cups, lightly packed)
   brown sugar
180 g (6 oz/2 cups) desiccated coconut
200 g (7 oz) butter, melted
2 eggs, at room temperature, lightly whisked
Icing (confectioners') sugar, to dust

Simple chocolate icing
155 g (5½ oz/1¼ cups) icing
   (confectioners') sugar
2 tablespoons unsweetened cocoa powder
30 g (1 oz) butter, at room temperature, diced
2 teaspoons boiling water

1 Preheat the oven to 170°C (325°F) or 150°C (300°F) fan-forced. Grease a shallow 20 cm x 30 cm (8 in x 12 in, base measurement) slice tin and line the base and the two long sides with one piece of baking paper, extending over the sides.

2 Sift the flour and cocoa powder into a large bowl. Stir in the brown sugar and coconut (a balloon whisk will make light work of this). Add the melted butter and eggs and use a wooden spoon and then your hands to mix until evenly combined.

3 Use your hands to press the mixture evenly into the prepared tin.

4 Bake for 30–35 minutes, or until a skewer inserted in the centre comes out clean. Leave to cool in the tin.

5 To make the Simple chocolate icing, sift together the icing sugar and cocoa powder into a medium bowl. Add the butter and boiling water and stir until smooth, adding a little more water if necessary to reach a thick spreadable consistency. Spread the icing over the slice in the tin and set aside for 30 minutes or until set.

6 Use the paper to lift the slice from the tin. Dust with icing sugar and cut into pieces to serve.

Baker's tip

● This slice will keep in an airtight container at room temperature for up to 4 days.

Variation

Chocolate & Berry Coconut Slice – Use your hands to press half the slice mixture over the base of the prepared tin to cover it evenly. Spread with 165 g (5¾ oz/½ cup) mixed berry jam (or berry jam of your choice). Spoon over and gently press the remaining slice mixture on top of the jam with your fingertips (quite roughly, if you like). Bake as directed and omit the Simple chocolate icing.

Simple Chocolate Cake

Everyone needs a recipe for the most simple of chocolate cakes. This one is a real crowd-pleaser and you will be asked to make it time and time again. To keep it completely fuss-free, forget about the chocolate icing and just dust with icing sugar.

SERVES: 8–10

Preparation time: 20 minutes (+ 1 hour cooling and 30 minutes standing time)   Baking time: 50 minutes

Melted butter, to grease
125 g (4½ oz) unsalted butter, cubed
220 g (7¾ oz/1 cup, firmly packed) brown sugar
185 ml (6 fl oz/¾ cup) milk (see Baker's tips)
2 eggs, at room temperature, lightly whisked
1½ teaspoons natural vanilla extract or essence
200 g (7 oz/1⅓ cups) self-raising flour
55 g (2 oz/½ cup) unsweetened cocoa powder
2 teaspoons baking powder
¼ teaspoon bicarbonate of soda (baking soda)
Chocolate Dollar 5s, to sprinkle (optional)

Chocolate icing
250 g (9 oz/2 cups) pure icing (confectioners') sugar
2 tablespoons unsweetened cocoa powder
2–2½ tablespoons water, at room temperature

1 Preheat the oven to 180°C (350°F) or 160°C (315°F) fan-forced. Grease a round 20 cm (8 in) cake tin with melted butter and line the base with baking paper.

2 Combine the butter, sugar and milk in a medium saucepan. Stir over medium heat until the butter melts, the sugar dissolves and the mixture is combined. Remove from the heat and use a fork to whisk in the eggs and vanilla.

3 Sift together the flour, cocoa powder, baking powder and bicarbonate of soda into a large bowl. Add the butter mixture and use a balloon whisk to stir until just combined.

4 Spoon the mixture into the prepared tin and use the back of a metal spoon to smooth the surface. Bake in the preheated oven for 50 minutes or until a skewer inserted in the centre of the cake comes out clean. Leave to stand in the tin for 5 minutes before turning out onto a wire rack to cool (this will take about 1 hour).

5 To make the Chocolate icing, sift the icing sugar and cocoa into a medium bowl. Use a wooden spoon to stir in 2 tablespoons of the water, adding the remaining ½ tablespoon water if necessary to mix to a very thick pouring consistency. Pour over the cooled cake, spreading it over the top of the cake and letting it run down the sides. Sprinkle with the Dollar 5s and set aside for 30 minutes for the icing to set before cutting.

Baker's tips

● You can use cooled coffee in place of the milk if you like a subtle mocha flavour.

● This cake will keep in an airtight container at room temperature for up to 3 days.

Muesli Bars

Simple additive-free muesli bars are far better than ones from a packet. If you like, swap in other dried fruits, nuts and seeds, depending on your preference.

MAKES: ABOUT 24

Preparation time: 15 minutes (+ cooling time)   Baking time: 55–60 minutes

300 g (10½ oz/3 cups) rolled (porridge) oats
45 g (1½ oz/½ cup) desiccated coconut
100 g (3½ oz) sultanas (golden raisins)
80 g (2¾ oz/½ cup) raw almonds, coarsely chopped (*see Baker's tips*)
40 g (1½ oz/¼ cup) pumpkin seeds (pepitas) or sunflower seeds
2 tablespoons sesame seeds
1½ teaspoons ground cinnamon
Finely grated zest of 1 orange
260 g (9¼ oz/180 ml/6 fl oz/¾ cup) good-quality honey or golden syrup (light treacle)
125 ml (4 fl oz/½ cup) sunflower oil or light olive oil
2 tablespoons brown sugar

1 Preheat the oven to 160°C (315°F) or 140°C (275°F) fan-forced. Lightly grease a shallow 20 cm x 30 cm (8 in x 12 in) baking tin and line the base and long sides with one piece of baking paper, cutting to fit.

2 Put the rolled oats, coconut, sultanas, almonds, pumpkin seeds, sesame seeds, cinnamon and zest in a large bowl and mix to combine evenly.

3 Put the honey or golden syrup, sunflower oil and sugar in a small saucepan over medium heat and stir until well combined and heated through.

4 Add the warm honey mixture to the rolled oats mixture and mix well until evenly combined. Use damp hands to press the mixture firmly into the lined tin(see Baker's tips). Then press the mixture with the back of a spoon or a palette knife to make the surface smooth and even.

5 Bake for 55–60 minutes or until the surface is deep golden all over. Leave to cool completely in the tin. Cut into bars or squares to serve.

Baker's tips

● You can leave the almonds out for a nut-free version if you wish.

● It's essential to press the mixture into the lined tin to prevent the bars crumbling when cut.

● These muesli bars will keep in an airtight container for up to 1 week.

Classic Walnut Brownies

Rich, decadent, totally addictive and, best of all, so easy to make – what else could you want from a brownie recipe? Try the variations below, too, for delicious twists on the classic.

MAKES: ABOUT 24

Preparation time: 15 minutes (+ cooling time)   Baking time: 35–40 minutes

Melted butter, to grease
250 g (9 oz) good-quality dark
   chocolate, chopped
150 g (5½ oz) butter, cubed
165 g (5¾ oz/¾ cup, firmly packed)
   brown sugar
3 eggs, at room temperature, lightly whisked
75 g (2½ oz/½ cup) plain (all-purpose) flour
2 tablespoons unsweetened cocoa powder
¾ teaspoon baking powder
150 g (5½ oz) walnuts, toasted
   (see Baker's tips)
Icing (confectioners') sugar or unsweetened
   cocoa powder, to dust (optional)

1 Preheat the oven to 180°C (350°F) or 160°C (315°F) fan-forced. Grease a 16 cm x 26 cm (6¼ in x 10½ in) shallow slice tin. Line the base and long sides with one piece of baking paper.

2 Place the chocolate and butter in a medium heatproof bowl over a saucepan of simmering water, making sure the base of the bowl doesn't touch the water. Stir occasionally until the chocolate and butter have melted and the mixture is smooth. Remove the bowl from the saucepan.

3 Add the brown sugar and eggs to the chocolate mixture and use a balloon whisk to stir until well combined.

4 Sift together the flour, cocoa powder and baking powder. Add to the chocolate mixture and stir until just combined. Stir in the toasted walnuts.

5 Pour the mixture into the prepared tin and spread evenly. Bake in the preheated oven for 35–40 minutes or until moist crumbs cling to a skewer inserted in the centre. Leave to cool in the tin.

6 Lift out the brownie from the tin using the baking paper. Cut into squares and serve dusted with icing sugar or cocoa powder, if desired.

Variations

Drunken Prune Brownies – Soak 150 g (5½ oz) halved, pitted prunes in 2 tablespoons warmed brandy for 30 minutes. Replace the walnuts with the soaked prunes and any remaining liquid.

Red Raspberry Brownies – Replace the walnuts with 150 g (5½ oz) frozen or fresh raspberries.

White Chocolate Chunk Brownies – Replace the walnuts with 150 g (5½ oz) coarsely chopped good-quality white chocolate.

Baker's tips

● To toast the walnuts, spread on a baking tray and toast in an oven preheated to 180°C (350°F) or 160°C (315°F) fan-forced for 8–10 minutes or until lightly golden and aromatic.

● These brownies will keep in an airtight container in a cool place (but not in the fridge) for up to 5 days.

Lesson 2

The Measure
& Beat Method

Just like the measure and mix method in Lesson 1, this is no-fuss, simple and quick. The ingredients are mixed together in an electric mixer until very well combined.

This method actually goes against the golden rule of not beating flour and liquid ingredients together unless you want to develop the gluten in the flour – such as when you are making pizza dough or bread.

Gluten development where it isn't wanted will result in a tough and/or heavy cake with an unpalatable texture. However, there are just a few cake recipes – those with a high proportion of butter and sugar – where this method works well. Why? The large amount of butter and sugar helps prevent the gluten developing and therefore compensates for the beating.

Interestingly, due to the beating, these cakes have a fine, less 'holey', crumb compared to those made with the creaming method (page 116), where the flour is folded in or beaten in until just combined at the final stage of mixing.

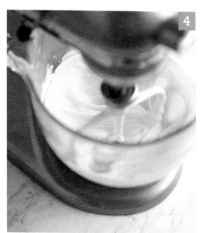

Step by step

1 Put all the dry ingredients in a mixing bowl.

2 Put the wet ingredients on top.

3 Use an electric mixer on low speed to beat until the ingredients are just combined. Beating on low first will mean the dry ingredients won't 'fly' out of the bowl before they have a chance to mix with the wet ingredients!

4 Increase the speed to high and beat for 2–3 minutes – the mixture will become paler in colour and lighter in texture as you beat.

5 When ready, the mixture will be well combined and have a smooth, silky texture, and it will be very pale in colour.

Keep in mind ...

- It is very important that the butter is quite soft (so you can easily make an imprint if you stick your finger into it) but not at melting point. If it is too hard, it won't combine with the other ingredients easily and will remain in small pieces – and you will end up with a tough-textured cake.
- As for most baking, the eggs are best at room temperature for this method.
- There is no need to lightly whisk the eggs before adding them – just crack them into a small bowl and throw them in!
- Use the paddle attachment if using a stand mixer and the standard beaters if using hand-held electric beaters.
- Beat the ingredients on low speed until just combined (so you don't get covered with flour!) and then increase the speed to high for the remaining beating time.
- If using hand-held electric beaters you may have to beat for a few more minutes than stated in the recipe to reach the desired consistency.

Now get baking!

This method is foolproof if you follow these simple tips. So, let's turn on the oven and see how incredibly easy it is to make the following recipes.

Easy Vanilla Cake with Passionfruit Buttercream

There is nothing quite like a simple vanilla cake. Another wonderful standby for almost any occasion, this cake is one to add to your baking repertoire. The lovely passionfruit 'measure and beat' buttercream icing tops it perfectly.

SERVES: 8–10

Preparation time: 15 minutes (+ 1½ hours cooling time)   Baking time: 45–50 minutes

Melted butter, to grease
150 g (5½ oz/1 cup) self-raising flour
35 g (1¼ oz/¼ cup) plain (all-purpose) flour
165 g (5¾ oz/¾ cup) caster (superfine) sugar
125 g (4½ oz) butter, cubed, at
    room temperature
80 ml (2½ fl oz/⅓ cup) milk
2 eggs, at room temperature
1½ teaspoons natural vanilla extract
    or essence

Passionfruit buttercream
125 g (4½ oz) butter, at room temperature
185 g (6½ oz/1½ cups) icing (confectioners')
    sugar, sifted
1 tablespoon passionfruit pulp,
    plus extra, to decorate

1 Preheat the oven to 180°C (350°F) or 160°C (315°F) fan-forced. Grease a round 20 cm (8 in) cake tin with melted butter and line the base with baking paper.

2 Place the self-raising and plain flours, sugar, butter, milk, eggs and vanilla in a large bowl. Use an electric mixer to beat on low speed until combined. Increase the speed to high and beat for 3 minutes or until the mixture is well combined and very pale in colour. Spoon the mixture into the prepared tin and smooth the surface with the back of a spoon.

3 Bake in the preheated oven for 45–50 minutes or until a skewer inserted in the centre comes out clean. Leave to cool in the tin for 5 minutes before turning out onto a wire rack to cool completely (this will take about 1½ hours).

4 To make the Passionfruit buttercream, use an electric mixer to beat the butter, icing sugar and passionfruit pulp in a medium bowl until pale and creamy.

5 Spread the buttercream over the top of the cooled cake and then spoon over the extra passionfruit pulp to decorate. Serve in wedges.

Baker's tips

● This cake will keep either iced or plain in an airtight container at room temperature for up to 2 days.

● You can freeze the un-iced cake for up to 1 month. Wrap well in plastic wrap and then seal in an airtight container or freezer bag before freezing. Thaw at room temperature.

Variation

Easy Citrus & Coconut Cake – Replace the vanilla with 1 tablespoon finely grated lemon or orange zest and add 45 g (1½ oz/½ cup) desiccated coconut with the flours. Replace the passionfruit pulp in the buttercream with 2 teaspoons finely grated lemon or orange zest and 2 teaspoons strained fresh lemon or orange juice.

Gluten-free Lamington Fingers

With these moist and flavoursome lamingtons, people with gluten or wheat intolerance won't have to miss out on this Australian classic, and no one else will notice they are gluten-free. These keep in an airtight container in the fridge for up to 2 days – stand them at room temperature for at least 30 minutes before serving.

MAKES: 12

Preparation time: 40 minutes (+ 40 minutes cooling time)   Baking time: 20 minutes

Melted butter, to grease
175 g (6 oz/1¼ cups) purchased gluten-free
    plain (all-purpose) flour mix
2½ teaspoons gluten-free baking powder
165 g (5¾ oz/¾ cup) caster (superfine) sugar
125 g (4½ oz) unsalted butter, at room
    temperature, cubed
2 eggs, at room temperature
80 ml (2½ fl oz/⅓ cup) milk
2 teaspoons natural vanilla extract
    or essence

Chocolate icing & coconut coating
500 g (1 lb 2 oz/4 cups) pure icing
    (confectioners') sugar
55 g (2 oz/½ cup) unsweetened
    cocoa powder
150 ml (5 fl oz) boiling water
½ teaspoon natural vanilla extract
    or essence
180 g (6 oz/2 cups) desiccated coconut,
    to coat

Variation

Gluten-free Vanilla Cupcakes – Bake the basic gluten-free butter cake (above) in a 12-hole 80 ml (2½ fl oz/⅓ cup) capacity muffin tin lined with cases for 20–25 minutes. Omit the Chocolate icing & coconut coating, and dust with pure icing (confectioners') sugar, or ice with an icing or buttercream of your choice made with pure icing sugar.

1 Preheat the oven to 180°C (350°F) or 160°C (315°F) fan-forced. Grease a 20 cm x 30 cm (8 in x 12 in, base measurement) shallow cake tin and line the base and two long sides with one piece of baking paper.

2 Put the flour, baking powder, sugar, butter, eggs, milk and vanilla in a large bowl. Use an electric mixer to beat on low speed until combined. Increase the speed to medium and beat for 3 minutes or until the mixture is well combined and very pale in colour. Spoon the mixture into the lined tin and spread evenly. Lightly tap the tin on the bench top to get rid of any excess air bubbles.

3 Bake for 20 minutes or until cooked when tested with a skewer. Leave to cool in the tin for 5 minutes, then turn out onto a wire rack to cool completely (this will take about 40 minutes).

4 To make the Chocolate icing, sift the icing sugar and cocoa powder into a medium bowl. Add the boiling water and vanilla and stir until smooth (it should be the consistency of pouring cream).

5 Trim the edges of the cooled cake with a sharp serrated knife then cut the cake into 12 fingers about 4.5 cm x 9.5 cm (1¾ in x 3¾ in) each.

6 Spread the coconut on a tray or plate. Rest a cake portion on a fork, dip into the Chocolate icing and then spoon the icing over the top and sides to completely coat (if the icing becomes too thick to handle, add a teaspoon of boiling water). Allow any extra icing to drip off. Roll the cake in the coconut to coat evenly. Place on a wire rack. Repeat with the remaining ingredients.

Rhubarb Sour Cream Crumble Cake

Every cake I make regularly has a history, this one included. On its first outing at a girls' weekend away it just kept on giving – dessert one night, afternoon tea the next day, morning tea the next. By the end of the weekend I thought everyone would have had enough, but they all wanted the recipe!

SERVES: 10–12

|||||||||||||||||||||||||||||||||||||||||||||||||||||||||||||||||||||||||||||||||||||||||||||||||||||||||||||||||||||||||||||||||||||||||||||||||||||||||||||||||

Preparation time: 25 minutes   Baking time: 1 hour 5 minutes–1 hour 10 minutes

Melted butter, to grease
185 g (6½ oz/1¼ cups) self-raising flour
165 g (5¾ oz) raw caster (superfine) sugar, plus 1 tablespoon extra
125 g (4½ oz) butter, at room temperature, cubed
85 g (3 oz/⅓ cup) sour cream
2 eggs, at room temperature
1½ teaspoons natural vanilla extract or essence
250 g (9 oz) trimmed rhubarb, washed and cut into 4 cm (1½ in) lengths
Icing (confectioners') sugar, to dust
Softly whipped cream or ice cream, to serve (optional)

Crumble topping
35 g (1¼ oz/¼ cup) plain (all-purpose) flour
55 g (2 oz/¼ cup, firmly packed) raw or brown sugar
1 teaspoon ground cinnamon
60 g (2¼ oz) chilled butter, cubed
50 g (1¾ oz/½ cup) flaked almonds

Baker's tips

● To line a spring-form cake tin, tear off a square of baking paper about 10 cm (4 in) larger than the tin, release the outside of the tin, place the paper over the base and then clamp the side of the tin around the base to hold the paper in place. Easy!

● This cake will keep in an airtight container at room temperature for up to 3 days.

1 Preheat the oven to 170°C (325°F) or 150°C (300°F) fan-forced. Grease a 22 cm (8½ in) spring-form cake tin with melted butter and line the base with baking paper (see Baker's tips).

2 To make the Crumble topping, put the flour, sugar and cinnamon in a medium bowl. Use your fingertips to rub in the butter until the mixture resembles coarse breadcrumbs. Stir in the almonds. Cover and put in the fridge while making the cake.

3 Place the flour, raw caster sugar, butter, sour cream, eggs and vanilla in a large bowl. Use an electric mixer to beat on low speed until combined. Increase the speed to high and beat for 3 minutes or until the mixture is well combined and very pale in colour. Spoon the mixture into the prepared tin and smooth the surface with the back of a spoon.

4 Toss the rhubarb pieces with the extra raw caster sugar. Scatter evenly over the top of the cake and then press gently into the batter. Sprinkle with the Crumble topping to cover.

5 Bake in the preheated oven for 1 hour 5 minutes–1 hour 10 minutes or until a skewer inserted in the centre comes out clean. Leave the cake to stand in the tin for 5 minutes before removing the side of the tin and transferring the cake, still on the base of the tin, to a wire rack. Serve warm or at room temperature, on its own or with cream or ice cream.

Gluten-free Baby Passionfruit Cakes with Raspberry Icing

I just love the combination of tart raspberries and aromatic passionfruit – it's where summer meets autumn. These 'baby' cakes (just a cute name for a small individual cake, really) are light, full of flavour and topped with an ever-so-stunning raspberry icing – coloured and flavoured with real raspberries.

MAKES: 12

Preparation: 20 minutes (+ 30 minutes cooling and 30 minutes standing time)   Baking time: 20–25 minutes

Melted butter, to grease
100 g (3½ oz/1 cup) almond meal
95 g (3¼ oz/½ cup) instant polenta
2 teaspoons gluten-free baking powder
125 g (4½ oz) unsalted butter, at room
   temperature, cubed
165 g (5¾ oz/¾ cup) caster (superfine) sugar
90 g (3¼ oz/⅓ cup) passionfruit pulp
   (about 4 medium passionfruit)
2 eggs, at room temperature

Raspberry icing
30 g (1 oz) fresh or frozen raspberries
125 g (4½ oz/1 cup) pure icing
   (confectioners') sugar, sifted
1½ teaspoons water

Baker's tip

● These cakes will keep in an airtight container at room temperature for up to 2 days.

1 Preheat the oven to 180°C (350°F) or 160°C (315°F) fan-forced. Brush a 12-hole 80 ml (2½ fl oz/⅓ cup) capacity muffin tin with melted butter to grease.

2 Combine the almond meal, polenta, baking powder, butter, sugar, passionfruit pulp and eggs in a large bowl. Use an electric mixer to beat on low speed until combined. Scrape down the side of the bowl and then beat on high speed for 3 minutes or until the mixture is well combined and very pale in colour. Spoon the mixture into the prepared muffin holes, dividing evenly.

3 Bake in the preheated oven for 20–25 minutes or until the cakes are golden and a skewer inserted in the centre comes out clean. Remove from the oven and leave to stand in the tin for 5 minutes before turning out onto a wire rack, bottom sides up, to cool. This will take about 30 minutes.

4 Meanwhile, to make the Raspberry icing, place the raspberries in a small saucepan and sprinkle with 2 tablespoons of the icing sugar. Heat over low heat, stirring occasionally, for 2 minutes or until the raspberries have broken down. Pass the raspberry mixture through a sieve, pressing with the back of a spoon to extract as much juice as possible. Discard any seeds. Stir the raspberry syrup with the water into the remaining icing sugar until smooth and well combined to make a thick, pourable icing.

5 Spoon 1 teaspoon of the Raspberry icing on top of each cake, spreading if necessary and allowing it to run down the sides. Set aside for 30 minutes or until the icing sets.

One-bowl Chocolate Cupcakes

With an uncanny ability to please and charm both kids and adults alike, these
chocolate cupcakes are heavenly, simple to make and perfect for any occasion.

MAKES: 12

Preparation time: 15 minutes (+ 30 minutes cooling and 30 minutes standing)   Baking time: 25–28 minutes

Melted butter, to grease
185 g (6½ oz/1¼ cups) self-raising flour
55 g (2 oz/½ cup) unsweetened cocoa
    powder, sifted
245 g (9 oz/1¼ cups, lightly packed)
    brown sugar
125 g (4½ oz) butter, at room
    temperature, cubed
2 eggs, at room temperature
2 teaspoons natural vanilla extract
    or essence
170 ml (5½ fl oz/⅔ cup) water
Chocolate shavings or curls (*see Baker's tips*),
    to decorate (optional)

Chocolate icing
250 g (9 oz/2 cups) pure icing
    (confectioners') sugar
2 tablespoons unsweetened cocoa powder
2–2½ tablespoons water, at
    room temperature

1 Preheat the oven to 180°C (350°F) or 160°C (315°F)
   fan-forced. Line a 12-hole 80 ml (2½ fl oz/⅓ cup)
   capacity muffin tin with paper cases.

2 Put all the dry ingredients and then the wet ingredients
   in a large bowl and use an electric mixer to beat on low
   speed until combined. Increase the speed to high and
   beat for 3–4 minutes or until paler in colour and silky
   smooth in texture.

3 Divide the mixture evenly among the lined muffin holes.
   Bake in the preheated oven for 25–28 minutes or until
   a skewer inserted in the centre of a cupcake comes out
   clean. Leave in the tin for 5 minutes before transferring
   to a wire rack to cool (this will take about 30 minutes).

4 Meanwhile, to make the Chocolate icing, sift the icing
   sugar and cocoa into a medium bowl. Use a wooden
   spoon to stir in 2 tablespoons of the water, adding the
   remaining ½ tablespoon water if necessary to mix to a
   thick spreading consistency. Spread the cooled cupcakes
   with the icing and decorate with chocolate curls. Set
   aside for 30 minutes for the icing to set before serving.

Variations

Raspberry-studded Chocolate Cupcakes – Gently fold
200 g (7 oz) frozen or fresh raspberries through the
cake mixture just before dividing among the muffin
holes to bake.

Mocha Cupcakes – Dissolve 1 tablespoon good-quality
coffee granules in 1 tablespoon hot water. Cool before
adding with all the other ingredients for beating.

Double Chocolate Cupcakes – Stir 100 g (3½ oz)
chopped good-quality dark chocolate through the
cake mixture just before dividing among the muffin
holes to bake.

Baker's tips

● To make chocolate curls or shavings, you will need a block
of dark or milk chocolate (milk chocolate is less brittle than
dark chocolate and is more suited to making curls, while the
dark chocolate is great for making shavings). Wrap the block
in baking paper to protect it from the warmth of your hand.
Run a vegetable peeler very firmly along the length of the
block (the wider the block of chocolate the larger the curls
or shavings will be) and let them drop onto a plate below.
If the day is warm keep them in the fridge until ready to use.

● This mixture can also be baked in a greased and base-
lined 20 cm (8 in) round cake tin at 170°C (325°F) or 150°C
(300°F) fan-forced for 50–55 minutes.

● These cupcakes will keep iced or un-iced in an airtight
container for up to 2 days.

Lemon & Coconut Syrup Cake

A simple butter cake made special by the addition of intensely fragrant and mouth-puckering lemon. Perfect on its own for morning or afternoon tea, or with cream or ice cream for dessert. Or you could even leave out the syrup and drizzle it with a simple lemon glaze icing.

SERVES: 10

Preparation time: 30 minutes (+ 1½ hours cooling time)   Baking time: 45 minutes

Melted butter, to grease
150 g (5½ oz/1 cup) self-raising flour
45 g (1½ oz/½ cup) desiccated coconut
150 g (5½ oz) butter, at room temperature, cubed
165 g (5¾ oz/¾ cup) caster (superfine) sugar
3 eggs, at room temperature
Finely grated zest and juice of 2 lemons

Lemon syrup
2 lemons
220 g (7¾ oz/1 cup) caster (superfine) sugar

Variations

Orange Poppy Seed Syrup Cake – Replace the lemons with oranges. Omit the coconut and increase the flour to 185 g (6½ oz/1¼ cups). Add 2 tablespoons poppy seeds with all the other ingredients before beating.

Mandarin & Coconut Syrup Cake – Replace the lemons with mandarins.

Baker's tip

● This cake will keep in an airtight container at room temperature for up to 3 days.

1 Preheat the oven to 170°C (325°F) or 150°C (300°F) fan-forced. Grease a 24 cm (9½ in, top measurement) or 2.5 litre (87 fl oz/10 cup) capacity fluted ring tin with melted butter, then dust with flour to lightly coat.

2 Combine the flour, coconut, butter, sugar, eggs, lemon zest and 1 tablespoon juice (reserve the remainder for later) in a large bowl. Use an electric mixer to beat on low speed until combined. Scrape down the side of the bowl and then beat on high speed for 3 minutes or until the mixture is well combined and very pale in colour. Spoon the mixture into the prepared tin and smooth the surface with the back of a spoon.

3 Bake for 45 minutes or until a skewer inserted in the cake comes out clean.

4 While the cake is baking, make the Lemon syrup. Use a vegetable peeler to remove the rind in wide strips from both lemons. Use a small sharp knife to remove any white pith from the rind. Juice both lemons and combine with the lemon juice left over from the cake. Measure and add enough water to make 250 ml (9 fl oz/1 cup). Pour into a small saucepan and add the rind strips and sugar. Stir over medium heat until the sugar has dissolved. Bring to a simmer and simmer for 5 minutes. Transfer the rind strips to a plate. Set aside.

5 Remove the cake from the oven and leave to stand for 5 minutes. Turn onto a wire rack set over a tray. Use a skewer to pierce the cake all over. Gradually and evenly pour the hot syrup over the hot cake. Pour any syrup that has collected in the tray back over the cake. Set aside to cool.

6 Transfer the cake to a serving plate, decorate with the lemon rind strips and serve.

Lesson 3

The Folding Method

The basic aim of the folding method is to combine two or more mixtures or ingredients while retaining any incorporated air. Muffins, soufflés and some cakes and puddings are the recipes that mainly use this method.

For this you will need either a spatula or a large metal spoon. Both these utensils are able to 'cut' through a mixture with their clean slicing edge as well as being able to 'scoop' and 'fold' the mixture gently and efficiently, so you don't knock out any of the precious incorporated air or mix too vigorously when combining the mixtures.

Often this method is used to gently incorporate flour into a butter/sugar/egg mixture (as in a butter cake) or combined wet ingredients into combined dry ingredients (as in a muffin, illustrated here) so as not to develop the gluten in the flour and to stop the finished product being 'tough'.

Sometimes it also involves a light and airy mixture (whisked egg whites or whisked eggs and sugar) being incorporated into a heavier, denser one (a fruit or chocolate mixture) such as when making a soufflé – which we will get to in Lesson 7, The Whisking Egg Whites Method (page 182).

Step by step

1 Combine the dry ingredients in a large bowl and make a well in the centre.

2 Add the combined wet ingredients.

3 Use a spatula or large metal spoon to first cut through the mixture to the base of the bowl.

4 Then, using a sweeping action, draw the mixture up and around the side of the bowl.

5 As you turn the spatula, fold the mixture on top of itself.

6 Turn the bowl a quarter turn and repeat the process a number of times, making sure you scrape the side and the base of the bowl with each fold.

7 Do this until the mixture is just combined, but evenly so. This principle is easily adapted to fold flour into a butter/sugar/egg mixture or to fold egg whites into heavier base mixtures.

Keep in mind ...

- The key to this mixing method is the technique – cutting through the mixture, and then lifting and turning the mixture on itself – and repeating it until the mixture is just combined.
- Remember not to start beating or stirring vigorously with the spatula or spoon, as this will only result in lost air and/or a tough mixture.
- If folding a lighter mixture, such as whisked egg whites, through a heavier mixture, such as a chocolate mixture, always add the lighter mixture to the heavier mixture. If the heavier mixture is thick you will need to add a large spoonful or two of the lighter mixture and fold this in first to 'lighten and loosen' it so that the remaining light mixture can be incorporated easily. Sometimes you will need to incorporate egg whites in a number of batches.

Now get baking!

Don't worry, this method will become clear once you are in the kitchen and have that spatula or spoon in your hand making the following recipes.

Zucchini, Parmesan & Basil Muffins

Savoury muffins are a great alternative to the sweet ones, especially when served as a snack or instead of bread alongside soup or salad. The zucchini in these makes them lovely and moist while adding substance.

MAKES: 12

Preparation time: 15 minutes (+ 5 minutes standing time)   Baking time: 25–30 minutes

Vegetable oil, to grease (optional)
150 g (5½ oz/1 cup) plain (all-purpose) flour
150 g (5½ oz/1 cup) wholemeal plain
   (all-purpose) flour
1 tablespoon baking powder
½ teaspoon salt
70 g (2½ oz/⅔ cup) finely grated
   parmesan cheese
65 g (2¼ oz/⅔ cup) coarsely grated
   vintage cheddar cheese
¼ cup chopped basil leaves
185 ml (6 fl oz/¾ cup) buttermilk
80 ml (2½ fl oz/⅓ cup) light olive oil
   or sunflower oil
2 eggs, at room temperature
2 zucchini (courgettes), about 100 g each,
   coarsely grated
40 g (1½ oz/¼ cup) pine nuts, to scatter
Cayenne pepper, to sprinkle

1 Preheat the oven to 190°C (375°F) or 170°C (325°F) fan-forced. Line a 12-hole 80 ml (2½ fl oz/⅓ cup) capacity muffin tin with paper cases or grease with a little vegetable oil.

2 Sift together the flours, baking powder and salt into a large bowl, returning any husks left in the sieve to the bowl. Season well with pepper and then gently stir in the parmesan, cheddar and basil. Make a well in the centre.

3 Use a fork to whisk together the buttermilk, olive oil and eggs in a bowl. Add the zucchini and mix to combine. Add to the flour mixture and use a spatula or large metal spoon to fold together until just combined. (Don't overmix – the batter should still be a little lumpy.)

4 Spoon the mixture into the prepared muffin holes, dividing evenly. Scatter over the pine nuts and sprinkle with a little cayenne pepper. Bake in the preheated oven for 25–30 minutes or until the muffins are golden and a skewer inserted in the centre comes out clean. Leave to cool in the tin for 5 minutes before transferring to a wire rack. Serve warm or at room temperature.

Baker's tip

● These muffins are best eaten the day they are baked, however they freeze well – wrap individually in plastic wrap and then seal in an airtight container or freezer bag. Freeze for up to 3 months. Thaw at room temperature.

Apple & Pecan Maple Muffins

I always say muffins should have substance – after all, they are muffins, not cake!
Dense with apple, sweet with spice, topped with pecans and glazed with maple syrup,
these muffins are a favourite of mine.

MAKES: 12

Preparation time: 20 minutes (+ 5 minutes standing time)   Baking time: 20–25 minutes

150 g (5½ oz/1 cup) plain (all-purpose) flour

150 g (5½ oz/1 cup) wholemeal plain
(all-purpose) flour

1 tablespoon baking powder

2 teaspoons ground cinnamon

150 g (5½ oz/¾ cup, lightly packed)
brown sugar

2 sweet eating apples (about 180 g/6 oz
each), such as golden delicious, pink lady
or royal gala, peeled and cut into 1.5 cm
(⅝ in) pieces

185 ml (6 fl oz/¾ cup) buttermilk
(see Baker's tips)

80 ml (2½ fl oz/⅓ cup) light olive oil
or sunflower oil

2 eggs, at room temperature

1½ teaspoons natural vanilla extract
or essence

75 g (2½ oz/¾ cup) pecans, coarsely chopped

60 ml (2 fl oz/¼ cup) pure maple syrup, plus
extra to serve (optional)

1 Preheat the oven to 190°C (375°F) or 170°C (325°F) fan-forced. Line a 12-hole 80 ml (2½ fl oz/⅓ cup) capacity muffin tin with paper cases.

2 Sift together the flours, baking powder and cinnamon into a large bowl, returning any husks left in the sieve to the bowl. Stir in the sugar and apple and make a well in the centre.

3 Use a fork to whisk together the buttermilk, olive oil, eggs and vanilla in a bowl. Add to the flour mixture and use a spatula or large metal spoon to fold together until just combined. (Don't overmix – the batter should still be a little lumpy.)

4 Spoon the mixture into the paper cases, dividing evenly. Scatter over the pecans and then drizzle with the maple syrup.

5 Bake in the preheated oven for 20–25 minutes or until the muffins are golden and a skewer inserted in the centre comes out clean. Leave to cool in the tin for 5 minutes, then transfer to a wire rack. Serve warm or at room temperature, drizzled with extra maple syrup, if desired.

Baker's tips

● If you don't have any buttermilk in the fridge you can replace it with 170 ml (5½ fl oz/⅔ cup) full-cream (whole) milk mixed with 2 teaspoons lemon juice.

● These muffins are best eaten the day they are baked, however they freeze well, too – wrap individually in plastic wrap and then seal in an airtight container or freezer bag. Freeze for up to 3 months. Thaw at room temperature.

Banana & Berry Muffins

The yoghurt in these fruit-laden muffins adds both moisture and a wonderful subtle flavour. You can also make them with gluten-free flours (see Variation, below).

MAKES: 12

Preparation time: 20 minutes (+ 5 minutes standing time)   Baking time: 25–30 minutes

300 g (10½ oz/2 cups) wholemeal plain (all-purpose) flour

1 tablespoon baking powder

2 teaspoons ground cinnamon

165 g (5¾ oz) raw caster (superfine) sugar

50 g (1¾ oz/⅔ cup) shredded coconut

200 g (7 oz) frozen mixed berries, raspberries, blackberries or blueberries (see Baker's tips)

200 g (7 oz/¾ cup) Greek-style natural yoghurt

80 ml (2½ fl oz/⅓ cup) light olive oil or sunflower oil

2 eggs, at room temperature

1½ teaspoons natural vanilla extract or essence

2 large ripe bananas (about 375 g/13 oz in total)

1 teaspoon icing (confectioners') sugar, to dust (optional)

1 Preheat the oven to 190°C (375°F) or 170°C (325°F) fan-forced. Line a 12-hole 80 ml (2½ fl oz/⅓ cup) capacity muffin tin with paper cases.

2 Sift the flour, baking powder and cinnamon into a large bowl, returning any husks left in the sieve to the bowl. Stir in the raw caster sugar and coconut. Gently stir in the frozen berries. Make a well in the centre.

3 Use a fork to whisk together the yoghurt, olive oil, eggs and vanilla in a bowl. Peel and mash the bananas and stir into the yoghurt mixture. Add to the flour mixture and use a spatula or large metal spoon to fold together until just combined. (Don't overmix – the batter should still be a little lumpy.)

4 Spoon the mixture into the paper cases, dividing evenly. Bake in the preheated oven for 25–30 minutes or until the muffins are golden and a skewer inserted in the centre comes out clean. Leave to cool in the tin for 5 minutes, then turn out onto a wire rack. Serve warm or at room temperature dusted with icing sugar, if desired.

Variation

Gluten-free Banana & Berry Muffins – Replace the wholemeal plain (all-purpose) flour with 200 g (7 oz) brown rice flour, 30 g (1 oz) quinoa flour and 30 g (1 oz) arrowroot.

Baker's tips

● There's no need to thaw the frozen berries before using them in this recipe.

● These muffins are best eaten the day they are baked, however they freeze well, too – wrap individually in plastic wrap and then seal in an airtight container or freezer bag. Freeze for up to 3 months. Thaw at room temperature.

Chilli & Cheddar Cornbread

This 'quick bread' is perfect to have warm with soups and stews, on its own or spread with lashings of butter. It is particularly good when cut into thick slices, instead of wedges, and toasted. It is super quick to make and you'll only use one bowl.

SERVES: 8–10

Preparation time: 15 minutes (+ 5 minutes standing time)   Baking time: 30 minutes

Melted butter, extra, to grease
150 g (5½ oz/1 cup) self-raising flour
190 g (6¾ oz/1 cup) instant
    polenta (cornmeal)
1 teaspoon dried chilli flakes, or to taste
1 teaspoon salt
100 g (3½ oz/1 cup) coarsely grated
    vintage or extra tasty cheddar cheese,
    plus 25 g (1 oz/¼ cup) extra, to sprinkle
310 ml (10¾ fl oz/1¼ cups) buttermilk
1 egg, at room temperature
125 g (4½ oz) butter, melted and cooled

1 Preheat the oven to 180°C (350°F) or 160°C (315°F) fan-forced. Grease a 20 cm (8 in) round cake tin with melted butter and then line the base with baking paper.

2 Combine the flour, polenta, chilli flakes and salt in a large bowl and stir to combine evenly. Stir through the grated cheese and season well with freshly ground black pepper. Make a well in the centre.

3 Whisk together the buttermilk and egg to combine and then whisk in the butter. Add to the dry ingredients and use a large metal spoon or spatula to fold together until just combined. Spoon into the prepared tin and then smooth the surface with the back of a spoon. Sprinkle with the extra cheddar.

4 Bake in the preheated oven for 30 minutes or until a skewer inserted in the centre comes out clean. Leave the cornbread to stand in the tin for 5 minutes before turning out onto a wire rack. Serve warm or at room temperature in wedges.

Variations

Cheddar & Bacon Cornbread – Omit the chilli and add 100 g (3½ oz, or about 2 slices) bacon, chopped and pan-fried until crisp, and a small handful of snipped chives, with the flour, polenta and salt.

Coriander & Cheddar Cornbread – Add a small handful of chopped coriander (cilantro) leaves with the flour, polenta, chilli and salt.

Chilli & Cheddar Cornbread Muffins – Spoon the mixture into a greased or paper case-lined 12-hole 80 ml (2½ fl oz/⅓ cup) capacity muffin tin. Bake in a preheated 190°C (375°F) or 170°C (325°F) fan-forced oven for 25 minutes or until a skewer inserted in the centre comes out clean.

Baker's tips

● This cornbread is best eaten the day it is made, however it freezes well, too, either whole or cut into wedges or slices – wrap well in plastic wrap and then seal in an airtight container or freezer bag. Label, date and freeze for up to 3 months. Thaw at room temperature.

● You can also bake this cornbread in a greased and base-lined 20 cm (8 in) square cake tin.

Cinnamon & Orange Carrot Cake

Satisfying and completely delicious, this cake has real substance. The combination of wholemeal flour, loads of carrot (which is the secret to its moist nature), cinnamon, orange zest and pecans for crunch is fabulous.

MAKES: ABOUT 16 PIECES

Preparation time: 15 minutes (+1 hour cooling)   Baking time: 50–55 minutes

Sunflower oil, extra, to grease

150 g (5½ oz/1 cup) wholemeal plain (all-purpose) flour (*see Baker's tips*)

120 g (4¼ oz) plain (all-purpose) flour (*see Baker's tips*)

2 teaspoons bicarbonate of soda (baking soda)

1 teaspoon baking powder

1½ teaspoons ground cinnamon

220 g (7¾ oz/1 cup) raw sugar or 200 g (7 oz) brown sugar

100 g (3½ oz/1 cup) pecans, coarsely chopped (*see Baker's tips*)

3 eggs, at room temperature

250 ml (9 fl oz/1 cup) sunflower oil or light olive oil

500 g (1 lb 2 oz/about 5 medium) carrots, peeled and coarsely grated

Finely grated zest of 2 oranges

Fine orange rind strips, to decorate (optional)

Orange cream cheese frosting

250 g (9 oz) cream cheese

Finely grated zest of 2 oranges

90 g (3¼ oz/¾ cup) icing (confectioners') sugar, sifted

1 Preheat the oven to 180°C (350°F) or 160°C (315°F) fan-forced. Brush a 20 cm (8 in) square cake tin with sunflower oil to grease. Line the base with baking paper.

2 Sift the flours, bicarbonate of soda, baking powder and cinnamon into a large bowl, returning any husks left in the sieve to the bowl. Add the raw sugar and pecans and stir to combine.

3 Put the eggs and sunflower oil in a medium bowl and use a fork to whisk until well combined. Stir in the grated carrot and orange zest. Add to the dry ingredients and use a large metal spoon or spatula to fold together until just combined.

4 Spoon the mixture into the prepared cake tin and smooth the surface with the back of a spoon. Bake in the preheated oven for 50–55 minutes or until a skewer inserted in the centre comes out clean. Leave the cake to stand in the tin for 5 minutes before turning out onto a wire rack to cool completely (this will take about 1 hour).

5 Meanwhile, to make the Orange cream cheese frosting, use an electric mixer to beat the cream cheese and orange zest until very smooth. Add the icing sugar and beat until well combined and very creamy. Spread the cooled cake with the frosting, decorate with orange rind strips, if using, and cut into portions to serve.

Baker's tips

● Both the wholemeal and white plain (all-purpose) flours can be replaced with 300 g (10½ oz) plain (all-purpose) wholemeal spelt flour.

● The pecans can be replaced with 100 g (3½ oz) coarsely chopped walnuts or 85 g (3 oz/½ cup) seedless raisins.

● The frosted cake will keep in an airtight container in the fridge for up to 4 days. Bring to room temperature to serve.

The Mixing in a Food Processor Method

With its ability to blend mixtures with great ease and efficiency, a food processor can be incredibly handy when you are baking. However, you need to remember that not all mixtures destined for the oven are suitable to mix with a food processor, so only use one if the recipe specifies.

This method is used in four main ways:

1 To combine wet and dry ingredients.
2 To incorporate butter into dry ingredients before blending with the wet ingredients (illustrated here).
3 To blend butter or other 'creamy' ingredients and soften them before blending with other ingredients.
4 To purée ingredients (like a whole orange in the Whole Orange Cake recipe, page 103).

The significant common element of recipes that use this method is they don't require extra air to be added to the mixture through beating or whisking, so they can easily be blended with the sharp cutting action of the blade of a food processor.

I recommend using a food processor with a medium to large bowl for this method, so large-volume cake and cheesecake mixtures can be handled easily and efficiently in one go.

Step by step

1 First put the dry ingredients into the bowl of a food processor and add the cubed butter.

2 Process until the butter is finely chopped and evenly distributed through the dry ingredients – it will appear uneven at first, with large chunks of butter still visible.

3 Continue to process until the butter becomes finely chopped and the mixture is more even in texture.

4 Add the wet ingredients.

5 Process using the pulse button until the mixture just comes together.

6 You may need to transfer the mixture to a bench top or a bowl to bring the mixture together with your hands before shaping and baking, depending on the recipe.

Keep in mind ...

- There is no need to sift dry ingredients (except unsweetened cocoa powder, pure icing (confectioners') sugar and bicarbonate of soda/baking soda) before adding them to the bowl – the blade of the food processor will break down any lumps in ingredients like flour.
- As in most baking, eggs are best used at room temperature when making recipes based on this method. There is no need to lightly whisk the eggs before adding them unless the recipe asks you to do so.
- Recipes made in the food processor can use chilled, room temperature or melted butter. Take note of which one and stick to the recipe.
- For mixtures that incorporate the butter into the dry ingredients before blending with the wet ingredients, make sure the butter is cut into evenly sized pieces so that it will be mixed evenly.
- Don't overprocess your mixture if the recipe states to 'process/blend until just combined', especially if the mixture contains flour. This could result in a heavy, dense and unpalatable mixture.

- Make good use of the pulse button (pulse action), which allows you to continuously turn the blade movement on and off. This allows any mixture that is on the side of the bowl to drop down onto the blade and the bottom of the bowl in the main blending area. It will also allow you to monitor how well and quickly your mixture is being blended, so that you are less likely to overprocess it.
- Make sure the bowl of your food processor suits the quantity of mixture you are making – there is nothing more frustrating than finding your bowl isn't large enough to hold all the ingredients and blend them efficiently. A medium to large bowl is a good size for the recipes that follow.

Now get baking!

Once you get into the kitchen and start whipping up the following recipes with your food processor, you'll realise how handy this appliance is when baking.

Gingernut Biscuits

Well known in the biscuit aisle of the supermarket (and said to be the most popular biscuit in New Zealand), wonderfully spicy and beautifully bullet-hard gingernuts are perfect for dunking in your tea. Now it's time to make and dunk your own.

MAKES: ABOUT 32

Preparation time: 20 minutes (+ cooling time)   Baking time: 20–22 minutes

250 g (9 oz/1⅔ cups) plain (all-purpose) flour
3 teaspoons ground ginger
1 teaspoon ground cinnamon
½ teaspoon bicarbonate of soda (baking soda)
185 g (6½ oz/1 cup, lightly packed) brown sugar
125 g (4½ oz) chilled unsalted butter, cubed
2 tablespoons golden syrup (light treacle)
2 tablespoons boiling water

1   Preheat the oven to 180°C (350°F) or 160°C (315°F) fan-forced. Line two large baking trays with baking paper.

2   Process the flour, spices, bicarbonate of soda, sugar and butter in a food processor until the mixture resembles fine breadcrumbs.

3   Stir together the golden syrup and boiling water in a small bowl until well combined. Add to the flour mixture and process using the pulse button until the mixture just comes together. Transfer to a medium bowl.

4   Roll tablespoonfuls of the mixture into balls and place about 5 cm (2 in) apart on the lined trays then flatten them slightly until about 1 cm (½ in) thick.

5   Bake in the preheated oven for 20–22 minutes, swapping the trays around halfway through baking, or until golden brown and firm to the touch. Leave the biscuits to cool on the trays.

Baker's tips

● Keep in an airtight container at room temperature for up to 2 weeks.

● These gingernut biscuits are also great finished with the Lemon glaze on page 57. Use the back of a teaspoon to spread a little of the glaze over the top of each biscuit and then set aside for about 30 minutes for the glaze to set before serving or storing.

Whole Orange Cake

It's not a printing error – a whole orange, skin and all, goes into this cake. Thin-skinned navel oranges, which are in season around winter and spring, are the best to use as they have no seeds and very little bitter pith. The syrup keeps this cake deliciously moist so there's no need to ice it – but if you do want to, a buttercream or glaze icing flavoured with finely grated orange zest would be perfect.

SERVES: 8–10

Preparation time: 15 minutes   Baking time: 50–60 minutes

Melted butter, extra, to grease
1 navel orange, quartered, cored
   and seeds removed
220 g (7¾ oz/1 cup) caster (superfine) sugar
125 g (4½ oz) butter, melted and cooled
2 eggs, at room temperature
225 g (8 oz/1½ cups) self-raising flour

Orange syrup
250 ml (9 fl oz/1 cup) strained freshly
   squeezed orange juice
160 g (5¾ oz/½ cup) orange marmalade
75 g (2½ oz/⅓ cup) caster (superfine) sugar

Variations

Whole Blood Orange Cake – Replace the whole navel orange with a blood orange.

Whole Orange & Walnut Cake – Replace the butter with 100 ml (3½ fl oz) light olive oil, and replace the self-raising flour with 150 g (5½ oz/1 cup) wholemeal self-raising flour and 100 g (3½ oz) walnuts, toasted and finely ground. Serve dusted with icing (confectioners') sugar.

1 Preheat the oven to 170°C (325°F) or 150°C (300°F) fan-forced. Grease a 20 cm (8 in) round cake tin with melted butter and line the base with baking paper.

2 Place the quartered orange, sugar, butter and eggs in the bowl of a food processor. Process until the orange is finely chopped. Add the flour and process until just combined.

3 Pour the mixture into the prepared tin and use the back of a spoon to smooth the surface. Bake in the preheated oven for 50–60 minutes or until a skewer inserted in the centre comes out clean. Remove from the oven and leave to stand for 5 minutes before turning out onto a wire rack. Stand the rack over a baking tray.

4 Meanwhile, to make the Orange syrup, place the orange juice, marmalade and sugar in a small saucepan. Stir over medium heat until the sugar has dissolved. Increase the heat to high and bring to the boil. Boil gently, uncovered and without stirring, for 5 minutes or until reduced slightly.

5 Use a skewer to prick the cake all over. Pour the hot syrup evenly over the hot cake, allowing it to soak in. Serve warm or cool to room temperature with any syrup caught on the tray in a jug on the side.

Baker's tip

● This cake will keep in an airtight container at room temperature for up to 4 days.

Roasted Nectarine & Almond Tart

I love this tart for many reasons, starting with how simple it is to make the pastry, thanks to the food processor, and how you just use your fingers to press it into the tin.

SERVES: 8–10

Preparation time: 25 minutes (+ 30 minutes cooling and 40 minutes chilling time)   Baking time: 50–55 minutes

35 g (1¼ oz/⅓ cup) flaked almonds
Icing (confectioners') sugar, to dust
Vanilla ice cream, cream or sweetened
   Greek-style natural yoghurt, to serve

Almond pastry
100 g (3½ oz) unsalted butter,
   at room temperature, cubed
55 g (2 oz/¼ cup) caster (superfine) sugar
1 teaspoon natural vanilla extract or essence
1 egg yolk, at room temperature
150 g (5½ oz/1 cup) plain (all-purpose) flour
35 g (1¼ oz/⅓ cup) almond meal
1½ teaspoons baking powder

Roasted nectarines
700 g (1 lb 9 oz) nectarines, stones removed
   and each cut into 8 wedges
2 tablespoons honey
1 teaspoon natural vanilla extract or essence
2 cinnamon sticks
20 g (¾ oz) butter, cubed

1 To make the Roasted nectarines, preheat the oven to 180°C (350°F) or 160°C (315°F) fan-forced. Combine the nectarines, honey and vanilla in a bowl and toss to coat. Arrange the nectarines in a single layer in an ovenproof dish. Pour the honey mixture over. Add the cinnamon sticks and dot with the butter. Cook in the preheated oven for 20 minutes or until the nectarines are just tender when tested with a skewer. Leave to cool to room temperature (about 30 minutes). Discard the cinnamon sticks.

2 Meanwhile, to make the Almond pastry, process the butter, sugar and vanilla in a food processor until pale and creamy. Add the egg yolk and process until well combined, scraping down the side of the bowl when necessary. Combine the flour, almond meal and baking powder in a separate bowl. Add to the butter mixture and pulse until the mixture just starts to come together. Turn the mixture into a bowl and bring together with your hands to form a soft dough. Take a quarter of the pastry (for the topping), shape into a disc and wrap in plastic wrap. Shape the remaining pastry into another disc and wrap in plastic wrap. Put both portions in the fridge to chill for 40 minutes.

3 Increase the oven temperature to 190°C (375°F) or 170°C (325°F) fan-forced. Remove the larger pastry portion from the fridge. Pinch off small amounts of the pastry and press into an ungreased round 23 cm (9 in, base measurement) tart (flan) tin with a removable base. Use your fingertips to flatten the pastry to about 5 mm (¼ in) thick. Place the tin on a baking tray. Drain the cooled Roasted nectarines, reserving any syrup for serving, and arrange the nectarines in the pastry case.

4 Take the remaining portion of chilled pastry from the fridge and coarsely grate it over the top of the nectarines to roughly cover. Scatter over the flaked almonds.

5 Bake in the preheated oven for 50–55 minutes or until the pastry is golden and cooked through. Leave to stand on a wire rack until cooled to room temperature.

6 Dust with icing sugar and serve in wedges with ice cream, cream or yoghurt, and reserved syrup in a jug on the side.

Baker's tips

● This tart can be served warm, however it will be a little fragile to handle, so use a spatula to help serve the slices.

● It will keep in an airtight container in the fridge for 3 days. Stand at room temperature for 20 minutes before serving.

Lemon & Blueberry Cheesecake

Bringing together sweet blueberries and sour lemons, this simple cheesecake
is light but luscious. It's the perfect end to a lazy summer meal.

Preparation time: 25 minutes (+ 1 hour cooling and 3 hours chilling time)   Baking time: 1 hour 10 minutes

Melted butter, extra, to grease
375 g (13 oz) cream cheese, at room
   temperature, cubed (*see Baker's tips*)
3 eggs, at room temperature
185 g (6½ oz/¾ cup) sour cream
125 ml (4 fl oz/½ cup) thin (pouring) cream
165 g (5¾ oz/¾ cup) caster (superfine) sugar
1 tablespoon finely grated lemon zest
2 tablespoons freshly squeezed lemon juice
200 g (7 oz) fresh or frozen blueberries
   (*see Baker's tips*)
Icing (confectioners') sugar, to dust

Biscuit base
100 g (3½ oz) plain sweet biscuits
60 g (2¼ oz) butter, melted

Variations

Orange & Raspberry Cheesecake – Replace the lemon
zest and juice with orange zest and juice. Replace the
blueberries with fresh or frozen raspberries.

Blueberry & White Chocolate Cheesecake – Replace the
lemon zest and juice with 1½ teaspoons natural vanilla
extract or essence. Melt 180 g (6 oz) good-quality white
chocolate and cool to room temperature. Add to the
bowl of the food processor just before transferring the
mixture to the tin and process until just combined.

Individual Lemon & Blueberry Cheesecakes – Line a
12-hole 80 ml (2½ fl oz/⅓ cup) capacity muffin tin with
paper cases. Divide the biscuit base, cream cheese
mixture and blueberries evenly among the cases.
Bake at 160°C (315°F) for 30 minutes. Cool as per the
recipe, then chill in the fridge for at least 1 hour before
removing the paper cases and serving.

1 Preheat the oven to 150°C (300°F). Line the base
of a 20 cm (8 in) spring-form cake tin with baking
paper. Brush the side of the tin with a little melted
butter to grease.

2 To make the Biscuit base, process the biscuits in a
food processor until finely crushed. Add the butter
and process until well combined. Sprinkle the mixture
over the base of the tin and use the back of a metal spoon
or the base of a glass to press down to cover evenly. Put
the tin on a baking tray and place in the fridge.

3 Clean the food processor bowl and process the cream
cheese until smooth. Add the eggs and process until
smooth. Add the sour cream, thin cream, sugar, lemon
zest and juice and process until well combined and
smooth, scraping down the side and base of the bowl
when necessary. Pour into the tin over the base.
Scatter the blueberries over the top.

4 Bake for 1 hour 10 minutes or until the cheesecake is
just set but the centre trembles slightly when the tin is
shaken gently. Turn off the oven, use a wooden spoon to
keep the oven door ajar and leave the cheesecake in the
oven for 1 hour (this helps prevent the cheesecake from
cracking). Transfer the cheesecake, still in the tin, to
the fridge and chill for at least 3 hours or until well chilled.
Dust with icing sugar and serve.

Baker's tips

● Having the cream cheese at room temperature means it
will easily become smooth and creamy in the food processor.
If you use it straight from the fridge it will take longer and
you'll need to scrape the side and base of the food processor
frequently so that no lumps are left after processing.

● If using frozen blueberries, use them straight from the
freezer – do not thaw.

Berry & Coconut Slice

You may know this type of slice – old-fashioned, simple and hard to beat. It is particularly good for morning or afternoon tea with a cuppa, on a picnic or as a cake stall offering. Feel free to use any berry jam you wish – blackberry, raspberry and dark cherry all work really well, too.

MAKES: ABOUT 15 PIECES

Preparation time: 20 minutes   Baking time: 48–55 minutes

Melted butter, to grease
320 g (11¼ oz/1 cup) mixed berry jam

Base
225 g (8 oz/1½ cups) plain (all-purpose) flour
75 g (2½ oz/⅓ cup) caster (superfine) sugar
80 g (2¾ oz) chilled butter, cubed
1 egg, at room temperature
1 teaspoon natural vanilla extract or essence

Topping
180 g (6 oz/2 cups) desiccated coconut
55 g (2 oz/¼ cup) caster (superfine) sugar
3 eggs, at room temperature, lightly whisked

Baker's tips

● You can roll a straight-sided glass over the base of the slice to ensure it is even.

● This slice will keep in an airtight container at room temperature for up to 5 days.

1 Preheat the oven to 200°C (400°F) or 180°C (350°F) fan-forced. Grease a 16 cm x 26 cm (6¼ in x 10½ in, base measurement) shallow slice tin with melted butter and line the base and sides with one piece of baking paper, cutting into the corners to fit.

2 To make the Base, combine the flour, sugar and butter in the bowl of a food processor and process until the mixture resembles fine breadcrumbs. Lightly whisk the egg with the vanilla. Add to the flour mixture and pulse until evenly combined and the mixture just starts to come together. Tip the base mixture into the prepared tin and use your hands to press it evenly over the base (see Baker's tips). Bake in the preheated oven for 18–20 minutes or until golden around the edge.

3 Meanwhile, to make the Topping, combine the coconut, sugar and egg in a bowl and use a fork to mix until evenly combined.

4 Remove the base from the oven and reduce the temperature to 170°C (325°F) or 150°C (300°F) fan-forced. Use the back of a spoon to spread the jam evenly over the base. Spoon the topping over the jam and use the back of a clean spoon to spread evenly to cover, pressing it down with the back of the spoon if you would like a smooth top.

5 Return the slice to the oven and bake for 30–35 minutes or until the topping is golden and the base is cooked through. Remove the slice from the oven, place the tin on a wire rack and leave to cool in the tin. Once cool, cut into portions to serve.

Almond & Mango Cake

If you are looking for a quick, easy and impressive cake, this is the one. Lots of clever shortcuts – such as using your food processor to make it – means this cake will be in the oven in 15 minutes or so.

SERVES: 8–10

Preparation time: 15 minutes (+ 5 minutes standing time)   Baking time: 40 minutes

Melted butter, to grease
100 g (3½ oz) chilled unsalted butter, cubed
110 g (3¾ oz/½ cup) caster (superfine) sugar
80 g (2¾ oz/¾ cup) almond meal
75 g (2½ oz/½ cup) plain (all-purpose) flour
1 teaspoon baking powder
2 eggs, at room temperature
1 firm ripe mango (about 350 g/12 oz), cheeks peeled and sliced (you will need about 150 g/5½ oz flesh)
25 g (1 oz/¼ cup) flaked almonds
Icing (confectioners') sugar, to dust

1 Preheat the oven to 180°C (350°F) or 160°C (315°F) fan-forced. Grease a 20 cm (8 in, base measurement) spring-form cake tin with the melted butter and line the base with baking paper.

2 Put the butter, caster sugar, almond meal, flour and baking powder in the bowl of a food processor. Process until well combined and the mixture resembles fine breadcrumbs. Add the eggs and pulse until smooth and just combined.

3 Spoon the mixture into the prepared tin and smooth the surface with the back of a spoon. Arrange the mango slices over the top then use the back of a clean spoon to press the mango into the cake mixture slightly. Scatter over the almonds.

4 Bake for 40 minutes or until golden and a skewer inserted in the centre comes out clean.

5 Leave the cake to stand in the tin for 5 minutes before removing the side of the tin and placing the cake (still on the base) on a wire rack. Serve warm or at room temperature, dusted with icing sugar.

Baker's tip

● This cake will keep in an airtight container in a cool place (but not in the fridge) for up to 3 days.

Quick-mix Almond Shortbread

The method used to make this shortbread is fast and simple. Basically all you need is a food processor to get the mixing done quickly. You do need to chill the dough before slicing it into the biscuit shapes – so it's a perfect make-ahead recipe and you can keep the dough in the fridge or freezer until you want to cook the shortbread.

MAKES: ABOUT 30

Preparation time: 15 minutes (+1 hour chilling and cooling time)   Baking time: 35 minutes

150 g (5½ oz) butter, cubed
110 g (3¾ oz/½ cup) caster (superfine) sugar, plus extra to sprinkle
150 g (5½ oz/1 cup) plain (all-purpose) flour, plus extra to dust
30 g (1 oz/¼ cup) cornflour (cornstarch)
70 g (2½ oz/⅔ cup) almond meal
1 teaspoon natural vanilla extract or essence

Variations

Quick-mix Almond & Citrus Shortbread – Replace the vanilla with 2 teaspoons finely grated lemon, orange or mandarin zest.

Quick-mix Chocolate & Hazelnut Shortbread – Replace 35 g (1¼ oz/¼ cup) plain (all-purpose) flour with 30 g (1 oz/¼ cup) sifted unsweetened cocoa powder and replace the almond meal with the same quantity of hazelnut meal.

Quick-mix Pistachio & Cardamom Shortbread – Replace the vanilla with ½ teaspoon ground cardamom. In step 2, add 70 g (2½ oz/½ cup) pistachio kernels, chopped, and mix in as you knead until evenly combined. Continue with the recipe.

1 Place all the ingredients in the bowl of a food processor and process for 1 minute or until the mixture starts to form a dough – be careful not to overmix.

2 Turn the mixture onto a lightly floured bench top and knead gently with your fingertips until smooth. Divide into 2 equal portions and roll into thick sausages 4 cm (1½ in) in diameter and 15 cm (6 in) long. Wrap in plastic wrap and place in the fridge for at least 1 hour or until ready to bake.

3 Preheat the oven to 160°C (315°F) or 140°C (275°F) fan-forced. Line two large baking trays with baking paper.

4 Unwrap the biscuit dough and slice into 1 cm (½ in) thick rounds. Place on the baking trays about 2 cm (1 in) apart to allow for spreading. Sprinkle each biscuit with a little extra caster sugar.

5 Bake for 35 minutes, swapping the trays halfway through baking, or until the shortbread is pale golden and cooked through. Leave the shortbread to cool on the trays.

Baker's tips

● The uncooked dough, rolled into logs and wrapped well in plastic wrap, can be kept in the fridge for up to 1 week. It can also be frozen, sealed in an airtight container or freezer bags, for up to 1 month. Thaw in the fridge before slicing and baking.

● These shortbread will keep in an airtight container or jar for up to 2 weeks.

Belgian Tart

I *love* this tart – a no-fuss slice-like affair of buttery shortbread layers filled with apricot jam and topped with peanuts. Research has revealed no reason why the tart is Belgian but it brings back vivid childhood memories of Mum making it in two enamel plates, throwing them in the oven and then, once cool, covering them with foil to take to a picnic or tennis day. I can picture it all so clearly when I make the same tart now (with a few small alterations) in my own kitchen.

SERVES: 8–10

Preparation time: 20 minutes (+ cooling time)   Baking time: 35 minutes

185 g (6½ oz) butter, slightly softened, cubed
150 g (5½ oz/⅔ cup) caster (superfine) sugar
1 teaspoon natural vanilla extract or essence
1 egg yolk, at room temperature
260 g (9¼ oz/1¾ cups) plain
   (all-purpose) flour
1 teaspoon baking powder
165 g (5¾ oz/½ cup) apricot jam
   (*see Baker's tips*)
70 g (2½ oz/½ cup) unsalted raw peanuts

1   Preheat the oven to 160°C (315°F) or 140°C (275°F) fan-forced.

2   Put the butter and sugar in the bowl of a food processor and process until well combined. Add the vanilla and the egg yolk and process to combine, scraping down the side of the bowl if necessary. Sift together the flour and baking powder. Add to the butter mixture and pulse until just combined and a soft dough forms.

3   Press half of the mixture evenly over the base of an ungreased 23 cm (9 in, base measurement) tart (flan) tin with a removable base. Spread evenly with the jam, leaving a 2 cm (¾ in) border. Press portions of the remaining dough between your hands to flatten and press over the jam to cover, patching where necessary. Scatter over the peanuts and press into the dough.

4   Place the tart tin on a baking tray and bake in the preheated oven for 35 minutes or until golden and cooked through. Leave the tart to cool in the tin. Serve in wedges.

Baker's tips

● Use any jam you like instead of the apricot jam – fig, blackberry and mixed berry all work well.

● This tart will keep in an airtight container at room temperature for up to 4 days.

Date & Orange Loaf

Moist, full of flavour and such a simple recipe, I know this loaf will
become a favourite after just the first mouthful.

Preparation time: 20 minutes (+ cooling time)   Baking time: 50 minutes

Melted butter, extra, to grease

1 orange, zest finely grated, and peeled,
   seeded and chopped

220 g (7¾ oz/1 cup, firmly packed)
   brown sugar

80 g (2¾ oz) butter, melted

1 egg, at room temperature

170 ml (5½ fl oz/⅔ cup) milk

100 g (3½ oz) dried pitted dates, chopped

150 g (5½ oz/1 cup) wholemeal plain
   (all-purpose) flour

75 g (2½ oz/½ cup) plain (all-purpose) flour

1½ teaspoons baking powder

½ teaspoon bicarbonate of soda
   (baking soda)

Icing (confectioners') sugar, to dust

1 Preheat the oven to 180°C (350°F) or 160°C (315°F)
   fan-forced. Grease a 9 cm x 19 cm (3½ in x 7½ in,
   base measurement) loaf (bar) tin with melted butter
   and line the base and two long sides with one piece
   of baking paper.

2 Put the orange zest and flesh, brown sugar, butter and
   egg in the bowl of a food processor and process until
   well combined and smooth. Add the milk and dates
   and process until just combined. Add the flours, baking
   powder and bicarbonate of soda and pulse until
   just combined.

3 Pour the cake batter into the prepared tin and smooth
   the surface. Bake in the preheated oven for 50 minutes
   or until a skewer inserted in the centre comes out clean.

4 Leave the loaf to stand in the tin for 5 minutes before
   turning out onto a wire rack to cool completely. Dust
   with icing sugar and serve in slices.

Baker's tip

● This loaf will keep in an airtight container at room
temperature for up to 5 days, but after the first day it
is best toasted and eaten plain or spread with butter.

Lesson 5

The Creaming Method

This method involves beating butter and sugar together using an electric mixer until they are 'creamed'. Eggs are then gradually beaten in, followed by the flour and other ingredients such as milk.

Creaming butter and sugar together, usually until the mixture is pale in colour and light or 'creamy' in consistency, adds to the lightness of the final result and makes it easier to incorporate other ingredients, such as eggs, milk and flour. How 'creamy' a butter and sugar mixture becomes depends on the proportions of ingredients used – the more sugar, the less 'creamy' it will become.

Recipes for a variety of cakes, biscuits, loaves, puddings and slices use this method. It is also used when making buttercream icing, so in the recipe on page 125 for Melting Moments you will be able to practise this method twice in one recipe.

You will need an electric mixer for this method – our grandmothers used a wooden spoon but it does take a lot of muscle to reach the right consistency this way. Either a stand mixer or hand-held beaters will do the trick.

Step by step

1 Use an electric mixer to beat the butter and sugar.

2 Scrape down the side of the bowl when necessary.

3 Keep beating until the mixture is pale and creamy and has increased slightly in volume, or until directed in the recipe. Don't rush this step – make sure you beat until the right consistency, as described in the recipe, is reached. Taking shortcuts will affect the final texture of your baked

item. Changes in consistency and colour are essential and can take some time.

4 Add the eggs, if using, one at a time.

5 Beat well after each addition until the mixture is smooth and creamy.

6 Use a spatula or large metal spoon to gently fold the dry ingredients into the butter mixture, or briefly beat on low speed using the electric mixer as directed, depending on the recipe.

7 Add the milk, or other liquid, with the dry ingredients as directed – the recipe may call for all the flour to be added and then the milk, or for portions of the flour and milk to be added alternately, and then folded, beaten or mixed in, using a wooden spoon or even your hands, until just combined.

8 Gently fold or beat in any remaining ingredients until just combined. The mixture is now ready to bake.

it is soft enough to spread is the best method to get the butter to the right consistency. But you can soften butter quickly by either cutting it into small cubes or coarsely grating it and leaving it to stand at room temperature for 5–10 minutes.

- Choose the paddle attachment if using a stand mixer and the standard beaters if using hand-held electric beaters.

- If you are using hand-held electric beaters you may have to beat the mixture for a few more minutes than stated in the recipe to reach the desired consistency.

- As with most baking, eggs are best used at room temperature when making recipes based on this method. There is no need to lightly whisk the eggs before adding them.

Now get baking!

Okay, let's get into the kitchen so you can familiarise yourself with the creaming method. There are plenty of recipes using this method on the following pages – from wonderfully scented butter cakes to completely indulgent chocolate cookies. There couldn't possibly be better reasons to master this technique.

Keep in mind ...

- The butter should always be at room temperature. If it is chilled too firm it will be hard to beat and to incorporate air into, and a light 'creamy' texture won't be achieved. Also, if the butter is too cold the mixture will curdle when the eggs are added, possibly resulting in a cake with a heavy, coarse and uneven texture.

- If you forget to take the butter out of the fridge ahead of time, don't put it in the microwave to soften it quickly,

as a microwave will often heat things unevenly so the butter may start to melt in some parts before others have softened. The structure of the butter changes if it is warmed too much and melts, making it almost impossible to incorporate air into. Using melted or partially melted butter in the creaming method will result in a heavy and 'greasy' baked product.

- Standing the butter at room temperature for around 1 hour (depending on the weather) or until

Pound Cake

Back in 18th-century England, this simple but by no means ordinary cake was made with equal quantities of butter, sugar, eggs and flour – a pound of each!

SERVES: 10

Preparation time: 20 minutes (+ cooling time)   Baking time: 50–55 minutes

Melted butter, to grease
250 g (9 oz) butter, at room temperature, cubed
220 g (7¾ oz/1 cup) caster (superfine) sugar
1½ teaspoons natural vanilla extract or essence
4 eggs, at room temperature
250 g (9 oz/1⅔ cups) plain (all-purpose) flour
2½ teaspoons baking powder
2 tablespoons milk
Icing (confectioners') sugar, to dust

1 Preheat the oven to 180°C (350°F) or 160°C (315°F) fan-forced. Grease a 20 cm (8 in, base measurement) round cake tin with melted butter and line the base with baking paper.

2 Using an electric mixer, beat the butter, sugar and vanilla in a large bowl until pale and creamy.

3 Add the eggs one at a time, beating well after each addition.

4 Sift together the flour and baking powder. Use a large metal spoon or spatula to fold half the flour mixture through the butter mixture. Fold in the milk and then the remaining flour mixture until just combined.

5 Spoon the batter into the prepared tin and smooth the surface with the back of a spoon. Bake in the preheated oven for 50–55 minutes or until a skewer inserted in the centre comes out clean.

6 Leave to stand in the tin for 5 minutes before turning out onto a wire rack to cool. Dust with icing sugar before serving in wedges.

Variations

Chocolate Pound Cake – Increase the caster sugar to 275 g (9¾ oz/1¼ cups). Reduce the plain (all-purpose) flour to 185 g (6½ oz/1¼ cups). Increase the milk to 125 ml (4 fl oz/½ cup) and mix to a smooth paste with 50 g (1¾ oz/½ cup) sifted unsweetened cocoa powder, and fold into the batter after the first addition of flour. Bake for 1 hour–1 hour 5 minutes.

Blackberry Pound Cake – Toss 150 g (5½ oz) fresh or frozen blackberries with 1 tablespoon of the flour. Fold these in after folding in all the flour. Bake for 1¼ hours.

Lemon Drizzle Pound Cake – Replace the vanilla with the finely grated zest of 1 lemon and replace the milk with 2 tablespoons freshly squeezed lemon juice. Combine 55 g (2 oz/¼ cup) caster (superfine) sugar and 2 tablespoons freshly squeezed lemon juice in a small saucepan and stir over medium heat until the sugar has dissolved. Remove the glaze from the heat and set aside until the cake is cooked. Brush the top of the cake with some lemon glaze immediately after removing from the oven. Brush the cake with the remaining glaze once removed from the tin. Set aside to cool.

Baker's tip

● This cake will keep in an airtight container at room temperature for up to 2 days.

Danish Apple Cake

Its simplicity is what makes this cake so special. A humble but delicious butter cake layered with sliced apples and a sprinkling of sugar and cinnamon, it will have you coming back time and time again.

SERVES: 10

Preparation time: 25 minutes (+ 10 minutes standing time)   Baking time: 55–60 minutes

Melted butter, to grease
185 g (6½ oz) butter, at room
    temperature, cubed
165 g (5¾ oz/¾ cup) caster (superfine) sugar,
    plus 75 g (2½ oz/⅓ cup) extra
2 teaspoons natural vanilla extract
    or essence
3 eggs, at room temperature
185 g (6½ oz/1¼ cups) plain
    (all-purpose) flour
1 teaspoon baking powder
2 teaspoons ground cinnamon
5 sweet eating apples (about 800 g/1 lb 12 oz
    in total), such as pink lady or royal gala,
    peeled, cored and each cut into 16 wedges

1 Preheat the oven to 180°C (350°F) or 160°C (315°F) fan-forced. Grease a 22 cm (8½ in, base measurement) spring-form cake tin with melted butter and line the base with baking paper.

2 Use an electric mixer to beat the butter, sugar and vanilla until pale and creamy. Add the eggs one at a time, beating well after each addition. Sift together the flour and baking powder. Add to the butter mixture and mix on low speed until just combined.

3 Combine the extra caster sugar and cinnamon and set aside. Spread half the cake batter over the base of the prepared tin. Arrange half the apples over the batter and sprinkle with half the cinnamon sugar. Repeat with the remaining cake batter, apples and cinnamon sugar.

4 Bake in the preheated oven for 55–60 minutes or until a skewer inserted in the centre comes out clean, covering with a piece of foil in the last 15 minutes of baking if the cake is browning too quickly. Leave to stand in the tin for 10 minutes before transferring to a wire rack. Serve warm or at room temperature, on its own or with thick cream or vanilla ice cream.

Baker's tip

● This cake will keep in an airtight container at room temperature for up to 2 days.

Melting Moments

My husband, Paul, is quite partial to these melt-in-the-mouth biscuits sandwiched with sweet buttercream. I am, too. My mum's version, which we called radio biscuits, contained custard powder and possibly came from the Country Women's Association cookbook she and I used a lot. Mine have orange zest in the filling for a citrus tang.

MAKES: ABOUT 18

Preparation time: 40 minutes   Baking time: 16–18 minutes

250 g (9 oz) butter, at room
    temperature, cubed
125 g (4½ oz/1 cup) icing (confectioners')
    sugar, sifted
1½ teaspoons natural vanilla extract
    or essence
250 g (9 oz/1⅔ cups) plain (all-purpose) flour
60 g (2¼ oz/½ cup) cornflour (cornstarch)

Orange buttercream filling
60 g (2¼ oz) butter, at room temperature
Finely grated zest of 1 orange
125 g (4½ oz/1 cup) icing (confectioners')
    sugar, sifted

1   Preheat the oven to 160°C (315°F) or 140°C (275°F) fan-forced. Line two large baking trays with baking paper.

2   Use an electric mixer to beat the butter, icing sugar and vanilla until pale and creamy, scraping down the side of the bowl when necessary.

3   Sift the flour and cornflour together over the butter mixture. Mix on low speed (or use your hands to mix) until just combined and a soft dough forms.

4   Use lightly floured hands to roll heaped teaspoonfuls of the mixture into balls and place on the lined trays, about 5 cm (2 in) apart (you should have about 36 balls). Dip a fork in flour and use it to flatten the balls to about 1 cm (½ in) thick and 4 cm (1½ in) in diameter.

5   Bake in the preheated oven for 16–18 minutes, swapping the trays after 8 minutes, or until the biscuits are pale golden and cooked through. Remove from the oven and cool on the trays.

6   While the biscuits are cooling, make the Orange buttercream filling. Use an electric mixer to beat the butter and orange zest in a small bowl until pale and creamy. Add the icing sugar and beat on low speed, scraping down the side of the bowl when necessary, until well combined and smooth.

7   Spread a little buttercream on the base of a cooled biscuit and sandwich together with another biscuit. Repeat with the remaining biscuits and filling.

Variations

Coffee Melting Moments – Replace the orange zest in the filling with 1 teaspoon instant coffee granules dissolved in 1 teaspoon boiling water, cooled before using.

Lemon Melting Moments – Replace the orange zest in the filling with the finely grated zest of 1 large lemon.

Passionfruit Melting Moments – Replace the orange zest in the filling with 1 tablespoon passionfruit pulp.

Baker's tip

● These biscuits will keep in a jar or airtight container in a cool place (but not in the fridge) for up to 4 days.

Chocolate Chunk & Walnut Fudge Cookies

Deliciously decadent cookies not for the faint-hearted, these are incredibly versatile too – try pecans, hazelnuts (toasted and peeled) or macadamias instead of the walnuts, or replace the 150 g (5½ oz) of dark chocolate chunks with milk or white chocolate, or even a mixture of all three!

MAKES: ABOUT 35

Preparation time: 25 minutes (+ 20 minutes cooling and 1 hour chilling)   Baking time: 10–12 minutes (per batch)

450 g (1 lb/3 cups) coarsely chopped good-quality dark chocolate

125 g (4½ oz) butter, at room temperature, cubed

110 g (3¾ oz/½ cup, firmly packed) brown sugar

2 eggs, at room temperature

225 g (8 oz/1½ cups) plain (all-purpose) flour

½ teaspoon baking powder

90 g (3¼ oz/¾ cup) coarsely chopped toasted walnuts

Variations

White Chocolate Chunk & Macadamia Fudge Cookies
Replace the 150 g (5½ oz/1 cup) chopped dark chocolate (added to the mixture in Step 4) with 150 g (5½ oz) chopped white chocolate and replace the walnuts with 95 g (3¼ oz/¾ cup) coarsely chopped toasted unsalted macadamia nuts.

Double Chocolate Fudge Cookies – Replace the 150 g (5½ oz/1 cup) chopped dark chocolate (added to the mixture in Step 4) with 150 g (5½ oz/1 cup) chopped milk chocolate. Omit the walnuts.

Baker's tip

● Keep these cookies in an airtight container in a cool place (but not in the fridge) for up to 2 weeks.

1 Put 300 g (10½ oz/2 cups) of the dark chocolate in a heatproof bowl over a saucepan of simmering water, making sure the base of the bowl doesn't touch the water. Use a metal spoon to stir over low heat until the chocolate is melted and smooth. Remove from the heat and set aside, stirring occasionally, for 20 minutes or until cooled to room temperature.

2 Use an electric mixer to beat the butter and sugar in a medium bowl, scraping down the side of the bowl when necessary, until just combined.

3 Add the eggs one at a time, beating well after each addition until well combined. Add the cooled chocolate and beat until combined.

4 Sift the flour and baking powder together over the cookie mixture. Add the remaining 150 g (5½ oz/1 cup) coarsely chopped dark chocolate and the walnuts. Use a wooden spoon to stir until evenly combined.

5 Cover the bowl with plastic wrap and place in the fridge for 1 hour or until the mixture is firm enough to roll into balls.

6 Preheat the oven to 180°C (350°F) or 160°C (315°F) fan-forced. Line a large baking tray with baking paper.

7 Roll heaped tablespoonfuls of the mixture into balls and place 5 cm (2 in) apart on the tray for the first batch. Return any remaining dough to the fridge. Use your hands to flatten the balls slightly, to about 4 cm (1½ in) in diameter. Bake in the preheated oven for 10–12 minutes or until the cookies are still slightly soft to touch.

8 Remove the cookies from the oven and leave to cool completely on the tray. Repeat with the remaining dough in two more batches.

Fig & Cranberry Christmas Cake

Traditional rich fruitcake is such a joy at Christmas time. Dense with brandy-soaked fruit and spices, a little goes a long way. Mine has the addition of cranberries and orange for a modern twist to an old favourite. The coarsely chopped nuts on top make a lovely fuss-free decoration.

MAKES: 20 CM (8 IN) SQUARE
OR 22 CM (8½ IN) ROUND CAKE
(ABOUT 30 PIECES)

Preparation time: 30 minutes (+ overnight soaking and overnight cooling)   Baking time: 3½–4 hours

300 g (10½ oz) dried figs
200 g (7 oz) pitted prunes
200 g (7 oz) seedless raisins
300 g (10½ oz) dried cranberries
200 g (7 oz) sultanas (golden raisins)
100 g (3½ oz) currants
110 g (3¾ oz/⅓ cup) fig jam
Finely grated zest and juice of 1 orange
185 ml (6 fl oz/¾ cup) brandy or orange
    liqueur, plus 60 ml (2 fl oz/¼ cup) extra
185 g (6½ oz) unsalted butter, at
    room temperature, cubed
110 g (3¾ oz/½ cup, firmly packed)
    brown sugar
1½ teaspoons natural vanilla extract
    or essence
4 eggs, at room temperature
200 g (7 oz) blanched almonds (optional),
    plus 160 g extra, coarsely chopped,
    to decorate (optional)
225 g (8 oz/1½ cups) plain (all-purpose) flour
50 g (1¾ oz/½ cup) almond or hazelnut meal
½ teaspoon baking powder
2 teaspoons ground cinnamon
1 teaspoon mixed spice
½ teaspoon ground ginger
2 tablespoons apricot jam or marmalade,
    warmed and sieved, to glaze

1 Chop the figs, prunes and raisins to the same size as the sultanas. Put in a large bowl with the cranberries, sultanas, currants, jam, orange zest and juice, and brandy. Cover and set aside at room temperature at least overnight (see Baker's tips, page 131).

2 Position the oven rack so the middle of the cake will sit in the centre of the oven, and preheat the oven to 150°C (300°F). Grease and line the base and sides of a 20 cm (8 in) square or 22 cm (8½ in) round cake tin with baking paper and wrap the tin to protect the cake (see Preparing a cake tin for a rich fruitcake, page 131).

3 Use an electric mixer to beat the butter, sugar and vanilla until pale and creamy. Add the eggs one at a time, beating well after each addition (the mixture will appear curdled). Use a wooden spoon to stir in the soaked fruit and almonds (if using).

4 In a separate bowl, whisk together the flour, almond meal, baking powder and spices to combine evenly. Add to the fruit mixture and use the wooden spoon and then your hands to mix lightly until well combined.

Recipe continued overleaf →

Baker's tips

● You can soak the fruit in Step 1 for up to 2 weeks, stirring occasionally.

● You can also serve this cake with vanilla ice cream as a festive dessert.

● The cake will keep wrapped in plastic wrap and then foil in an airtight container for up to 6 weeks. If you omit the whole almonds in the mixture and the chopped almonds on top, it will keep for up to 3 months.

● You can use this mixture to make five small individual cakes – the perfect size for gifts. Grease and line the base and side of 5 x 10 cm (4 in) round or square cake tins with baking paper (no need to wrap them in newspaper). Divide the mixture among the tins, cover with foil and bake for 1 hour. Remove the foil and bake for another 45 minutes, or until a skewer inserted in the centre of a cake comes out clean.

5 Spoon the mixture into the prepared tin and press firmly into the corners. Lift and gently drop the tin on the bench top 4–5 times to get rid of any air pockets. Smooth the surface and decorate with the extra chopped almonds (if using). Put the tin on the magazine on the tray (see instructions below) and cover the cake with a piece of foil. Bake in the preheated oven for 2 hours. Remove the foil and continue to bake for a further 1½–2 hours or until a skewer inserted in the centre comes out clean.

6 Pour the extra brandy evenly over the top of the hot cake. Trim any overhanging paper, cover the tin with foil and then wrap in two tea towels (dish towels). Leave to cool overnight.

7 Unwrap the cake, brush the top with the warmed and sieved jam, and cut into slices.

Preparing a cake tin for a rich fruitcake

I was taught this method many years ago by CWA judge Norma Allen. It is far quicker than using multiple layers of brown paper and will effectively protect your cake during the long, slow baking – the aim being to stop the outside from browning too much before the centre of the cake is cooked.

● Grease the cake tin and line the base and side with baking paper, allowing the paper to reach about 5 cm (2 in) above the top of the tin.

● Lay 4 sheets of newspaper on top of one another. Fold the paper lengthways into thirds (you will end up with a 12-layer strip of paper). Repeat with another 4 sheets of newspaper. Wrap one of the newspaper strips around the outside of the tin, then wrap the other strip around the other side so the whole tin is covered. Keep them in place with ovenproof sticky tape and secure firmly with several rounds of kitchen string, tied tightly.

● Place an old magazine on a baking tray and sit the lined tin on top ready for baking.

Sticky Toffee Pudding

Hailing from the 1970s and reaching peak popularity in the '90s, this pudding now sits alongside the likes of lemon delicious, rice pudding and chocolate fondants as a classic. Sweet, sticky and completely addictive, it is always a crowd-pleaser.

SERVES: 8

Preparation time: 20 minutes (+ 25 minutes cooling time)   Baking time: 30 minutes

200 g (7 oz) fresh dates, pitted and chopped
250 ml (9 fl oz/1 cup) water
1 teaspoon bicarbonate of soda
   (baking soda)
100 g (3½ oz) unsalted butter,
   at room temperature, cubed
165 g (5¾ oz/¾ cup, firmly packed)
   brown sugar
2 eggs, at room temperature
150 g (5½ oz/1 cup) self-raising flour
Vanilla ice cream or cream, to serve

Toffee sauce
100 g (3½ oz) unsalted butter, cubed
220 g (7¾ oz/1 cup, firmly packed)
   brown sugar
250 ml (9 fl oz/1 cup) thin (pouring) cream

Baker's tips

● In Step 2 you can put the date mixture in the fridge to cool it more quickly.

● Any leftover pudding and sauce will keep in separate airtight containers in the fridge for up to 4 days. Reheat both separately in the microwave on medium in 1-minute bursts until warmed through.

1 Preheat the oven to 180°C (350°F) or 160°C (315°F) fan-forced. Grease a 16 cm x 26 cm (6¼ in x 10½ in) shallow cake tin with melted butter and line the base and two long sides with one piece of baking paper, allowing the paper to overhang the sides.

2 Put the dates and water in a small saucepan over medium heat. Bring to the boil, reduce the heat and simmer for 3–5 minutes, or until pulpy. Stir in the bicarbonate of soda and set aside for 20 minutes, or until cooled to room temperature (see Baker's tips).

3 Use an electric mixer to beat the butter and sugar in a medium bowl until pale and creamy. Add the eggs one at a time, beating well after each addition. Use a large metal spoon or spatula to fold in the cooled date mixture. Add the flour and fold in until just combined.

4 Spoon the mixture into the prepared tin and smooth the surface with the back of a spoon. Bake in the preheated oven for 30 minutes, or until a skewer inserted in the centre of the pudding comes out clean.

5 Meanwhile, to make the Toffee sauce, put the butter, sugar and cream in a medium saucepan over medium heat. Stir until the butter has melted and the sugar has dissolved. Bring just to the boil, reduce the heat and simmer for 3 minutes.

6 Remove the pudding from the oven, leave in the tin and pour over a quarter of the hot Toffee sauce. Set aside for 5 minutes. Remove the warm pudding from the tin and cut into portions. Serve drizzled with the remaining warm Toffee sauce, and ice cream or cream on the side.

Cinnamon Teacake

I started making cinnamon teacakes for my dad on Sundays when I was about seven. They were his favourite so I've made many in my time. Just a word of advice – a cinnamon teacake is made to be eaten warm. Truly.

SERVES: 8

Preparation time: 20 minutes   Baking time: 30 minutes

Melted butter, to grease
100 g (3½ oz) butter, at room
    temperature, cubed
110 g (3¾ oz/½ cup) caster (superfine) sugar
1 teaspoon natural vanilla extract or essence
1 egg, at room temperature
150 g (5½ oz/1 cup) self-raising flour
80 ml (2½ fl oz/⅓ cup) milk

Cinnamon topping
1 tablespoon caster (superfine) sugar
½ teaspoon ground cinnamon
20 g (¾ oz) butter, melted

1　Preheat the oven to 180°C (350°F) or 160°C (315°F) fan-forced. Grease a shallow 20 cm (8 in) round cake tin with melted butter and line the base with baking paper.

2　Use an electric mixer to beat the butter, sugar and vanilla until pale and creamy. Add the egg and beat until well combined. On low speed, beat in half the flour, then the milk, and then the remaining flour until just combined.

3　Spoon into the prepared tin and use the back of a spoon to smooth the surface.

4　Bake in the preheated oven for 30 minutes or until golden and a skewer inserted in the centre comes out clean. Leave the cake to stand in the tin for 5 minutes before transferring to a wire rack or serving plate.

5　To make the Cinnamon topping, combine the sugar and cinnamon. Brush the top of the warm cake with the melted butter. Sprinkle the cinnamon sugar evenly over the top of the cake. Serve warm or at room temperature. This cake is best eaten the day it is made.

Honey & Oat Banana Bread

Based on a recipe developed for *The Low GI Family Cookbook* (Hachette), this has become a favourite in our house and I love it as much as the kids do. It includes many ingredients that help lower the GI of the loaf, such as honey, bananas, buttermilk and oat bran, and a slice will ensure the kids are getting something delicious that provides sustained energy for their busy days.

MAKES: 20 PIECES

Preparation time: 15 minutes   Baking time: 45–50 minutes

Melted unsalted butter, to grease
100 g (3½ oz) unsalted butter, at room temperature, cubed
175 g (6 oz/½ cup) single-origin floral honey
2 eggs, at room temperature
2 large (about 400 g/14 oz in total) very ripe bananas
80 ml (2½ fl oz/⅓ cup) buttermilk
110 g (3¾ oz/¾ cup) plain (all-purpose) flour (*see Baker's tips*)
75 g (2½ oz/½ cup) wholemeal plain (all-purpose) flour (*see Baker's tips*)
1 teaspoon baking powder
½ teaspoon bicarbonate of soda (baking soda)
1½ teaspoons ground cinnamon
65 g (2¼ oz/½ cup) unprocessed oat bran

1 Preheat the oven to 180°C (350°F) or 160°C (315°F) fan-forced. Grease an 11 cm x 21 cm (4¼ in x 8¼ in, base measurement) loaf (bar) tin with melted butter and line the base and two long sides with one piece of baking paper.

2 Use an electric mixer to beat the butter and honey in a large mixing bowl until well combined, pale and creamy.

3 Add the eggs one at a time, beating well after each addition until well combined.

4 Mash the bananas and stir into the mixture with the buttermilk using a spatula or large metal spoon.

5 Sift the flours, baking powder, bicarbonate of soda and cinnamon together into a bowl and return any husks in the sieve to the bowl. Add the oat bran and stir to combine. Add to the banana mixture and using a large metal spoon or spatula, fold in until just combined.

6 Spoon into the prepared loaf tin and smooth the surface with the back of a spoon. Bake in the preheated oven for 45–50 minutes or until a skewer inserted in the centre comes out clean. Leave the loaf to stand in the tin for 5 minutes before turning out onto a wire rack to cool.

Baker's tips

● The plain and wholemeal (all-purpose) flours can be replaced by 180 g (6 oz/1¼ cups) wholemeal spelt flour.

● Keep the banana bread in an airtight container in a cool place (but not in the fridge) for up to 3 days.

● To freeze, wrap individual slices in plastic wrap and seal in an airtight container or freezer bag. Thaw the slices at room temperature or toast straight from the freezer.

Banana & Lemon Cake

Moist with banana, subtly spiced with cinnamon and finished with a no-fuss
lemon cream cheese icing, there is so much to love about this cake!

SERVES: 16

Preparation: 20 minutes (+ 1 hour cooling time)   Baking time: 55–60 minutes

Melted butter, to grease
185 g (6½ oz) butter, at room
    temperature, cubed
165 g (5¾ oz/¾ cup, firmly packed)
    brown sugar
1½ teaspoons natural vanilla extract
    or essence
3 eggs, at room temperature
4 very ripe bananas
    (about 800 g/1 lb 12 oz in total)
300 g (10½ oz/2 cups) self-raising flour
2 teaspoons ground cinnamon

Lemon cream cheese frosting
250 g (9 oz) cream cheese, at room
    temperature, cubed
50 g (1¾ oz) unsalted butter, at room
    temperature, cubed
185 g (5½ oz/1½ cups) icing (confectioners')
    sugar mixture, sifted
Finely grated zest and juice of 1 lemon

1   Preheat the oven to 180°C (350°F) or 160°C (315°F)
    fan-forced. Grease a 20 cm (8 in) square cake tin with
    melted butter and line the base with baking paper.

2   Use an electric mixer to beat the butter, sugar and
    vanilla in a large bowl until pale and creamy, scraping
    down the side of the bowl when necessary. Add the
    eggs one at a time, beating well after each addition
    until well combined.

3   Use a fork to mash the bananas on a plate. Add to the
    butter mixture and beat until just combined.

4   Sift together the flour and cinnamon. Add the flour
    mixture to the butter mixture and, on the lowest possible
    speed, beat until just combined.

5   Spoon the mixture into the prepared tin and smooth
    the surface with the back of the spoon. Bake in the
    preheated oven for 55–60 minutes, or until a skewer
    inserted in the centre comes out clean. Leave the cake to
    stand in the tin for 5 minutes before turning out onto a
    wire rack to cool completely (this will take about 1 hour).

6   To make the Lemon cream cheese frosting, use an
    electric mixer to beat the cream cheese and butter until
    pale, creamy and completely smooth. With the motor
    running, gradually add the icing sugar, a tablespoonful
    at a time, until well combined. Beat in the lemon zest
    and 2 teaspoons of the lemon juice until just combined.

7   Spread the frosting over the top and sides of the cooled
    cake. Serve in slices.

Baker's tip

● This iced cake will keep in an airtight container in
the fridge for up to 2 days. Stand at room temperature
for 30 minutes before serving.

Cinnamon Pear Crumble Cakes

Enriched with sour cream and studded with chunks of pear, these cakes have a delicious nutty, cinnamon-spiced crumble surprise filling as well. They are perfect to serve at room temperature for afternoon tea or warm with cream or ice cream for dessert. Use a ripe pear that is still a little firm for the best results, avoiding very soft ones.

MAKES: 8

Preparation time: 30 minutes (+ 5 minutes standing time)   Baking time: 25–30 minutes

Melted butter, to grease
60 g (2¼ oz) butter, at room temperature
75 g (2½ oz/⅓ cup) caster (superfine) sugar
½ teaspoon natural vanilla extract
   or essence
1 egg, at room temperature
100 g (3½ oz) sour cream
100 g (3½ oz/⅔ cup) plain (all-purpose) flour
¾ teaspoon baking powder
1 firm ripe poaching or baking pear (about
   220 g/7¾ oz), such as williams, packham
   or beurre bosc, peeled, cored and cut into
   2 cm (¾ in) chunks
Cream or vanilla ice cream,
   to serve (optional)

Crumble filling
55 g (2 oz/¼ cup, firmly packed) brown sugar
2 tablespoons plain (all-purpose) flour
½ teaspoon ground cinnamon
30 g (1 oz) chilled butter, cubed
50 g (1¾ oz) walnuts or pecans, toasted
   and coarsely chopped

1 Preheat the oven to 190°C (375°F) or 170°C (325°F) fan-forced. Line 8 holes of an 80 ml (2½ fl oz/⅓ cup) capacity muffin tin with paper cases.

2 To make the Crumble filling, put the sugar, flour and cinnamon in a medium bowl. Use your fingertips to rub in the butter until the mixture resembles coarse breadcrumbs. Stir in the walnuts.

3 To make the cake, use an electric mixer to beat the butter, sugar and vanilla in a medium bowl until pale and creamy. Add the egg and beat well. Add the sour cream and beat until just combined. Sift together the flour and baking powder. Add to the butter mixture and beat on low speed until just combined. Use a spatula or large metal spoon to fold in the pear until evenly combined.

4 Divide half the cake mixture among the paper cases, spreading to cover the bases. Sprinkle each with the Crumble filling and then spoon over the remaining cake mixture to cover.

5 Bake in the preheated oven for 25–30 minutes or until a skewer inserted in the centre of a cake comes out clean. Leave the cakes to stand in the tin for 5 minutes before transferring to a wire rack. Serve warm or at room temperature, on their own or with cream or ice cream.

Baker's tips

● You can also make the Crumble filling using a food processor. Put the sugar, flour, cinnamon and butter in a food processor and process until the mixture resembles coarse breadcrumbs. Transfer to a bowl and stir in the nuts.

● These cakes will keep in an airtight container at room temperature for up to 2 days.

Classic Chocolate Chip Cookies

These good old-fashioned cookies are simple to make and even easier to devour!
Either dark or milk chocolate (or a combination of the two) will work well – just take
your pick. Eat them with a glass of cold milk.

MAKES: ABOUT 30

Preparation time: 15 minutes (+ 30 minutes cooling time)   Baking time: 20 minutes

125 g (4½ oz) butter, at room
temperature, cubed

220 g (7¾ oz/1 cup, firmly packed)
brown sugar

1 teaspoon natural vanilla extract
or essence

2 eggs, at room temperature

300 g (10½ oz/2 cups) plain
(all-purpose) flour

1 teaspoon baking powder

200 g (7 oz) good-quality dark or milk
chocolate, chopped, or chocolate chips

1 Preheat the oven to 180°C (350°F) or 160°C (315°F)
fan-forced. Line two large baking trays with
baking paper.

2 Use an electric mixer to beat the butter, sugar and
vanilla until pale and creamy. Add the eggs one at a time,
beating well after each addition. Sift together the flour
and baking powder, add to the butter mixture and use
a wooden spoon or spatula to mix until well combined.
Mix in the chocolate.

3 Roll tablespoonfuls of the mixture into balls and place
on the oven trays, leaving about 5 cm (2 in) between
each for spreading. Flatten each ball to about 5 cm (2 in)
in diameter.

4 Bake in the preheated oven for 20 minutes, swapping
the trays around halfway through baking, or until light
golden and cooked through. Leave the cookies on the
trays until cool (about 30 minutes).

Baker's tip

● These cookies will keep in an airtight container
at room temperature for up to 1 week.

Jam Drops

I remember making these old-fashioned favourites often as a child. They are
the perfect biscuits to make with kids because there's a lot of rolling and poking
involved. Use any jam you like or have on hand – apricot, strawberry, mixed berry,
blackberry and plum all work well – and make it homemade if you can.

MAKES: ABOUT 22

Preparation time: 20 minutes (+ cooling time)   Baking time: 20 minutes

125 g (4½ oz) butter, at room
   temperature, cubed
75 g (2½ oz/⅓ cup) caster (superfine) sugar
1 teaspoon natural vanilla extract or essence
185 g (6½ oz/1¼ cups) plain
   (all-purpose) flour
35 g (1¼ oz/¼ cup) custard powder
½ teaspoon baking powder
2 tablespoons milk
85 g (3 oz/¼ cup) raspberry jam
   or jam of your choice

1 Preheat the oven to 180°C (350°F) or 160°C (315°F)
   fan-forced. Line two large baking trays with
   baking paper.

2 Use an electric mixer to beat the butter, sugar and vanilla
   in a medium bowl until pale and creamy. Sift together
   the flour, custard powder and baking powder. Add to
   the butter mixture with the milk and beat on the lowest
   possible speed until a soft dough just forms.

3 Roll tablespoonfuls of the biscuit dough into balls and
   place them about 5 cm (2 in) apart on the lined trays.
   Flatten each ball to about 1 cm (½ in) thick and
   4 cm (1½ in) in diameter. Use your finger or the round
   end of a wooden spoon to make a 2 cm (¾ in) diameter
   indent in the centre of each biscuit. Fill each indent
   with about ½ teaspoon of jam.

4 Bake in the preheated oven for 20 minutes, swapping
   the trays around halfway through baking, or until
   the biscuits are lightly golden and cooked through.
   Leave to cool on the baking trays.

Baker's tip

● These biscuits will keep in an airtight jar at room
temperature for up to 1 week.

Caramelised Apple & Hazelnut Puddings

The combination of sweet caramelised apple and earthy hazelnuts is heavenly in these puddings. Serve them topped with a generous dollop of cream or a scoop of vanilla ice cream for a truly comforting winter dessert.

SERVES: 6

Preparation time: 25 minutes (+ 5 minutes standing time)   Baking time: 25 minutes

Melted butter, to grease
185 g (6½ oz) unsalted butter, at room
   temperature, cubed
165 g (5¾ oz/¾ cup) raw sugar
1½ teaspoons natural vanilla extract
   or essence
3 eggs, at room temperature
110 g (3¾ oz/1 cup) hazelnut meal
   (see Baker's tips)
100 g (3½ oz/⅔ cup) self-raising flour
Vanilla ice cream or cream, to serve

Caramelised apples
3 cooking or eating apples (about 540 g/1 lb
   3 oz in total), such as golden delicious,
   granny smith or pink lady
2 teaspoons freshly squeezed lemon juice
40 g (1½ oz) unsalted butter, cubed
165 g (5¾ oz/¾ cup) raw sugar

Baker's tips

● You can replace the hazelnut meal with almond meal if you like.

● These puddings are best served straight from the oven but they are also delicious served at room temperature.

1 Preheat the oven to 180°C (350°F) or 160°C (315°F) fan-forced. Brush six 250 ml (9 fl oz/1 cup) capacity ramekins or ovenproof dishes with melted butter.

2 To make the Caramelised apples, peel, core and quarter the apples. Cut each quarter into 4 wedges and put in a bowl. Sprinkle with the lemon juice and toss to coat. Melt the butter in a medium frying pan or wide-based saucepan over high heat until foaming. Add the apple, sprinkle with the sugar and stir for 3–5 minutes, or until it starts to caramelise. Reduce the heat to medium and cook for a further 5 minutes, or until the apple is just tender and a syrup has formed. Remove from the heat and set aside to cool slightly.

3 Meanwhile, use an electric mixer to beat the butter, sugar and vanilla until pale and creamy. Add the eggs one at a time, beating well after each addition. Combine the hazelnut meal and flour. Add to the butter mixture and beat on the lowest possible speed until just combined.

4 Divide evenly and arrange the Caramelised apples over the base of the greased ramekins. Drizzle with any syrup remaining from cooking. Spoon the pudding mixture, dividing evenly, over the top. Smooth the surface with the back of the spoon.

5 Place the ramekins on a baking tray and bake in the preheated oven for 25 minutes or until a skewer inserted in the centre comes out clean.

6 Remove from the oven and leave the puddings in the ramekins to cool slightly for 5 minutes. Run a palette knife around the outside of the puddings and invert onto serving plates. Serve warm with ice cream or cream.

Lesson 6

The Rubbing-in Method

This method is used for making scones, shortcrust pastry and some biscuits and slices. Butter is 'rubbed' into flour (and sometimes other dry ingredients) with your fingertips until it is crumbly and the butter is evenly distributed. Wet ingredients are then stirred through and the mixture forms a dough.

With this method, you use your fingertips to evenly distribute small pieces of butter through the mixture that eventually melt when baked and leave little air pockets. This is what gives a tender crumb to a scone, flakiness to pastry and that characteristic buttery 'shortness' to a biscuit.

The amount of butter plays a big part in recipes using this method, and different types of recipes will use varying amounts of butter. For example, a basic scone recipe may only have 60 g (2¼ oz) butter for every 300 g (10½ oz/2 cups) flour, while a shortcrust pastry (as illustrated here) can have around 200 g (7 oz) butter for the same amount of flour. Both recipes use the same technique for combining these ingredients but there are three main differences: the consistency of the mixture; the amount of liquid required; and the resulting texture.

The consistency of the mixture after rubbing in the butter and before adding the liquid ingredients will be vastly different depending on the amount of butter that is used. The scone mixture, with the smaller amount of butter, will be drier and the butter will be distributed in fine pieces. The pastry mixture, however, will be moist and will have larger chunks of butter through it.

The amount of liquid required to bring the butter/flour mixture together

in a dough versus a pastry will vary. Obviously the more butter used, as for pastry, the less liquid will be needed.

The amount of butter will affect the resulting texture – just compare scones with pastry. A pastry will have a rich,

flaky texture, due to its high butter content, while the scones will be more like cake or bread, with the butter only contributing slightly to determining the final texture.

Step by step

1 Put the flour and any other dry ingredients into a bowl as directed and add the cubed butter. The butter is often chilled, but not always, so make sure you follow the instructions in the recipe.

2 With your palms facing upwards, and working quickly and lightly, use your fingertips to rub the butter into the flour.

3 The mixture will at first appear to be uneven, with large chunks of butter.

4 As you continue to rub, the mixture will become finer and more even in texture.

5 Continue to rub until the mixture resembles fine breadcrumbs, with some larger pieces of butter still visible.

6 Stir in any other dry ingredients, such as sugar, as directed, then pour or sprinkle the combined wet ingredients evenly over the dry ingredients.

7 Use a round-ended knife (like a butter knife) to mix using a 'cutting' action.

8 Continue to mix with a cutting action until the dough starts to come together.

Steps continued overleaf →

9 Press a little of the mixture between your fingers – if it holds together easily, it is ready. If not, add a little more liquid, mix in and test again. The mixture should be soft but not sticky.

10 Bring the dough together with your hands and turn onto a lightly floured bench top.

11 Using your fingertips, knead the dough briefly and lightly about six times or until it comes together and is almost smooth.

12 Your dough/pastry is now ready to shape, chill, roll and bake as directed.

Keep in mind ...

- When rubbing in butter, a wide, shallow bowl is most suitable, as it allows you to get your hands in and work with your palms facing upwards without being cramped.

- Take note whether the recipe requires the butter to be at room temperature or chilled. I find that slightly softened butter (letting it stand at room temperature for 15–30 minutes) works better in scone-like mixtures, while pastry dough definitely needs to be made with well-chilled butter.

- The butter should be cut into small, even cubes; this will help you incorporate it into the flour more quickly and evenly.

- Work quickly – the faster you can rub in the butter and the less you handle the mixture, the lighter your final product will be.

- Only use your fingertips, not your whole hands. The palms are the warmest part of your hands and the butter is more likely to melt if it touches your palms when you are rubbing it in, which can result in a heavy texture.

- Keep the palms of your hands facing upwards and lift the flour high out of the bowl when rubbing in the butter, as this will aerate the mixture and help give it a lighter texture when baked.

Now get baking!

It's time to get into the kitchen and make the following recipes – whether it's a batch of biscuits, a delicious quick bread or a luscious lemon tart – all of which are perfect for you to practise the rubbing-in method.

Cream Scones

I have vivid memories of baking batches of scones at shearing time. I would bundle
them together in a tea towel to keep them warm and take them up to the shearing
shed where they would be devoured at 'smoko'. Nowadays, scones are what I whip
up if time is short – they are simple, fast and everyone loves them.

MAKES: 9

Preparation time: 10 minutes   Baking time: 12 minutes

Melted butter, to grease
300 g (10½ oz/2 cups) self-raising flour,
　　plus extra, to dust
Pinch of salt
60 g (2 oz) butter, at room
　　temperature, cubed
2 tablespoons caster (superfine) sugar
80 ml (2½ fl oz/⅓ cup) milk
125 ml (4 fl oz/½ cup) thin (pouring) cream,
　　plus extra, to glaze
1 teaspoon natural vanilla extract or essence
Berry jam and whipped cream, to serve

Variations

Sultana Scones – Add 100 g (3½ oz) sultanas
(golden raisins) with the sugar in Step 2.

Cinnamon & Date Scones – Add 1 teaspoon ground
cinnamon with the flour and salt, and add 100 g
(3½ oz) chopped pitted fresh or dried dates with
the sugar in Step 2.

Cheese Scones – Add 25 g (1 oz/¼ cup) finely grated
parmesan cheese and 50 g (1¾ oz/½ cup) finely
shredded vintage cheddar cheese to the flour mixture
after rubbing in the butter. Omit the sugar and vanilla,
and add the milk and cream as directed. Sprinkle with
25 g (1 oz/¼ cup) extra finely shredded vintage cheddar
cheese after brushing the tops of the scones with
cream. Serve split and spread with butter.

1 Preheat the oven to 220°C (425°F) or 200°C (400°F)
fan-forced. Lightly grease a baking tray with melted
butter. Lightly dust with flour and shake off any excess.

2 Sift the flour and salt together into a large bowl. With
your palms facing upwards, use your fingertips to rub in
the butter until the mixture resembles fine breadcrumbs
and the butter is evenly incorporated. Stir in the sugar
and make a well in the centre.

3 Combine the milk, cream and vanilla. Add the milk
mixture to the flour mixture and use a round-ended
knife to mix with a cutting action until the dough
comes together in clumps.

4 Use lightly floured hands to bring the dough together –
it will be soft, but not sticky. Place on a lightly floured
bench top and knead lightly and briefly (only about
six times) to bring it together in a ball.

5 Use the palm of your hand to flatten the dough into a
15 cm (6 in) square about 2 cm (¾ in) thick. Using a
floured knife, cut the dough into 9 portions and place
them on the prepared tray, about 2 cm (¾ in) apart.

6 Use a pastry brush to lightly brush the top of each scone
with a little extra cream. Dust with a little extra flour.

7 Bake in the middle of the preheated oven for
12 minutes, or until the scones are lightly golden and
cooked through; they are ready if they sound hollow
when you tap them on the base. Serve warm or at room
temperature, split and topped with jam and cream.
These scones are best eaten on the day they are made.

Blueberry & Buttermilk Scones

There is something quite deliciously wholesome yet wonderfully wicked about these
scones. It's worth making them to discover what I mean ...

MAKES: 8

Preparation time: 15 minutes   Baking time: 30 minutes

300 g (10½ oz/2 cups) wholemeal plain
   (all-purpose) flour, plus extra, to dust
2½ teaspoons baking powder
1½ teaspoons ground cinnamon
Pinch of salt
100 g (3½ oz) butter, at room
   temperature, cubed
55 g (2 oz/¼ cup) raw sugar, plus
   1 tablespoon extra, to sprinkle
125 g (4½ oz) fresh blueberries
125 ml (4 fl oz/½ cup) buttermilk
60 ml (2 fl oz/¼ cup) milk, plus extra,
   to brush
1½ teaspoons natural vanilla extract
   or essence
Thick (double) cream, mascarpone
   or butter, to serve

1 Preheat the oven to 200°C (400°F) or 180°C (350°F)
   fan-forced. Line a baking tray with baking paper.

2 Put the flour, baking powder, cinnamon and salt in
   a large bowl. With your palms facing upwards, use
   your fingertips to rub in the butter until the mixture
   resembles fine breadcrumbs and the butter is evenly
   incorporated. Stir in the sugar and blueberries.
   Make a well in the centre.

3 Combine the buttermilk, milk and vanilla. Add to the
   flour mixture and use a round-ended knife to mix with a
   cutting action until the dough comes together in clumps.

4 Use lightly floured hands to bring the dough together –
   it will be soft, but not sticky. Place on a lightly floured
   bench top and knead lightly and briefly (only about
   six times) to bring it together into a ball.

5 Shape the dough into a 20 cm (8 in) round about 2.5 cm
   (1 in) thick and place on the lined tray. Use a floured
   large sharp knife to cut the round into 8 wedges, leaving
   it as a round. Use a pastry brush to lightly brush the top
   with a little extra milk, and sprinkle with the extra sugar.

6 Bake in the middle of the preheated oven for 30 minutes,
   until the scones are lightly golden and cooked through;
   they are ready if they sound hollow when you tap them
   on the base. Serve warm or at room temperature with
   cream, mascarpone or butter. These scones are best
   eaten on the day they are made.

Oat Biscuits

Reminiscent of good old digestives, these biscuits easily swing between savoury and sweet. Serve them with blue cheese or dip them in dark chocolate to suit your flavour preference.

MAKES: ABOUT 25

Preparation time: 25 minutes (+ cooling time) Baking time: 18–20 minutes

150 g (5½ oz/1 cup) wholemeal plain (all-purpose) flour, plus extra, to dust
130 g (4½ oz/1 cup) oat bran
75 g (2½ oz/⅓ cup, firmly packed) brown sugar
1 teaspoon baking powder
½ teaspoon salt
125 g (4½ oz) chilled unsalted butter, cubed
60 ml (2 fl oz/¼ cup) milk

1 Preheat the oven to 180°C (350°F) or 160°C (315°F) fan-forced. Line two baking trays with baking paper.

2 Combine the flour, oat bran, sugar, baking powder and salt in a large bowl. With your palms facing upwards, use your fingertips to rub in the butter until the mixture resembles fine breadcrumbs and the butter is evenly incorporated.

3 Sprinkle the milk over the flour mixture and use a round-ended knife to mix with a cutting action until the dough comes together in clumps. Bring together with your hands to form a dough.

4 Turn the dough onto a lightly floured bench top and divide into 2 portions. Use a lightly floured rolling pin to roll out 1 portion until about 5 mm (¼ in) thick. Use a 6 cm (2½ in) round cutter to cut the dough into discs and place them on the lined trays about 3 cm (1¼ in) apart. Prick the tops of each biscuit twice with a fork. Re-roll any offcuts and cut out more biscuits. Repeat with the remaining dough portion.

5 Bake in the preheated oven for 18–20 minutes or until the biscuits are golden around the edges, aromatic and cooked through. Leave to cool on the trays.

Baker's tips

● You can also make these biscuits using a food processor. Process the flour, oat bran, sugar, baking powder, salt and butter in a food processor until the mixture resembles breadcrumbs. Sprinkle the mixture with the milk and use the pulse button to process until the mixture starts to come together as a dough. Transfer to a bowl and bring together with your hands. Continue with the recipe from Step 4.

● These biscuits will keep in an airtight container at room temperature for up to 1 week.

Cheese & Bacon Scrolls

A world away from the commercially made ones, these scrolls are great as a snack or with a warming winter soup. Feel free to try flavour variations, such as chopped herbs instead of the mustard powder or prosciutto instead of the bacon.

MAKES: 12

Preparation time: 30 minutes Cooking time: 25–30 minutes

3 trimmed bacon slices (about
    160 g/5¾ oz in total), chopped
300 g (10½ oz/2 cups) self-raising flour,
    plus extra, to dust
½ teaspoon dry mustard powder
Pinch of salt
50 g (1¾ oz) butter, at room
    temperature, cubed
25 g (1 oz/¼ cup) finely grated
    parmesan cheese
250 ml (9 fl oz/1 cup) milk
100 g (3½ oz/1 cup) finely shredded vintage
    cheddar cheese, plus 25 g (1 oz/¼ cup)
    extra, to sprinkle

1 Preheat the oven to 190°C (375°F) or 170°C (325°F) fan-forced. Line a large baking tray with baking paper.

2 Cook the bacon in a frying pan over medium–high heat for 5 minutes, or until crisp. Set aside.

3 Put the flour, mustard powder and salt in a medium bowl. With your palms facing upwards, use your fingertips to rub in the butter until the mixture resembles fine breadcrumbs and the butter is evenly incorporated. Stir in the parmesan cheese and make a well in the centre.

4 Add the milk to the flour mixture and use a round-ended knife to mix with a cutting action until the dough comes together in clumps. Use lightly floured hands to bring the dough together – it will be soft, but not sticky. Place on a lightly floured bench top and knead lightly and briefly (only about six times) to bring it together into a ball.

5 Use a lightly floured rolling pin to roll the dough out on a lightly floured bench top to a 25 cm x 30 cm (10 in x 12 in) rectangle. Sprinkle evenly with the bacon and then the cheddar cheese. Starting at a long end, roll up the dough into a log. Use a sharp serrated knife to cut the roll into 12 even slices. Place the scrolls on the lined tray about 2 cm (¾ in) apart and sprinkle with the extra cheddar. Bake in the preheated oven for 25–30 minutes, or until the scrolls are golden and cooked through. Serve warm or at room temperature.

Baker's tip

● These scrolls are best eaten the day they are made. They can, however, be frozen in a sealed airtight container or freezer bag. Thaw at room temperature and reheat on a lined baking tray in an oven preheated to 160°C (315°F) or 140°C (275°F) fan-forced for 10–15 minutes.

Apple, Rhubarb & Blackberry Crumble

There's nothing better in winter than a soul-warming pudding for dessert. This delicious crumble brings together fresh apples and rhubarb with frozen blackberries – a memorable combination and a dessert you'll make often. The leftovers are pretty good for breakfast topped with natural yoghurt, too.

SERVES: 8

Preparation time: 20 minutes   Cooking time: 50–60 minutes

3 large cooking apples (about 600 g/1 lb 5 oz in total), such as granny smith, peeled, cored and cut into thin wedges
2 teaspoons freshly squeezed lemon juice
1½ teaspoons natural vanilla extract or essence
300 g (10½ oz) trimmed rhubarb, cut into 2.5 cm (1 in) lengths
250 g (9 oz) frozen blackberries
75 g (2½ oz/⅓ cup) caster (superfine) sugar
65 g (2¼ oz/⅓ cup, firmly packed) brown sugar
Vanilla ice cream or cream, to serve

Crumble topping
75 g (2½ oz/¾ cup) rolled (porridge) oats
100 g (3½ oz/⅓ cup) plain (all-purpose) flour
110 g (3¾ oz/½ cup, firmly packed) brown sugar
1 teaspoon ground cinnamon
100 g (3½ oz) chilled unsalted butter, cubed
80 g (2¾ oz/¾ cup) flaked almonds

1 Preheat the oven to 180°C (350°F) or 160°C (315°F) fan-forced.

2 Put the apple wedges in a large bowl, sprinkle with the lemon juice and vanilla, and toss to coat the apple. Add the rhubarb, blackberries and the sugars, and toss to combine evenly. Transfer to a 2 litre (70 fl oz/8 cup) capacity ovenproof dish.

3 To make the Crumble topping, combine the rolled oats, flour, sugar and cinnamon in a medium bowl. Add the butter and, with your palms facing upwards, use your fingertips to rub it into the flour mixture until well combined. Stir through the flaked almonds. Sprinkle evenly over the apple mixture.

4 Place the dish on a baking tray lined with baking paper. Bake in the preheated oven for 50–60 minutes, or until the fruit is tender when tested with a skewer and the topping is golden and crisp.

5 Serve warm with vanilla ice cream or cream.

Baker's tip

● This crumble can also be cooked in eight 250 ml (9 fl oz/1 cup) capacity ovenproof dishes or ramekins. Bake at the same temperature for 35 minutes.

Variation

Apple, Rhubarb & Strawberry Crumble – Replace the frozen blackberries with 250 g (9 oz/1⅔ cups) fresh strawberries, hulled and halved.

Basic Shortcrust Pastry

A really good homemade pastry is the secret to a fabulous pie or tart (flan), and it is easy to achieve when you have a good recipe. So stash the packet, follow my basic recipe, variations and tips, and make your own!

Preparation time: 15 minutes (+ 20 minutes chilling time)

MAKES: enough for a 23 cm (9 in) round tart (flan) case, a 24 cm (9½ in) square tart case, 10 x 6 cm (2½ in) individual tart cases, a 12 cm x 35 cm (4½ in x 14 in) tart case or 24 tartlet cases (1 tablespoon capacity)

225 g (8 oz/1½ cups) plain (all-purpose) flour
A good pinch of salt
150 g (5½ oz) chilled unsalted butter, cubed
3–3½ tablespoons iced water

1 Combine the flour and salt in a large bowl. Add the chilled butter. With your palms facing upwards, use your fingertips to rub in the butter until the mixture resembles fine breadcrumbs with some larger pieces of butter still visible.

2 Sprinkle 3 tablespoons of the iced water over the flour and butter mixture. Use a round-ended knife in a cutting motion to mix until evenly combined and the mixture starts holding together. Press a little of the mixture between your fingers – if it holds together easily, there is no need to add more water; if it doesn't, add the remaining ½ tablespoon water and combine. The pastry should be soft but not sticky.

3 Bring the pastry together with your hands and transfer to a cool, lightly floured bench top. Lightly and briefly knead the pastry with your fingertips for about 30 seconds, or until just smooth and soft. Shape the pastry into a disc, wrap well in plastic wrap and place in the fridge for 20 minutes to rest, then use as directed.

Variations

Parmesan Shortcrust Pastry – Combine 50 g (1¾ oz/½ cup) finely grated parmesan cheese with the flour and salt before rubbing in the butter.

Mustard Shortcrust Pastry – Add 1½ teaspoons dry mustard powder to the flour and salt before rubbing in the butter.

Sweet Shortcrust Pastry – Add 2 tablespoons sifted icing (confectioners') sugar or caster (superfine) sugar to the flour and salt before rubbing in the butter.

Chocolate Shortcrust Pastry – Reduce the flour to 200 g (7 oz/1⅓ cups). Sift 2 tablespoons unsweetened cocoa powder and 2 tablespoons icing (confectioners') sugar with the flour and salt, then rub in the butter.

Making pastry ahead of time

Homemade shortcrust pastry will keep well in the fridge or freezer.

Refrigerating uncooked pastry – This pastry (and all the variations) can be made up to 3 days ahead. Wrap well in plastic wrap and refrigerate. Leave to stand at room temperature for about 1 hour (depending on the weather) until softened slightly and pliable enough to roll easily.

Freezing uncooked pastry – Shape into a disc, wrap well in plastic wrap, seal in an airtight container or freezer bag and freeze for up to 1 month. Transfer to the fridge to thaw completely (this will take about 1 day). Leave to stand at room temperature for about 1 hour (depending on the weather) until softened slightly and pliable enough to roll easily.

Freezing uncooked pastry cases – Place the pastry case, still in the tin, in the freezer. Once frozen, leave the pastry in the tin or remove and seal in an airtight container or freezer bag. Freeze for up to 1 month. Bake directly from the freezer or transfer to the fridge to thaw completely (this will take about 1 day) and bake as directed.

Tips for perfect pastry

How to make shortcrust pastry in a food processor

1 Put the flour, salt (and/or sugar, if using) and chilled butter in the bowl of a food processor. Pulse until the mixture resembles breadcrumbs (coarse or fine, depending on the recipe – the more butter, the coarser the mixture will be).

2 Sprinkle over the water and/or whisked egg yolk and pulse briefly until the mixture just starts to cling together (don't let it form a ball).

3 Turn the dough out onto a cool, lightly floured bench top. Lightly knead the pastry with your fingertips for about 30 seconds, or until smooth and soft. Shape the pastry into a disc, wrap well in plastic wrap and put in the fridge for 20 minutes to rest.

How to line a tart tin with shortcrust pastry

1 Unwrap the pastry and place on a cool, lightly floured bench top. Pat the pastry with the palm of your hand to flatten it slightly. Use a lightly floured rolling pin to roll the pastry into a disc 3–5 mm ($^1/_8$–$^1/_4$ in) thick. Always roll from the centre of the pastry outwards and in the same direction, giving the pastry a quarter turn after each roll so that it rolls evenly and doesn't stick to the bench top. Do not use too much flour or the pastry will become dry.

2 Carefully roll the pastry loosely around the rolling pin. Place it over a tart (flan) tin with a removable base and then unroll the pastry, being careful not to stretch it. Gently lift the edge of the pastry and ease it into the tart tin to line the base and side, and settle it into the join. Use your fingertips to press it gently into the corners without stretching it. Then, working around the tin, press the pastry into the side using your thumb.

3 Roll the rolling pin over the top of the tart tin to trim away any overhanging pastry. Use as directed.

How to blind bake shortcrust pastry

A shortcrust tart (flan) shell or pie crust will often need to be partially or fully cooked to help it stay crisp and prevent it from becoming soggy after the filling is added. This is called blind baking.

1 Preheat the oven to 200°C (400°F) or 180°C (350°F) fan-forced. Place the uncooked pastry case in the tart (flan) tin (or small tart tins) on a baking tray. Prick the base with a fork (about 12 times for a 23 cm/9 in round case). This will help the pastry case from 'bubbling' too much during baking.

2 Line the pastry case with baking paper or foil and fill with pastry weights, dried beans or uncooked rice, pressing them into the join and fluting. Bake in the preheated oven for 15 minutes.

3 Remove from the oven and use the paper or foil to lift out the weights. Return the pastry case to the oven and cook for a further 10–15 minutes for a partially cooked pastry case or 15–25 minutes for a fully cooked one. Remove from the oven and cool in the tin on a wire rack, or add the filling and return to the oven as directed.

Roasted Pumpkin, Tomato & Oregano Tart

An impressive tart with its combination of roasted pumpkin and tomatoes, Persian feta and a parmesan shortcrust pastry base, it is surprisingly simple to put together. Great to serve at lunch when you're entertaining.

SERVES: 6–8

Preparation time: 30 minutes (+ pastry-making)   Baking time: 55 minutes–1 hour 5 minutes

1 quantity Parmesan Shortcrust Pastry
   (page 162), shaped into a rectangle
   before wrapping and chilling as directed
150 g (5½ oz) drained marinated Persian
   feta cheese, coarsely crumbled

Filling
500 g (1 lb 2 oz) pumpkin (winter squash),
   such as jap or butternut, peeled,
   de-seeded, cut into 1 cm (½ in) thick
   slices and then 5 cm (2 in) wide wedges
1 red onion, cut into thin wedges
2 tablespoons oregano leaves
2 tablespoons extra virgin olive oil, plus
   extra, to drizzle
250 g (9 oz) cherry or grape tomatoes,
   halved (quartered if large)
½ teaspoon sugar

1 To make the Filling, preheat the oven to 220°C (425°F) or 200°C (400°F) fan-forced. Place the pumpkin, onion, 1 tablespoon of the oregano leaves and 1½ tablespoons of the oil in a bowl. Season well with salt and freshly ground black pepper, and toss to coat evenly. Spread over two-thirds of a large non-stick baking tray in a single layer. Toss the tomatoes with the remaining oil and the sugar, and season well with salt. Spread over the remaining one-third of the oven tray. Bake in the preheated oven for 25–30 minutes or until tender and lightly golden. Remove from the oven and set aside.

2 Reduce the oven temperature to 200°C (400°F) or 180°C (350°F) fan-forced. Unwrap the pastry and place on a cool, lightly floured bench top. Pat the pastry with the palm of your hand to flatten it slightly. Use a lightly floured rolling pin to roll the pastry into a rectangle about 3 mm (⅛ in) thick.

3 Carefully roll the pastry loosely around the rolling pin. Place it over a 12 cm x 35 cm (4½ in x 14 in, base measurement) tart (flan) tin with a removable base (see Baker's tips) and then unroll the pastry, being careful not to stretch it. Gently lift the edge of the pastry and ease it into the tart tin to line the base and sides and settle it into the corners. Use your fingertips to press it gently into the corners without stretching it. Then, working around the tin, press the pastry into the side using your thumb or finger. Roll the rolling pin over the top of the tart tin to trim away any overhanging pastry.

4 Place the tart tin on a baking tray. Prick the pastry base with a fork 12 times. Line the pastry case with baking paper or foil and fill with pastry weights, dried beans or uncooked rice, pressing them into the corners to fill the case. Bake in the preheated oven for 15 minutes.

5 Remove the pastry case from the oven and use the paper or foil to lift out the weights. Return the base to the oven and bake for a further 15–20 minutes, or until cooked through and golden brown. Remove from the oven.

6 Scatter half the feta over the base of the warm pastry case. Combine the roasted vegetables and tomatoes and toss gently to combine. Spoon into the pastry case and scatter over the remaining feta and oregano leaves. Drizzle with a little extra oil and sprinkle with pepper, if desired. Serve warm or at room temperature.

Baker's tips

● If you don't have a 12 cm x 35 cm (4½ in x 14 in, base measurement) rectangular tin you can use a 23 cm (9 in, base measurement) round tart tin with a removable base instead.

● This tart will keep in an airtight container in the fridge for up to 2 days. Bring to room temperature to serve.

Asparagus & Gruyère Tart

The best time to make this tart is in spring – when asparagus is young, flavoursome and inexpensive. A wedge of this delicious tart served with a simple leaf salad makes a wonderful light lunch or starter.

SERVES: 8–10

Preparation time: 30 minutes (+ pastry-making)   Baking time: 1 hour

1 quantity Basic Shortcrust Pastry (page 162), shaped into a disc before wrapping and chilling as directed
6 eggs, at room temperature
300 ml (10½ fl oz) thin (pouring) cream
2 bunches thin asparagus, trimmed, cut into 5 cm (2 in) lengths and blanched
160 g (5¾ oz/2 cups, loosely packed) gruyère cheese (*see Baker's tips*), finely shredded
1 tablespoon chopped flat-leaf (Italian) parsley or 2 teaspoons thyme leaves

Baker's tip

● The gruyère can be replaced with another Swiss-style cheese such as Jarlsberg.

1 Preheat the oven to 200°C (400°F) or 180°C (350°F) fan-forced.

2 Unwrap the pastry and place it on a cool, lightly floured bench top. Pat the pastry with the palm of your hand to flatten it slightly. Use a lightly floured rolling pin to roll out into a disc about 3 mm (⅛ in) thick. Carefully roll the pastry around the rolling pin and gently ease it into a 23 cm (9 in, base measurement) tart (flan) tin with a removable base. Press the pastry into the join and fluted side using your fingertips. Roll the rolling pin over the top of the tart to trim away any excess pastry.

3 Place the pastry case on an oven tray and prick the base 12 times with a fork. Line the pastry case with baking paper or foil and fill with pastry weights, dried beans or uncooked rice, pushing them into the join and fluting. Bake in the preheated oven for 20 minutes.

4 Remove the tart case from the oven and use the paper to lift the weights out of the case. Return the case to the oven and bake for a further 10 minutes, or until the pastry is just cooked through and looks dry.

5 Meanwhile, put the eggs and cream in a medium bowl and whisk together using a fork. Season well with freshly ground black pepper. Remove the tart case from the oven and scatter the asparagus over the base. Sprinkle evenly with the cheese and parsley. Pour over the egg mixture.

6 Reduce the oven temperature to 170°C (325°F) or 150°C (300°F) fan-forced. Bake for a further 25–30 minutes or until just set. Serve warm or at room temperature.

Peach Tart with Yoghurt Cream

Gorgeous summer peaches encased in a sweet, easy-as-they-come pastry, no real structure and charmingly rustic – this tart is simplicity at its best. Use yellow or white peaches, or a combination of the two, or even a mixture of stone fruit such as peaches, plums, nectarines and pitted cherries.

SERVES: 8–10

Preparation time: 25 minutes (+ pastry-making)   Baking time: 50–55 minutes

1 quantity Sweet Shortcrust Pastry
   (page 162), shaped into a disc before
   wrapping and chilling as directed
25 g (1 oz/¼ cup) almond meal
700 g (1 lb 9 oz) firm but ripe peaches,
   stones removed, cut into thick wedges
2 tablespoons raw sugar
Icing (confectioners') sugar, to dust (optional)

Yoghurt cream
200 g (7 oz/¾ cup) Greek-style
   natural yoghurt
125 ml (4 fl oz/½ cup) thin (pouring) cream
1 tablespoon icing (confectioners') sugar,
   or to taste
1 teaspoon natural vanilla extract or essence

1 Preheat the oven to 200°C (400°F) or 180°C (350°F) fan-forced.

2 Use a lightly floured rolling pin to roll out the pastry on a piece of baking paper into a round 3 mm (⅛ in) thick, about 33 cm (13 in) in diameter.

3 Use the paper to transfer the pastry to a large baking tray. Sprinkle the almond meal over the pastry leaving a 5 cm (2 in) border around the edge. Spread the peaches over the almond meal. Fold the pastry border up over the fruit. Sprinkle the upturned border and fruit with the raw sugar.

4 Bake in the preheated oven for 50–55 minutes or until the pastry is golden and crisp.

5 Meanwhile, to make the Yoghurt cream, use a balloon whisk to whisk the yoghurt, cream, icing sugar and vanilla in a medium bowl until it thickens slightly. Cover and refrigerate until required.

6 Serve the tart warm or at room temperature, dusted with icing sugar if desired, cut into wedges and with the Yoghurt cream on the side.

Baker's tip

● This tart is best served warm but it is also great served at room temperature. It will keep covered in the fridge for up to 2 days. Leave it to stand at room temperature for about 30 minutes before serving.

Chicken & Mushroom Pie

Homemade chicken pies are the ultimate in comfort food, made even better when they are topped with a deliciously crisp, buttery homemade pastry.

Preparation time: 1 hour 20 minutes (+ pastry-making and 1½ hours chilling time) Baking time: 35–40 minutes

1 quantity Basic Shortcrust Pastry (page 162), shaped into a disc before wrapping and chilling as directed

1 egg yolk whisked with 2 teaspoons milk, to glaze

2 teaspoons sesame seeds

Leafy herb salad, to serve (optional)

Filling

1 tablespoon olive oil, plus 2 teaspoons extra

8 chicken thigh fillets, trimmed

1 litre (35 fl oz/4 cups) chicken stock

1 brown onion, chopped

1 leek, pale section only, thickly sliced

130 g (4½ oz) bacon slices (about 4 thin), trimmed and chopped

60 g (2¼ oz) butter

400 g (14 oz) mushrooms, wiped, stems trimmed, sliced

12 thyme sprigs, leaves picked

200 ml (7 fl oz) milk

35 g (1¼ oz/¼ cup) plain (all-purpose) flour

2 teaspoons dijon mustard

Small handful of flat-leaf (Italian) parsley, leaves chopped

1 To make the Filling, heat the olive oil in a deep frying pan or large saucepan over medium–high heat. Cook the chicken fillets for 1–2 minutes on each side. Add the stock and bring to a gentle simmer. Reduce the heat to low and poach gently for 20 minutes. Remove the chicken from the stock and set aside to cool slightly. Skim any excess fat from the top of the stock with a large metal spoon. Transfer the stock to a heatproof jug.

2 Heat the extra olive oil in the frying pan over medium heat. Add the onion, leek and bacon and cook, stirring occasionally, for 10 minutes, or until the onion is just soft. Transfer to a bowl and set aside. Meanwhile, shred the chicken into bite-sized pieces.

3 Melt 20 g (¾ oz) of the butter in the frying pan over medium–high heat. Add the mushrooms and thyme and cook, stirring, for 5 minutes or until tender. Add to the onion mixture.

Recipe continued overleaf →

4 Combine 250 ml (9 fl oz/1 cup) of the reserved stock and the milk. Heat the remaining 40 g (1½ oz) butter in a medium saucepan over medium heat until melted. Add the flour and stir with a balloon whisk while it bubbles for about 1 minute. Remove the saucepan from the heat and gradually add the stock and milk mixture, stirring constantly, until smooth and well combined. Return the saucepan to a medium heat and stir constantly until thickened and simmering. Stir in the mustard.

5 Transfer the sauce to a large heatproof bowl. Add the chicken, the onion and mushroom mixture and the parsley. Season well with salt and mix to combine. Refrigerate for 1½ hours or until at room temperature.

6 Preheat the oven to 200°C (400°F) or 180°C (350°F) fan-forced. You will need a 1.5 litre (52 fl oz/6 cup) capacity ovenproof dish to cook the pie.

7 Unwrap the pastry and place it on a cool, lightly floured bench top. Pat the pastry with the palm of your hand to flatten it slightly. Use a lightly floured rolling pin to roll it out to the shape of the dish until about 3 mm (⅛ in) thick. Spoon the chicken mixture into the dish. Brush the edge of the dish with a little egg wash. Place the pastry over the filling then run a small sharp knife around the edge on a slight angle to trim the pastry. Press around the edge with a fork to seal it. Cut a cross in the top. Brush some egg wash over the pastry. Sprinkle with the sesame seeds.

8 Place the dish on a baking tray and bake in the preheated oven for 35–40 minutes or until the pastry is dark golden, crisp and cooked through. Serve immediately with a leafy salad on the side, if desired.

Baker's tip

● This pie will keep covered with plastic wrap in the fridge for up to 2 days. Reheat in an oven preheated to 160°C (315°F) or 140°C (275°F) fan-forced for 20–25 minutes, or until heated through.

Parmesan & Poppy Seed Biscuits

Don't think you are going to eat just one of these melt-in-the-mouth biscuits because they are totally addictive! Serve them on a cheese plate or package them up and give them as a thoughtful gift.

MAKES: ABOUT 45

Preparation time: 15 minutes (+ 1 hour chilling and cooling time)   Baking time: 12–15 minutes

150 g (5½ oz/1 cup) plain (all-purpose) flour, plus extra, to dust

½ teaspoon salt

35 g (1¼ oz/⅓ cup) finely grated parmesan cheese

30 g (1 oz/⅓ cup) coarsely grated vintage cheddar cheese

125 g (4½ oz) unsalted butter, at room temperature, cubed

2 tablespoons poppy seeds

1 Put all the ingredients except the poppy seeds in a large bowl. With your palms facing upwards, use your fingertips to rub the butter in until a dough forms. Bring the dough together with your hands.

2 Divide the dough into 2 portions and roll each into a log about 4 cm (1½ in) in diameter. Spread the poppy seeds on a plate and roll the logs in the poppy seeds to coat the outside surface. Wrap in plastic wrap and place in the fridge to chill for 1 hour or until firm enough to slice.

3 Preheat the oven to 160°C (315°F) or 140°C (275°F) fan-forced. Line two large baking trays with baking paper.

4 Slice the logs into 5 mm (¼ in) thick slices and place on the lined trays, leaving a little space between each one.

5 Bake in the preheated oven for 12–15 minutes or until the biscuits are pale golden and cooked through. Leave them to cool on the trays.

Baker's tips

● You can also use a food processor to make these biscuits. Put the flour, salt, cheeses and butter in the food processor and pulse, scraping down the side of the bowl if necessary, until the mixture begins to come together and is evenly combined. Transfer the mixture to a lightly floured bench top and bring the dough together with your hands. Continue with the recipe from Step 2.

● The uncooked dough, rolled into logs and wrapped well in plastic wrap, can be kept in the fridge for up to 1 week. It can also be frozen, sealed in an airtight container or freezer bag, for up to 1 month. Stand at room temperature for 30 minutes or until soft enough to slice and then bake for 14–17 minutes.

● These biscuits will keep in an airtight container for up to 1 week.

Leek & Goat's Cheese Tartlets

These tartlets, and the variations, are lovely little morsels to serve as an appetiser. You will need two 12-hole mini (1 tablespoon capacity) muffin tins to make them.

MAKES: 24

Preparation time: 35 minutes (+ pastry-making and 30 minutes freezing time)   Baking time: 18–23 minutes

1 quantity Basic Shortcrust Pastry (page 162), divided into 2 portions before wrapping and chilling as directed

1 leek, pale section only, outer layer removed, halved lengthways and thinly sliced

15 g (½ oz) unsalted butter

1 egg yolk, at room temperature

60 ml (2 fl oz/¼ cup) thickened (whipping) cream

30 g (1 oz) soft goat's cheese, crumbled

Variations

Leek, Ricotta & Thyme Tartlets – Replace the goat's cheese with 2 tablespoons finely grated parmesan or pecorino and 30 g (1 oz) fresh ricotta cheese crumbled into pea-sized pieces. Garnish each tartlet with a small sprig of fresh thyme before baking.

Leek & Blue Cheese Tartlets – Replace the goat's cheese with 25 g (1 oz) crumbled blue cheese (such as Stilton).

1 Use a lightly floured rolling pin to roll out 1 portion of pastry on a lightly floured bench top until about 3 mm (⅛ in) thick. Use a 6.5–7 cm (2½–2¾ in) round cutter to cut out circles. Carefully ease the dough circles into an ungreased 12-hole mini (1 tablespoon capacity) muffin tin, crimping the pastry 4–5 times to help shape it if necessary. Repeat with the remaining pastry to make 24 tartlet cases in total. Use a fork to prick the base of each tartlet case twice. Place in the freezer for at least 30 minutes or until ready to bake.

2 Preheat the oven to 200°C (400°F) or 180°C (350°F) fan-forced.

3 Meanwhile, to make the filling, place the leek and butter in a medium saucepan over low heat. Cover and cook for 15–20 minutes, stirring occasionally, or until very soft. Remove from the heat and allow to cool.

4 Use a fork to whisk the egg yolk, cream and goat's cheese together. Stir in the cooled leek mixture and season well with freshly ground black pepper.

5 Bake the tartlet cases in the preheated oven straight from the freezer for 12–15 minutes or until golden. Fill each tartlet case with a small amount of the filling. Return to the oven for 6–8 minutes, or until the filling is just set.

6 Serve warm or at room temperature.

Baker's tip

● You can make these tartlets up to 2 days ahead of serving. Cool and store in an airtight container in the fridge. Place the tartlets back in the tins before reheating in an oven preheated to 160°C (315°F) or 140°C (275°F) fan-forced for 10 minutes or until heated through.

Egg & Bacon Pies

This classic combination of egg and bacon in little pies works for picnics or brunch.
If you like, you can substitute chopped chives for some or all of the parsley.

MAKES: 6

Preparation time: 25 minutes (+ pastry-making)   Baking time: 18–22 minutes

1 quantity Mustard Shortcrust Pastry
   (page 162), divided into 2 portions
   and shaped into discs before wrapping
   and chilling as directed
150 g (5½ oz) bacon slices, rind and
   fat trimmed, chopped
25 g (1 oz/⅓ cup) finely shredded
   parmesan cheese
25 g (1 oz/¼ cup) finely shredded
   vintage cheddar cheese
Small handful of flat-leaf (Italian)
   or curly parsley, chopped
6 large eggs
1 egg yolk whisked with 1 teaspoon
   water, to glaze

1 On a lightly floured bench top, use a lightly floured rolling pin to roll out 1 portion of the pastry until 3 mm (⅛ in) thick. Use an upturned 13 cm (5 in) saucer or bowl as a guide to cut out 2 circles. Re-roll the pastry and cut out a third circle. Line three holes of a 6-hole 185 ml (6 fl oz/¾ cup) capacity muffin tin with the pastry rounds, pressing them in gently. Repeat with the remaining pastry to make 6 pastry cases in total. Place in the fridge to chill.

2 Meanwhile, preheat the oven to 190°C (375°F) or 170°C (325°F) fan-forced.

3 Cook the bacon in a small frying pan over medium heat for 5 minutes, or until crisp. Drain on paper towel and leave to cool to room temperature.

4 Combine the bacon, cheeses and parsley. Scatter half of the mixture over the base of the pastry cases.

5 Crack an egg into a ramekin and gently tip it into one of the pastry cases, being careful not to break the yolk. Repeat with the remaining eggs. Sprinkle with freshly ground pepper. Top with the remaining bacon mixture. Brush the pastry with the egg glaze.

6 Bake in the preheated oven for 18–22 minutes, or until the pastry is cooked through and the yolks are still a little soft. Leave the pies to stand in the tin for a few minutes before using a palette knife to lift them out onto serving plates. Serve warm or at room temperature.

Baker's tip

● These pies will keep in an airtight container in the fridge for up to 2 days. Leave them to stand at room temperature for at least 15 minutes before serving.

Chocolate Macadamia & Orange Tart

Rich, slightly decadent and faultlessly smooth, that's how I like my chocolate tart. This one is spiked with orange and studded with salted macadamias, and I challenge you to stop at just one slice.

SERVES: 8–10

Preparation time: 20 minutes (+ pastry-making and 15 minutes cooling time)   Baking time: 43–45 minutes

1 quantity Chocolate Shortcrust Pastry (page 162), shaped into a rectangle before wrapping and chilling as directed
Unsweetened cocoa powder or icing (confectioners') sugar, to dust
Vanilla ice cream or cream, to serve

Filling
75 g (2½ oz/1 cup) chopped good-quality dark chocolate
75 g (2½ oz) unsalted butter, cubed
90 g (3¼ oz/¼ cup) golden syrup (light treacle)
1 egg, at room temperature
1 egg yolk, at room temperature
Finely grated zest of 1 orange
155 g (5½ oz/1 cup) halved salted roasted macadamia nuts

1 Preheat the oven to 200°C (400°F) or 180°C (350°F) fan-forced.

2 Use a lightly floured rolling pin to roll out the pastry on a lightly floured bench top to a rectangle about 3 mm (⅛ in) thick. Carefully roll the pastry loosely around the rolling pin. Place it over a rectangular 10 cm x 34 cm (4 in x 13½ in, base measurement) tart (flan) tin with a removable base and then unroll the pastry, being careful not to stretch it. Gently lift the edge of the pastry and ease it into the tart tin to line the base and side and settle it into the join. Use your fingertips to press it gently into the join without stretching it. Then, working around the tin, press the pastry into the side using your thumb or finger. Roll the rolling pin over the top of the tart tin to trim away any overhanging pastry.

3 Place the pastry case on a baking tray and use a fork to prick the base 12 times. Line the pastry case with baking paper or foil and fill with pastry weights, dried beans or uncooked rice, making sure to press the weights into the corners and fill the case. Bake in the preheated oven for 15 minutes.

4 Remove the tart case from the oven and use the paper or foil to lift the weights out of the case. Return the case to the oven and bake for a further 10 minutes, or until the pastry is just cooked through and looks dry.

5 Meanwhile, make the Filling. Put the chocolate, butter and golden syrup in a small saucepan over low heat. Stir until melted and smooth. Remove from the heat.

6 Place the egg, egg yolk and orange zest in a medium bowl and whisk until combined. Stir in the chocolate mixture and transfer to a jug. Spread the macadamias evenly over the base of the warm tart case and then pour over the filling.

7 Reduce the oven temperature to 180°C (350°F) or 160°C (315°F) fan-forced and bake for 18–20 minutes, or until the filling is just set and slightly firm to touch in the centre.

8 Remove the tart from the oven and set aside for 15 minutes to cool slightly. Serve warm or at room temperature. Dust with cocoa powder or icing sugar and serve with ice cream or cream.

Baker's tip

● This tart will keep in an airtight container in the fridge for up to 3 days. Stand at room temperature for 30 minutes before serving.

Lemon Tart

A good lemon tart makes your mouth pucker – in the nicest possible way.
This one is sweet, smooth, silky and seductive, and sure to become a favourite.

SERVES: 8

Preparation time: 25 minutes (+ pastry-making)   Baking time: 50–55 minutes

1 quantity Sweet Shortcrust Pastry
(page 162), shaped into a disc before
wrapping and chilling as directed
Icing (confectioners') sugar, to dust
Cream or ice cream, to serve

Filling

3 eggs
165 g (5¾ oz/¾ cup) caster (superfine) sugar
185 ml (6 fl oz/¾ cup) thin (pouring) cream
150 ml (5 fl oz) strained freshly squeezed
lemon juice

Baker's tip

● This tart will keep in an airtight container in
the fridge for up to 2 days, although the pastry
will soften slightly. Bring to room temperature
to serve.

1 Preheat the oven to 200°C (400°F) or 180°C (350°F)
fan-forced.

2 Unwrap the pastry and place on a cool, lightly floured
bench top. Pat the pastry with the palm of your hand to
flatten it slightly. Use a lightly floured rolling pin to roll
out into a disc about 3 mm (⅛ in) thick. Carefully roll
the pastry around the rolling pin and gently ease it into
a 23 cm (9 in, base measurement) tart (flan) tin with a
removable base, pressing it into the join and fluted side
using your fingertips and thumb. Roll the rolling pin
over the top of the tart tin to trim away any excess pastry.

3 Place the pastry case on a baking tray and prick the base
12 times with a fork. Line the pastry case with baking
paper or foil and fill with pastry weights, dried beans or
uncooked rice, pushing them into the join and fluting.
Bake in the preheated oven for 20 minutes.

4 Remove the tart case from the oven and use the paper
or foil to lift out the weights. Return the case to the oven
and bake for a further 10 minutes or until the pastry is
cooked through and looks dry.

5 Meanwhile, to make the Filling, put the eggs, sugar,
cream and lemon juice in a medium bowl and whisk
with a fork until well combined. Strain the mixture
into a jug. Pour the filling into the hot pastry case
while still in the oven. Reduce the oven temperature
to 160°C (315°F) or 140°C (275°F) fan-forced and bake
for a further 20–25 minutes, or until the filling has just
set in the centre but still wobbles slightly when gently
shaken. Leave the tart to cool in the tin.

6 Dust with icing sugar and serve with cream or ice cream.

Lesson 7

The Whisking
Egg Whites
Method

Egg whites have this amazing ability to transform from thick liquid into a soft foam when whisked. Then, when folded through a base mixture for a cake, pudding or soufflé, this foam lends a beautifully light, airy texture.

Egg whites are usually whisked until they reach either 'soft' or 'firm' peaks, depending on the recipe.

'Soft' peaks describes the point at which the egg white mixture becomes thick enough that, when the whisk is lifted, the mixture forms a peak that then falls on itself.

'Firm' peaks is the next stage the egg whites will reach with more whisking. The mixture will become thicker and, when the whisk is lifted, a peak will form that will stand up and hold its shape. It is important not to whisk any longer once the stage of firm peaks is reached, as the whites can become dry and lose a lot of their volume if overwhisked.

Once you get the hang of this method, you'll know instinctively when the mixture is about to reach soft peaks or firm peaks. Practice makes perfect.

Step by step

1 Put the egg whites in a clean, dry mixing bowl. Often the recipe will say to add a pinch of salt or an acidic ingredient such as cream of tartar to help stabilise the egg whites and make them easier to whisk to a foam and harder to overwhisk.

2 Use a balloon whisk or an electric mixer with a whisk attachment to whisk the egg whites (on medium or medium–high speed if using an electric mixer) until they reach the desired consistency as stated in the recipe.

3 The egg whites have reached the 'soft peak' stage when the mixture forms a peak that folds in on itself.

4 If you continue whisking, the egg whites will reach the 'firm peak' stage – the mixture will form a peak that holds its shape.

5 Add some of the whisked egg whites (this may be just a spoonful or up to half the quantity) to the base mixture.

6 Use a spatula or large metal spoon to gently fold in the egg whites until they are evenly

combined, and the base mixture has 'loosened' and is of a thinner consistency.

7 Add the remaining egg whites and gently fold the two mixtures together.

8 Fold until the egg whites are just incorporated. The mixture is now ready to bake.

- Choose the whisk attachment if using an electric stand mixer or hand-held electric beaters. If your beaters don't have a whisk attachment, use the standard beaters.
- If using a balloon whisk, keep in mind it will take you a lot longer to get to the desired consistency than if using an electric mixer.
- Whisk the egg whites on medium or medium–high speed – not high speed – to produce the tiny, even air bubbles you want.
- Watch the egg whites closely, checking the consistency often, as it can change very quickly – soft and foamy one second to dry and unusable the next.

Now get baking!

So, let's get into the kitchen and really see how egg whites can be transformed into a very useful foam when baking soufflés and some cakes and desserts.

Keep in mind ...

- The egg whites are best used at room temperature when whisking – they have a greater ability to hold more air at room temperature than if chilled.
- Remember that any trace of fat, including egg yolk, will stop the egg whites from foaming and increasing in volume when whisked. Make sure all equipment – bowl, whisk and spatula or large metal spoon – are super clean and completely dry, as moisture will have the same negative effect.

- Never use a plastic bowl when whisking egg whites because traces of fat can be trapped in the surface of the bowl and, as mentioned in the previous point, fat is exactly what you don't need. Stainless steel, glass, ceramic or copper bowls are the best to use when whisking egg whites.
- Always separate your eggs into a small dish before adding the white to the mixing bowl so that if any yolk gets in it is easily removed and you won't have to throw away the whole batch.

Flourless Chocolate & Hazelnut Cake

Rich but light at the same time, this cake is indulgent without being overwhelmingly so, thanks to the light texture provided by the egg whites. My sort of chocolate cake, it makes a perfect dessert served with thick cream or ice cream and fresh berries when in season. However don't underestimate how blissfully suitable a slice in the afternoon with tea or coffee can be.

SERVES 8–10

Preparation time: 20 minutes   Baking time: 40–45 minutes

Melted butter, to grease
150 g (5½ oz/1 cup) chopped good-quality
    dark chocolate
100 g (3½ oz) butter, cubed
4 eggs, at room temperature, separated
110 g (3¾ oz/½ cup) caster (superfine) sugar
110 g (3¾ oz/1 cup) hazelnut meal
2 tablespoons unsweetened cocoa
    powder, sifted
2 tablespoons sherry, brandy or Frangelico
Icing (confectioners') sugar, or unsweetened
    cocoa powder, extra, to dust
Cream and berries, to serve (optional)

Variations

Flourless Chocolate, Orange & Almond Cake –
Replace the hazelnut meal with almond meal. Replace the sherry with 2 tablespoons orange liqueur such as Grand Marnier or Cointreau. Add 1 tablespoon finely grated orange zest with the egg yolks.

Flourless Chocolate & Prune Cake – Replace the sherry with 2 teaspoons instant coffee granules dissolved in 2 tablespoons water. Add 100 g (3½ oz) pitted prunes, chopped, to the chocolate mixture after adding the egg yolks, caster (superfine) sugar, hazelnut meal, cocoa powder and coffee, and stir to combine.

1 Preheat the oven to 150°C (300°F) or 130°C (250°F) fan-forced. Grease a 22 cm (8½ in, base measurement) spring-form cake tin with melted butter. Line the base and side with baking paper.

2 Combine the chocolate and butter in a medium heatproof bowl over a saucepan of simmering water, making sure the base of the bowl doesn't touch the water. Stir occasionally until the chocolate and butter have melted and the mixture is smooth. Remove the bowl from the saucepan.

3 Add the egg yolks, sugar, hazelnut meal, cocoa and sherry to the chocolate mixture and use a balloon whisk to stir until well combined. Transfer to a large bowl.

4 Use an electric mixer with a whisk attachment to whisk the egg whites on medium or medium–high speed in a clean, dry medium bowl until firm peaks form. Add a spoonful of egg white to the chocolate mixture and use a large metal spoon or spatula to fold it in to 'loosen' the mixture. Add the remaining egg white and fold in until just combined.

5 Pour the mixture into the prepared tin. Bake in the preheated oven for 40–45 minutes, or until the top of the cake feels set and crumbs cling to a skewer inserted in the centre. Remove the cake from the oven, place on a wire rack and leave to cool completely in the tin.

6 Remove from the tin, dust with icing sugar or cocoa powder, and serve with cream and berries, if desired.

Baker's tip

● This cake will keep in an airtight container at room temperature for up to 4 days.

Egg White Cake with Strawberry Icing

This cake really seems to have its method all mixed up but I promise you
it works – and works beautifully, at that!

SERVES: 10

Preparation time: 20 minutes (+ 1 hour cooling and 40 minutes standing time)   Baking time: 30 minutes

Melted butter, extra, to grease
220 g (7¾ oz/1 cup) caster (superfine) sugar
150 g (5½ oz/1 cup) plain (all-purpose) flour
1½ tablespoons cornflour (cornstarch)
1 teaspoon baking powder
6 egg whites, at room temperature
100 g (3½ oz) unsalted butter, melted
    and cooled

Strawberry icing
125 g (4½ oz/1 cup) pure icing
    (confectioners') sugar
1½ tablespoons smooth strawberry jam
2–2¼ teaspoons water

1 Preheat the oven to 180°C (350°F) or 160°C (315°F)
   fan-forced. Brush a 2.5 litre (87 fl oz/10 cup) capacity
   fluted ring (bundt) tin with melted butter to grease.

2 Sift together the sugar, flour, cornflour and baking powder.

3 Use an electric mixer with a whisk attachment to whisk
   the egg whites on medium or medium–high speed in
   a clean dry bowl until soft peaks just form.

4 Sift the dry ingredients again over the egg whites and
   use a large metal spoon or spatula to fold until just
   combined. Pour over the melted butter and fold in until
   just combined.

5 Pour the mixture into the greased tin and smooth the
   surface with the back of a spoon. Bake in the preheated
   oven for 30 minutes, or until a skewer inserted in the
   cake comes out clean. Leave the cake to stand in the
   tin for 10 minutes before turning out onto a wire rack
   to cool for about 1 hour.

6 To make the Strawberry icing, sift the icing sugar into
   a medium bowl. Combine the jam and 2 teaspoons of the
   water, add to the icing sugar and stir until smooth and
   a thick coating consistency, adding the remaining
   ¼ teaspoon water if needed.

7 Spoon the icing over the cooled cake, allowing it to
   dribble down the sides. Set aside for about 30 minutes,
   or until the icing is set. Serve in slices.

Baker's tips

● This cake will keep in an airtight container at room
temperature for up to 3 days.

● You can replace the strawberry jam with another jam of
your choice – blackberry, raspberry and plum all work well.

Lemon Delicious Pudding

The magic in this old-fashioned pudding lies in the way it goes into the oven as one mixture and emerges as a gorgeous light sponge sitting over a creamy, mouth-enlivening sauce. This is one pudding that will always please.

SERVES: 6–8

Preparation time: 25 minutes   Baking time: 30–35 minutes

Melted butter, to grease
125 g (4½ oz) unsalted butter,
    at room temperature, cubed
220 g (7¾ oz/1 cup) caster (superfine) sugar
2 teaspoons finely grated lemon zest
4 eggs, at room temperature, separated
80 ml (2½ fl oz/⅓ cup) strained freshly
    squeezed lemon juice
75 g (2½ oz/½ cup) plain (all-purpose) flour
310 ml (10¾ fl oz/1¼ cups) milk
Icing (confectioners') sugar, to dust
Cream or vanilla ice cream, to serve

Baker's tips

● For a Lemon & Lime Delicious, replace half the lemon juice with freshly squeezed lime juice.

● The depth of your dish will dictate the baking time of this pudding. If using a quite shallow dish it will take less time, so check it after 25 minutes.

● This pudding is best eaten straight from the oven while the sauce still lies beneath the sponge topping. It can be served at room temperature, although the luscious sauce will be absorbed by the sponge as it stands.

1 Preheat the oven to 180°C (350°F) or 160°C (315°F) fan-forced. Lightly grease a 2 litre (70 fl oz/8 cup) capacity ovenproof dish (see Baker's tips) with melted butter.

2 Use an electric mixer to beat the butter, caster sugar and lemon zest in a medium bowl until pale and creamy. Add the egg yolks one at a time, beating well after each addition. Beat in the lemon juice (the mixture will curdle at this stage but it will be fine). On the lowest possible speed, beat in the flour and then the milk (the mixture will be a thin batter consistency).

3 Using an electric mixer with a whisk attachment on medium or medium–high speed, or a balloon whisk, whisk the egg whites in a clean, dry medium bowl until firm peaks form. Use a large metal spoon or spatula to fold half the whisked egg whites through the butter mixture to 'loosen' it. Then fold through the remaining egg whites until just combined.

4 Pour the mixture into the greased dish and place in a roasting tin or larger ovenproof dish. Add enough boiling water to the roasting tin to reach halfway up the side of the dish. Bake in the preheated oven for 30–35 minutes, until the pudding is puffed and a creamy sauce has formed under the sponge topping.

5 Remove from the oven, dust with icing sugar and serve immediately with cream or ice cream.

Mocha Roll

Another of my favourite desserts I know you will want to make again and again. It's rich but not sickly sweet, and much easier to make than you'd expect. Prepare for an avalanche of requests to bake this!

SERVES: 8

Preparation time: 30 minutes (+ 30 minutes cooling and 2 hours chilling time)   Baking time: 18–20 minutes

Melted butter, to grease
180 g (6 oz) good-quality dark
    chocolate, chopped
60 ml (2 fl oz/¼ cup) espresso coffee
    or strong freshly brewed coffee
5 eggs, at room temperature, separated
75 g (2½ oz/⅓ cup) caster (superfine) sugar
185 ml (6 fl oz/¾ cup) thickened
    (whipping) cream
1 tablespoon Frangelico or liqueur
    of your choice
1 tablespoon unsweetened cocoa powder
Berries, to serve (optional)

1 Preheat the oven to 180°C (350°F) or 160°C (315°F) fan-forced. Brush a 20 cm x 30 cm (8 in x 12 in, base measurement) Swiss roll tin (jelly roll tin) or shallow slice tin with melted butter to grease. Line the base and sides with one piece of baking paper, cutting into the corners to fit.

2 Melt the chocolate with the coffee and water in a medium heatproof bowl over a saucepan of simmering water, making sure the base of the bowl doesn't touch the water, and stir until smooth. Remove the bowl from the saucepan.

3 Put the egg yolks and sugar in a large bowl and use an electric mixer with a whisk attachment to whisk on high speed until very thick and pale and a ribbon trail forms. Use a large metal spoon or spatula to fold in the chocolate mixture until just combined.

4 Clean the whisk attachment and use the electric mixer to whisk the egg whites on medium or medium–high speed

in a clean, dry large bowl until soft peaks form. Add a large spoonful of the egg whites to the chocolate mixture and fold in to 'loosen' the mixture. Add the remaining egg white and fold until evenly combined. Pour into the prepared tin and smooth the surface.

5 Bake in the preheated oven for 18–20 minutes, or until a skewer inserted in the centre comes out clean. Remove the cake from the oven and cover immediately with a piece of baking paper and a damp tea towel (dish towel). Set aside for 30 minutes or until cooled completely.

6 Meanwhile, whisk the cream and liqueur using an electric mixer with a whisk attachment on medium speed until firm peaks form.

7 Dust another piece of baking paper evenly with the cocoa powder. Remove the tea towel and baking paper from the cake. Carefully invert the cake onto the cocoa-dusted paper. Remove the baking paper on top. Spread the cake with the liqueur cream, leaving a 1 cm (½ in) border. Starting at the longer side closest to you and using the baking paper as a guide, firmly roll up the cake. Wrap the baking paper firmly around the roll and place, seam side down, on a tray. Chill for at least 2 hours before serving with fresh berries, if you like.

Baker's tips

● The mocha flavour is subtle but you can replace the coffee with just water if you prefer.

● This roll will keep covered with plastic wrap or in an airtight container in the fridge for up to 2 days.

Three-cheese Soufflés

Having enjoyed my mum's soufflé for Sunday lunch frequently over the years, it wasn't until I got to college to study Home Economics that I discovered making one was thought to be a little frightening. But that's not necessarily the case. Soufflés can be simple and if you have never made one, now is the time!

SERVES: 4–6

Preparation time: 40 minutes   Baking time: 20 minutes

Melted butter, to grease
2 tablespoons dried breadcrumbs, to coat
50 g (1¾ oz) vintage cheddar cheese, finely shredded
50 g (1¾ oz/⅔ cup) finely shredded gruyère cheese
50 g (1¾ oz/½ cup) finely grated parmesan cheese
50 g (1¾ oz) butter
2½ tablespoons plain (all-purpose) flour
250 ml (9 fl oz/1 cup) milk
2 teaspoons dijon mustard
½ teaspoon cayenne pepper
2 tablespoons chopped chives
Handful of flat-leaf (Italian) parsley, leaves chopped
4 eggs, at room temperature, separated
Pinch of salt

1 Preheat the oven to 190°C (375°F) or 170°C (325°F) fan-forced. Brush four individual 250 ml (9 fl oz/1 cup) or six 185 ml (6 fl oz/¾ cup) capacity ramekins or soufflé dishes with melted butter to grease well. Sprinkle with the breadcrumbs, turning the dishes to coat well, and tapping out any excess breadcrumbs. Place on a baking tray.

2 Combine the cheeses, and set 2 tablespoons of the mixture aside to top the soufflés later.

3 Melt the butter in a medium saucepan over medium heat until foaming. Add the flour and stir with a balloon whisk for about 1 minute, until the mixture is bubbling and leaves the side of the pan.

4 Remove the pan from the heat and gradually add half the milk, stirring constantly with the whisk until smooth. Gradually add the remaining milk, stirring until smooth. Return the pan to medium heat and stir constantly with the whisk until the sauce thickens and starts to simmer. Reduce the heat to low and simmer, stirring frequently, for 2 minutes.

5 Transfer the sauce immediately to a heatproof bowl and stir in the cheese mixture, mustard, cayenne pepper, chives and parsley. Season well with salt and freshly ground black pepper. Add the egg yolks and stir until well combined.

6 Use an electric mixer with a whisk attachment to whisk the egg whites with a pinch of salt on medium or medium–high speed in a clean, dry bowl until firm peaks form. Add about a quarter of the whisked egg whites to the cheese sauce and use a large metal spoon or spatula to fold together until just combined to 'loosen' the mixture. Fold in the remaining egg white until just combined (this mixture will appear to have streaks of egg whites through it but there should be no large clumps of egg white).

7 Divide the mixture evenly among the prepared dishes. Sprinkle with the reserved 2 tablespoons of cheese mixture. Bake in the preheated oven for 20 minutes, or until the soufflés are well risen and cooked through (they should still wobble slightly when the dishes are tapped and a skewer inserted in the centre should come out clean but slightly moist). Serve immediately.

Lesson 8

The Whisking Egg Whites & Sugar Method

When whisked with sugar, egg whites can do spectacular things – think crisp-shelled, snowy-white meringues and you'll get the picture immediately.

As with the whisking egg whites method in the previous lesson, this method also incorporates air into egg whites through whisking. But the addition of sugar changes the consistency of the mixture completely – it becomes very thick, incredibly glossy and has a spreadable consistency that can only be described as heavenly. It is also far more stable than whisked egg whites on their own.

This mixture can either be cooked as it is, or folded through another base mixture to add body and volume to it before baking. When folded through another mixture it also adds stability and structure – something egg whites on their own can't do.

You can also use a balloon whisk for this method, but keep in mind it will take you about four times longer to get to the desired consistency than if you use an electric mixer.

Step by step

1 Put the egg whites in a clean, dry bowl.

2 Use an electric mixer with a whisk attachment to whisk on medium or medium–high speed until the egg whites are frothy. Small amounts of other ingredients, such as cornflour (cornstarch), are sometimes added at this point.

3 Continue to whisk the egg whites until 'soft peaks' form (when the whisk is lifted the mixture forms a peak that falls on itself).

4 Reduce the mixer speed to medium and start adding the sugar gradually, a large spoonful at a time, whisking constantly for about 45 seconds after each addition.

5 The mixture will start to become thicker and glossier in appearance as you whisk in more sugar.

6 Once all the sugar has been incorporated the mixture should be very thick and glossy.

7 Continue to whisk for a further 2–3 minutes, or until the sugar has dissolved completely. You can check if it has dissolved by rubbing a little between your fingertips. If you can still feel definite grains of sugar, whisk for another minute before checking again. Your mixture is now ready to fold into another base mixture or simply shape and bake as it is.

Keep in mind ...

- It's not a good idea to make meringues on hot and humid or rainy days. Moisture in the air can stop the meringue from drying properly and becoming crisp, and can also make the meringue 'weep' either during or after cooking. You also need to make sure the bowl and equipment you are using is completely dry before coming into contact with the egg whites.
- Use egg whites from eggs at room temperature, as they will hold more air than chilled ones when whisked.
- Caster (superfine) sugar is best used for this mixing method, as it will dissolve more readily than regular granulated sugar.
- Any trace of fat, including egg yolk, will stop egg whites from foaming and increasing in volume when whisked, so all your equipment – bowl, whisk and spatula or large metal spoon – must be super clean. All equipment should also be completely dry, to avoid the negative effects of moisture. And never use a plastic bowl when whisking egg whites – stainless steel, glass, ceramic or copper bowls are best as they won't trap fat.
- Always separate each egg into a small dish before adding the white to the mixing bowl so if any yolk gets into the white it's easily removed and you don't have to throw away the whole batch.

- Choose the whisk attachment if using a stand mixer or hand-held electric beaters. If your hand-held beaters don't have a whisk attachment, just use the standard beaters.
- Whisk the egg whites on their own on medium or medium–high speed just until 'soft peaks' form before starting to add the sugar.
- When you start to add the sugar, do it gradually, a large spoonful at a time. And make sure you whisk on medium speed until the sugar is well combined before adding the next lot.
- Continue to whisk until the sugar dissolves completely (rub a little mixture between your thumb and finger to test this). When you lift the whisk, a long trailing peak should form.
- Whisking on medium will ensure the mixture will be a thick, smooth (not foamy) consistency.
- Don't continue to whisk once this point is reached. If overwhisked there is a chance the mixture will collapse during cooking and beads of liquid sugar will form on the surface.

Now get baking!

The recipes in this Lesson using the whisking egg whites and sugar method range from the perfect pavlova to cute little powder puffs and are all a great way to master this technique.

Summer Berry Pavlova

My mum used to make pavlova often. I remember her making many of them for my dad's surprise 40th birthday – every time he left the house to go to the paddocks she would whip up another one, wrap it carefully and then hide it somewhere around the house so he wouldn't suspect anything. One even ended up under my bed! Mum chose the right dessert for a large party – pavlova is definitely a crowd-pleaser.

SERVES: 8–10

Preparation time: 30 minutes (+ 2 hours cooling time) Baking time: 1 hour 15 minutes

Melted butter, to grease

4 egg whites, at room temperature

Pinch of salt

1 teaspoon white vinegar

2 teaspoons cornflour (cornstarch), plus extra, to dust

220 g (7¾ oz/1 cup) caster (superfine) sugar

1½ teaspoons natural vanilla extract or essence

500 g (1 lb 2 oz) fresh mixed berries (such as raspberries, blueberries and hulled small strawberries, halved if large)

1 tablespoon icing (confectioners') sugar

Raspberry cream

300 g (10½ oz) frozen raspberries, thawed

30 g (1 oz/¼ cup) icing (confectioners') sugar, sifted

200 ml (7 fl oz) thickened (whipping) cream, whipped to firm peaks

130 g (4½ oz/½ cup) Greek-style natural yoghurt

1 Place the oven rack in the lower third of the oven and preheat to 110°C (225°F). Lightly grease a rectangular ovenproof serving platter (see Baker's tips) with melted butter and dust lightly with extra cornflour.

2 Use an electric mixer with a whisk attachment to whisk the egg whites in a clean, dry large bowl on medium speed until foamy. Add the salt, vinegar and cornflour, and whisk on medium speed until soft peaks form (about 1 minute).

3 With the motor running, add the sugar a spoonful at a time, whisking well after each addition, until all the sugar has dissolved and the mixture is very thick and glossy (this will take 4–5 minutes). Add the vanilla and whisk to combine. Use a spatula to stir the meringue mixture to 'loosen' it slightly (to get rid of any excess air in the mixture and give it a smoother, less 'foamy' texture).

4 Spread the meringue mixture onto the prepared serving platter to make a 16 cm x 28 cm (6¼ in x 11¼ in) rectangle. Make a shallow well down the centre. Bake in the lower third of the preheated oven for 1 hour 15 minutes, until the meringue is crisp and hard to the touch, but not coloured.

Recipe continued overleaf →

Variations

Individual Summer Berry Pavlovas – Instead of spreading the meringue mixture on the rectangular platter, spoon 6 large ovals of mixture on a large baking tray lined with baking paper. Use the back of a metal spoon to make an indent in the centre of each. Reduce the baking time to 50–60 minutes. Divide the raspberry cream and macerated berries among the individual pavlovas to serve.

Mango, Raspberry & Passionfruit Pavlova – Replace the macerated berries with the pulp of 4 passionfruit, the flesh of 2 firm but ripe mangoes (cut into thin slices) and 125 g (4½ oz) fresh raspberries. Just before serving, spoon half the passionfruit over the cream and top with the mango slices and raspberries. Finish with the remaining passionfruit pulp.

Pomegranate & Fig Pavlova – Replace the macerated fresh berries with 1 pomegranate, seeds removed and any juice reserved, and 600 g (1 lb 5 oz) firm but ripe figs, cut into quarters. Combine the pomegranate seeds and reserved juice, figs and 1 teaspoon rosewater (optional), and toss gently to combine. Replace the raspberry cream with 300 ml (10½ fl oz) thickened (whipping) cream, whipped to soft peaks. Spoon the pomegranate and fig and the juices over the cream just before serving.

5 Turn off the oven, leave the door slightly ajar (see Baker's tips) and let the meringue cool completely in the oven (about 2 hours).

6 To macerate the fresh berries, place them in a bowl, sprinkle with the 1 tablespoon of icing sugar, stir gently and set aside for 30 minutes.

7 To make the Raspberry cream, place the frozen raspberries and the icing sugar in a small food processor (or use a hand/stick blender) and process until puréed. Press the raspberry purée through a sieve, discarding the seeds. Fold together the whipped cream and yoghurt. Swirl a quarter of the purée through the whipped cream mixture.

8 Spoon the raspberry cream into the centre of the pavlova and top with the macerated fresh berries. Serve immediately with the remaining raspberry purée on the side.

Baker's tips

● If you don't have a rectangular ovenproof serving platter, bake the pavlova shell on a baking tray lined with baking paper and transfer to a platter to fill and serve.

● Use a wooden spoon to keep the oven door ajar if it won't stay slightly open on its own when cooling the pavlova shell.

● The unfilled pavlova shell will keep in an airtight container in a cool place (but not in the fridge) for up to 1 day.

Powder Puffs

I had my first ever powder puff at the kitchen tea before my wedding some 20 years ago. It was light, delicate and heavenly – and I can't believe it took me that long to experience such a gorgeous treat! These start out slightly crisp and then take on a sponge-like texture once filled with jam and cream – a mini sponge cake just for one.

MAKES: ABOUT 14

Preparation time: 20 minutes (+ 2–3 hours standing time)   Baking time: 10–12 minutes (per batch)

2 eggs, at room temperature, separated
Pinch of salt
75 g (2½ oz/⅓ cup) caster (superfine) sugar
½ teaspoon natural vanilla extract
  or essence
35 g (1¼ oz/¼ cup) plain (all-purpose) flour
30 g (1 oz/¼ cup) cornflour (cornstarch)
½ teaspoon baking powder
100 ml (3½ fl oz) thickened
  (whipping) cream
115 g (4 oz/⅓ cup) raspberry jam
Icing (confectioners') sugar, to dust

Baker's tip

● The unfilled sponge rounds will keep in an airtight container at room temperature for up to 2 days. The filled powder puffs will keep in an airtight container in the fridge for up to 2 days. Leave the powder puffs to stand at room temperature for 30 minutes before serving.

1 Preheat the oven to 190°C (375°F) or 170°C (325°F) fan-forced. Line three large baking trays with baking paper.

2 Use an electric mixer with a whisk attachment to whisk the egg whites and salt on medium–high speed in a clean, dry bowl until soft peaks form. With the motor running, gradually add the sugar, a spoonful at a time, whisking well after each addition, until all the sugar has dissolved completely and the mixture is thick and glossy. Whisk in the vanilla. Add the egg yolks one at a time, whisking after each addition until well combined.

3 Sift together the flour, cornflour and baking powder over the egg mixture and whisk until just combined (be careful not to overwhisk).

4 Spoon heaped teaspoonfuls of the mixture onto the trays about 3 cm (1¼ in) apart to allow room for spreading, to make about 28. Use the back of the teaspoon to flatten each one slightly to a round about 5 cm (2 in) in diameter and 1 cm (½ in) thick.

5 Bake one tray of powder puffs in the centre of the preheated oven for 10–12 minutes or until the rounds are pale golden and slightly puffed. Remove from the oven and cool on the tray. Bake the remaining trays of mixture in two more batches.

6 Use a clean whisk attachment or balloon whisk to whisk the cream until soft peaks form. Spread the underside of half the cooked sponge rounds with a little jam, dividing evenly. Spread the remaining sponge rounds with the whipped cream, dividing evenly, and then sandwich the jam rounds with the cream rounds. Serve immediately or set aside for 2–3 hours, or until the sponge rounds soften slightly, dusted with icing sugar.

Angel Food Cake

A type of sponge cake originating in the US back in the 1800s, this has a light, chiffon-like texture and goes so well with whipped cream and ripe fresh strawberries. You'll need a special angel food cake tin for this recipe – basically a deep ring tin (21 cm/8¼ in, base measurement) with a removable base.

SERVES: 8–10

Preparation time: 25 minutes (+ 1 hour cooling time)   Baking time: 40 minutes

150 g (5½ oz/1 cup) plain (all-purpose) flour
275 g (9¾ oz/1¼ cups) caster (superfine) sugar
12 egg whites, at room temperature
1½ teaspoons cream of tartar
1½ teaspoons natural vanilla extract or essence
Strawberries and whipped cream, to serve
Icing (confectioners') sugar, to dust

Baker's tips

● This angel food cake is best cut with a sharp non-serrated knife.

● It will keep for up to 3 days in an airtight container at room temperature.

1 Preheat the oven to 180°C (350°F) or 160°C (315°F) fan-forced. Have an ungreased 21 cm (8¼ in, base measurement) angel food cake tin ready.

2 Sift the flour and 55 g (2 oz/¼ cup) of the caster sugar twice onto a piece of baking paper.

3 Use an electric mixer with a whisk attachment to whisk the egg whites and cream of tartar on medium speed in a clean, dry bowl, until soft peaks form. With the motor running, gradually add the remaining 220 g (7¾ oz/1 cup) of caster sugar, a spoonful at a time, whisking well after each addition, until all the sugar has dissolved completely and the mixture is thick and glossy. Whisk in the vanilla.

4 Sift one-third of the flour and sugar mixture over the egg white mixture and use a large metal spoon or spatula to fold until just combined. Repeat with the remaining flour and sugar mixture in two more batches.

5 Spoon the mixture into the ungreased tin and gently smooth the surface with the back of a metal spoon. Bake for 40 minutes, or until well risen, pale golden, and a skewer inserted in the centre comes out clean.

6 Immediately turn the cake upside down on a wire rack and set aside, still in the tin, for 1 hour or until completely cool.

7 To remove the cake, gently shake the tin to release it then invert onto a serving plate. Serve with strawberries and whipped cream and dust with icing sugar.

Giant Marbled Chocolate Meringues

The ability of egg whites to go from a translucent liquid to snowy-white clouds when whisked with sugar is one of the most wonderful transformations to show children in the kitchen. Kids will adore making these playful over-sized meringues with chocolate swirls, almost as much as they will love eating them!

MAKES: ABOUT 8 LARGE

Preparation time: 20 minutes (+ cooling time)   Baking time: 2 hours

4 egg whites, at room temperature
A good pinch of salt
220 g (7¾ oz/1 cup) caster (superfine) sugar
1 teaspoon natural vanilla extract or essence
1½ tablespoons unsweetened cocoa powder

Variation

Bite-sized Marbled Chocolate Meringues – For smaller meringues use teaspoons to spoon the mixture onto the lined trays. This will make about 40 meringues that should be baked for 1 hour then cooled in the same way as the giant versions.

1 Preheat the oven to 120°C (235°F). Line two large baking trays with baking paper.

2 Put the egg whites and salt in a clean, dry large bowl and use an electric mixer with a whisk attachment to whisk on medium or medium–high speed until soft peaks form. Gradually add the sugar, a spoonful at a time, whisking well after each addition on medium speed until well combined. After the last of the sugar has been added, continue to whisk for 1–2 minutes, or until the mixture is very thick and glossy and the sugar has dissolved completely. (You can tell if the mixture is ready by rubbing a little between your fingers – if it still feels grainy then continue to whisk for a little longer.) Whisk in the vanilla.

3 Sift the cocoa powder over the meringue mixture. Use a spatula or a large metal spoon to fold the meringue 3–4 times, or until the cocoa powder is streaked through the mixture.

4 Use 2 tablespoons to spoon the mixture into 8 large meringues on the lined trays. Place the trays in the oven, reduce the temperature to 90°C (195°F) and bake for 2 hours, or until the meringues are crisp on the outside.

5 Turn off the heat and allow the meringues to cool completely in the oven.

Baker's tip

● Keep these meringues in an airtight container at room temperature for up to 2 days.

Coconut Macaroons

The similar names often cause confusion, but even though macaroons and macarons (page 219) have egg whites and deliciousness in common, they are based on different concepts. These coconut macaroons are a lovely and simple, slightly chewy Italian biscuit made with egg whites and coconut and/or almond meal. They shouldn't be confused with the crisp, very sweet, sandwiched French macarons.

MAKES: ABOUT 30

Preparation time: 20 minutes   Baking time: 18 minutes

2 egg whites, at room temperature
Pinch of salt
80 g (2¾ oz/⅓ cup) caster (superfine) sugar
1 teaspoon natural vanilla extract or essence
135 g (4¾ oz/1½ cups) desiccated coconut
50 g (1¾ oz/½ cup) almond meal

Variations

Citrus Coconut Macaroons – Add the finely grated zest of 1 orange to the egg white mixture with the vanilla.

Chocolate Coconut Macaroons – Fold 120 g (4¼ oz) finely chopped dark chocolate through the egg white mixture with the coconut and almond meal.

Raspberry Coconut Macaroons – Use a teaspoon to make an indent in the top of each macaroon and add a little raspberry jam before baking.

1 Preheat the oven to 170°C (325°F) or 150°C (300°F) fan-forced. Line two large baking trays with baking paper.

2 Use an electric mixer with a whisk attachment to whisk the egg whites and salt on medium–high speed in a clean, dry bowl until soft peaks form. Gradually add the sugar, a spoonful at a time, whisking well after each addition, until very thick and glossy and the sugar has dissolved. Whisk in the vanilla.

3 Combine the coconut and almond meal. Add to the egg white mixture and use a large metal spoon or spatula to fold until just combined.

4 Spoon teaspoonfuls of the mixture onto the lined trays about 2 cm (¾ in) apart. Bake in the preheated oven for 18 minutes, swapping the trays around halfway through baking, or until golden and cooked through (they will still be a little soft to the touch). Leave the macaroons to cool on the trays.

Baker's tip

● These biscuits will keep in an airtight container at room temperature for up to 1 week.

Almond Bread

More like a biscuit, this wafer-thin almond bread is crispy, subtly sweet and studded with nuts. If you wrap the cooled loaf in plastic wrap and then foil and store it in the fridge for 1–2 days, it will be easier to cut into its characteristically thin slices. If you have one, an electric knife (remember those from the '70s?) makes slicing easier.   MAKES: ABOUT 50

Preparation time: 15 minutes (+ 1 hour cooling time)   Baking time: 50–55 minutes

Melted butter, to grease
3 egg whites, at room temperature
Pinch of salt
110 g (3¾ oz/½ cup) caster (superfine) sugar
1 teaspoon natural vanilla extract or essence
150 g (5½ oz/1 cup) plain (all-purpose) flour
150 g (5½ oz) natural almonds

Baker's tips

● The cooled loaf can be wrapped in plastic wrap and then foil and kept in the fridge for up to 1 week, then sliced and baked for the second time.

● An electric knife is great to use when cutting this loaf into wafer-thin slices.

● This almond bread will last for up to 1 month in an airtight jar or container at room temperature.

1 Preheat the oven to 180°C (350°F) or 160°C (315°F) fan-forced. Grease a 9 cm x 19 cm (3½ in x 7½ in, base measurement) loaf (bar) tin with melted butter and line the base and two long sides with one piece of baking paper.

2 Use an electric mixer with a whisk attachment to whisk the egg whites and salt on medium–high speed in a clean, dry bowl until soft peaks form. With the motor running, gradually add the sugar, a spoonful at a time, whisking well after each addition, until all the sugar has dissolved completely and the mixture is thick and glossy. Whisk in the vanilla.

3 Use a large metal spoon or spatula to fold in the flour and almonds until evenly combined. Spoon the mixture into the prepared tin and smooth the surface with the back of a metal spoon.

4 Bake in the preheated oven for 30 minutes or until golden and a skewer inserted in the centre comes out clean. Remove from the oven and leave the loaf in the tin on a wire rack for 1 hour or until cool. (See Baker's tips.)

5 Reduce the oven temperature to 150°C (300°F) or 130°C (250°F) fan-forced. Line two large baking trays with baking paper.

6 Use a very sharp knife (see Baker's tips) to cut the loaf into wafer-thin slices about 3 mm thick. Arrange the slices in a single layer on the lined baking trays (it is fine if they are close together). Bake in the preheated oven for 20–25 minutes, swapping the trays halfway through baking, or until lightly golden and crisp. Leave the wafers to cool on the trays.

Chocolate Soufflé Pudding

I have been baking this gluten-free pudding for years. Not only is it completely heavenly, it is also very clever and can be baked as a cake when you want.

SERVES: 8

Preparation time: 20 minutes (+ 5 minutes standing time)   Baking time: 55–60 minutes

Melted butter, to grease

Unsweetened cocoa powder, sifted, to dust

200 g (7 oz/1⅓ cups) chopped good-quality dark chocolate (70 per cent cocoa is good)

125 g (4½ oz) unsalted butter, cubed

2 tablespoons marsala wine or freshly brewed strong coffee

165 g (5¾ oz/¾ cup) caster (superfine) sugar

5 eggs, at room temperature, separated

Icing (confectioners') sugar, to dust

Cream or vanilla ice cream, to serve

Variation

Chocolate Soufflé Cake – Bake the mixture in a 22 cm (8½ in, base measurement) spring-form cake tin that has been base-lined with baking paper, and then greased and dusted with unsweetened cocoa powder. Bake at the same temperature for 55–60 minutes. Leave the cake to cool in the tin. Cut into wedges to serve.

1 Preheat the oven to 170°C (325°F) or 150°C (300°F) fan-forced. Brush a 2 litre (70 fl oz/8 cup) capacity ovenproof dish (about 20 cm/8 in diameter) with melted butter to grease. Lightly dust with cocoa powder, tapping out any excess.

2 Place the chocolate and butter in a medium heatproof bowl over a saucepan of simmering water, making sure the base of the bowl doesn't touch the water, and stir until melted and smooth. Transfer the mixture to a large bowl and stir in the marsala, 110 g (3¾ oz/½ cup) of the caster sugar and the egg yolks.

3 Use an electric mixer with a whisk attachment to whisk the egg whites in a clean, dry large bowl on medium speed until soft peaks form. Add the remaining 55 g (2 oz/¼ cup) caster sugar and whisk until thick and glossy. Add one-third of the egg white mixture to the chocolate mixture and use a large metal spoon or spatula to fold together. Fold through the remaining egg white mixture until just combined.

4 Pour the mixture into the prepared dish. Bake in the preheated oven for 55–60 minutes, or until crumbs cling to a skewer inserted in the centre.

5 Remove the pudding from the oven and set aside for 5 minutes. Dust with icing sugar and serve in scoops with cream or ice cream.

Baker's tips

● This pudding is also delicious served at room temperature. Leave to cool in the dish before serving.

● Any leftover pudding will keep covered in the fridge for up to 3 days. Leave to stand at room temperature for at least 30 minutes before serving.

Individual Berry Queen of Puddings

I've taken the idea of the retro British queen of puddings – custard, cake and jam with meringue baked on top – but made individual ones and added fresh berries.

SERVES: 8

Preparation time: 25 minutes (+ 30 minutes cooling time)   Baking time: 23–28 minutes

250 ml (9 fl oz/1 cup) milk
250 ml (9 fl oz/1 cup) thin (pouring) cream
1 vanilla bean, split lengthways
5 egg yolks, at room temperature
55 g (2 oz/¼ cup) caster (superfine) sugar
150 g (5½ oz/2½ cups, lightly packed) fresh white breadcrumbs
Finely grated zest of 2 lemons
2 tablespoons mixed berry jam
250 g (9 oz) fresh mixed berries (such as raspberries, blueberries and blackberries)
1 tablespoon icing (confectioners') sugar, to dust

Meringue topping
4 egg whites, at room temperature
Pinch of salt
165 g (5¾ oz/¾ cup) caster (superfine) sugar
1 teaspoon natural vanilla extract or essence

Baker's tips

● You can cover the bottom of the roasting tin with a folded tea towel (dish towel) to stop the ramekins sliding around when transferring them to and from the oven.

● If you want to make the puddings ahead of time, follow the recipe to the end of Step 3 up to 2 days before serving. Leave the puddings to stand at room temperature for 30 minutes before continuing with the recipe.

● You can caramelise the meringue topping with a blowtorch after baking, as we have, for a more 'dramatic' effect.

1 Preheat the oven to 160°C (315°F) or 140°C (275°F) fan-forced. Place eight 185 ml (6 fl oz/¾ cup) capacity ramekins or ovenproof dishes in a roasting tin.

2 Combine the milk and cream in a medium saucepan. Scrape the seeds from the vanilla bean and add the seeds and bean to the saucepan. Bring slowly to a simmer.

3 Meanwhile, use a balloon whisk or an electric mixer with a whisk attachment to whisk together the egg yolks and caster sugar in a large heatproof bowl until pale and creamy. Slowly whisk the hot milk mixture into the egg yolk mixture. Whisk in the breadcrumbs and lemon zest. Divide the custard evenly between the ramekins.

4 Add enough boiling water to the roasting tin to reach halfway up the sides of the ramekins to create a water bath (bain marie). Bake in the preheated oven for 15–18 minutes or until the custard has just set. Remove from the oven and transfer the ramekins to a wire rack. Set aside for 30 minutes or until cool.

5 Increase the oven temperature to 190°C (375°F) or 170°C (325°F) fan-forced.

6 To make the Meringue topping, use an electric mixer with a whisk attachment to whisk the egg whites and salt on medium speed until soft peaks form. With the motor running, gradually add the sugar, a spoonful at a time, and whisk until the sugar has dissolved completely and the mixture is thick and glossy. Whisk in the vanilla.

7 Warm the jam in a small saucepan over low heat, stirring often. Carefully spread over the top of the custards then divide the berries evenly between the ramekins. Top with the meringue mixture, swirling as desired.

8 Bake in the preheated oven for 8–10 minutes, or until the meringue is lightly browned. Serve immediately.

Meringue Kisses

Crisp and chewy, large and small, plain and with sprinkles – meringues were a big part of my childhood, especially at parties. They are a great thing to learn to make and are always popular with big and little kids alike.

MAKES: 45

Preparation time: 30 minutes (+ 2 hours cooling time) Baking time: 1 hour

2 egg whites, at room temperature
Pinch of salt
110 g (3¾ oz/½ cup) caster (superfine) sugar
1½ teaspoons natural vanilla extract
    or essence
2 teaspoons cornflour (cornstarch),
    plus extra, to dust
Natural food colouring or gel of
    your choice (optional)
Sprinkles of your choice (optional)

Baker's tips

● If your oven doesn't stay slightly ajar on its own, stick a wooden spoon in the top opening.

● For chewy rather than crisp meringues, cool them at room temperature.

● These meringue kisses will keep in an airtight container or jar at room temperature for up to 1 week.

1 Preheat the oven to 110°C (225°F). Line two large baking trays with baking paper.

2 Use an electric mixer with a whisk attachment to whisk the egg whites and salt in a clean, dry large bowl on medium or medium–high speed until soft peaks form.

3 With the motor running on medium speed, add the sugar a spoonful at a time, whisking well after each addition, until all the sugar has dissolved and the mixture is very thick and glossy (4–5 minutes). Add the vanilla and cornflour and whisk to combine. Use a spatula to stir the meringue mixture to 'loosen' it slightly.

4 For striped meringues, use a wide paintbrush to lightly brush vertical lines of liquid or gel food colouring, evenly spaced, on the inside of a large piping (icing) bag fitted with a plain 1.7 cm (⅔ in) nozzle. Use a large metal spoon or spatula to spoon the meringue mixture into the piping bag. Twist the end of the piping bag and pipe small 'kisses' about 3 cm (1¼ in) in diameter on the lined baking trays about 2 cm (¾ in) apart. Alternatively, you can spoon the plain meringue onto the trays and scatter over sprinkles. Bake in the preheated oven for 1 hour, swapping the trays halfway, or until the meringues are crisp and hard to touch, but without any golden tinges.

5 Turn off the oven, leave the door slightly ajar (see Baker's tips) and leave the meringues to cool completely in the oven (about 2 hours).

White Chocolate & Orange Macarons

French macarons – the darlings of the confectionery world – are unashamedly sweet and have been made with both classic and the most unlikely of flavourings. This recipe is far easier than the classic technique but produces similar results.

MAKES: ABOUT 16

Preparation time: 25 minutes (+ 30 minutes standing and 1 hour chilling time)   Baking time: 15–20 minutes

80 g (2¾ oz/¾ cup) almond meal
125 g (4½ oz/1 cup) pure icing (confectioners') sugar, sifted
2 egg whites, at room temperature
2 tablespoons caster (superfine) sugar

White chocolate ganache
200 g (7 oz) good-quality white chocolate, finely chopped
60 ml (2 fl oz/¼ cup) thin (pouring) cream
1 teaspoon orange blossom water, or to taste
Finely grated zest of 2 oranges

1 Combine the almond meal and icing sugar in a bowl and use a balloon whisk to stir until they are evenly combined with no lumps. Set aside.

2 Use an electric mixer with a whisk attachment to whisk the egg whites and caster sugar on medium or medium–high speed in a clean, dry large bowl until the sugar has dissolved and the mixture is thick and glossy. Use a large metal spoon or spatula to gently fold the almond meal and icing sugar mixture through the meringue until just combined.

3 Spoon half the macaron mixture into a piping (icing) bag fitted with a 1 cm (½ in) nozzle (see Baker's tips). Pipe 3 cm (1¼ in) rounds on the lined trays about 2 cm (¾ in) apart (see Baker's tips). Tap the trays lightly on the bench top to help settle the mixture. Refill the piping bag with the remaining meringue and repeat.

4 Leave the macarons to stand at room temperature for 30 minutes or until a skin forms on the top of each one.

5 Preheat the oven to 150°C (300°F). Line two large baking trays with baking paper (see Baker's tips).

6 Bake the macarons in the preheated oven, swapping the trays halfway through cooking, for 15–20 minutes or until the macarons are crisp on the outside. Remove from the oven and leave to cool on the trays.

7 To make the White chocolate ganache, place the chocolate and cream in a small heatproof bowl over a saucepan of simmering water, making sure the base of the bowl doesn't touch the water. Stir frequently until the chocolate has just melted and the mixture is smooth. Stir in the orange blossom water and orange zest. Refrigerate for 1 hour, stirring occasionally, until the mixture is thick and spreadable.

8 Spread a cooled macaron with a little ganache and sandwich with another macaron. Repeat with the remaining macarons and ganache.

Baker's tips

● You can draw 3 cm (1¼ in) circles, 2 cm (¾ in) apart on the baking paper before using it, marked side down, to line the baking trays. This makes it easier to pipe the macarons in a consistent size.

● If you don't want the fuss of piping the meringues, you can simply put teaspoonfuls of the mixture onto the trays. It won't create perfect rounds but will still give a good result.

● The unfilled macarons will keep in an airtight container at room temperature for up to 1 week. Once filled they will keep in an airtight container at room temperature for up to 3 days.

Hazelnut & Chocolate Tortes

An elegant take on the notion of a torte, these little individual treats are deceptively simple to make. Bake, layer and impress!

SERVES: 8

Preparation time: 30 minutes (+ 2 hours cooling and 10 minutes chilling)   Baking time: 1 hour 40 minutes

60 g (2¼ oz) good-quality dark chocolate
  (70 per cent cocoa), chopped
2 tablespoons thin (pouring) cream
Extra coarsely chopped hazelnuts, to serve

Hazelnut meringue
150 g (5½ oz) toasted and peeled hazelnuts
  (*see Baker's tips*)
4 egg whites, at room temperature
Pinch of salt
220 g (7¾ oz/1 cup) caster (superfine) sugar
1½ teaspoons natural vanilla extract
  or essence

Chocolate ganache
150 g (5½ oz/1 cup) chopped good-quality
  dark chocolate (70 per cent cocoa)
125 ml (4 fl oz/½ cup) thin (pouring) cream

1 Preheat the oven to 100°C (200°F). Draw a 20 cm (8 in) square on three pieces of baking paper. Line three baking trays with the paper, pencil marks facing down.

2 To make the Hazelnut meringue, process 100 g (3½ oz) of the hazelnuts in a food processor until finely ground. Coarsely chop the remaining hazelnuts.

3 Use an electric mixer with a whisk attachment to whisk the egg whites and salt on medium speed in a clean, dry bowl until soft peaks form. With the motor running, gradually add the sugar, a spoonful at a time, and whisk until the sugar has dissolved completely and the mixture is thick and glossy. Whisk in the vanilla. Use a large metal spoon or spatula to fold the ground hazelnuts into the meringue.

4 Divide the meringue evenly among the marked squares on the baking trays and use the back of a spoon to spread evenly to fill each. Bake in the preheated oven for 1 hour and

40 minutes, swapping the trays between shelves every 30 minutes, or until the meringue is crisp. Turn off the oven and leave the meringue in the oven, with the door shut, for 2 hours or until cooled to room temperature.

5 To make the Chocolate ganache, combine the chocolate and cream in a small saucepan. Stir frequently over low heat until the chocolate has melted and the mixture is smooth. Transfer to a medium bowl, cover and set aside at room temperature until a thin spreadable consistency.

6 Spread half the ganache over one of the meringue layers still on the tray. Top with another meringue sheet. Continue to layer with the remaining chocolate ganache and meringue layers, finishing with a meringue layer. Cover with plastic wrap and refrigerate for 10 minutes.

7 Place the 60 g (2¼ oz) chocolate and 2 tablespoons cream in a small heatproof bowl over a saucepan of simmering water, making sure the base doesn't touch the water. Stir occasionally until the chocolate has just melted and the mixture is smooth. Remove the bowl from the saucepan.

8 Carefully transfer the layered meringue to a cutting board. Use a sharp knife to trim the edges and then cut into 8 portions about 5 cm x 10 cm (2 in x 4 in). Drizzle each one with the chocolate mixture and scatter over the chopped hazelnuts to serve.

Baker's tips

● To toast and peel the hazelnuts, spread on a baking tray and place in an oven preheated to 180°C (350°F) or 160°C (315°F) fan-forced for 10 minutes, shaking the tray occasionally, until lightly golden and the skins start peeling away from the nuts. Set aside to cool. Place the hazelnuts in a clean tea towel (dish towel) and rub to remove the skins.

● These tortes will keep in an airtight container at room temperature for up to 2 days.

Lesson 9

The Whisking Eggs & Sugar Method

Baked products that have a light and airy texture, such as sponge cakes, use this mixing method. It's also often used in biscotti, slices, some brownies, and puddings such as chocolate fondant puddings.

This method is used when you want to incorporate air into whole eggs to lighten a mixture. Recipes using the whisking method usually contain little or no butter or raising agent and therefore the main way to lighten the mixture is by whisking the eggs with sugar.

Sometimes the whisking eggs and sugar method is done in a bowl over a saucepan of simmering water (without the bowl actually touching the water). In this technique the eggs cook gently as they are whisked and as a result will thicken and form a more stable mixture. You will need hand-held electric beaters or a balloon whisk if a recipe asks for you to do this, as you can't use a stand mixer. Make sure you check the recipe before you start.

Step by step

1 Put the whole eggs in a mixing bowl.

2 Use an electric mixer with a whisk attachment on high speed or a balloon whisk to whisk the whole eggs until they are frothy.

3 With the motor running, add the sugar a spoonful at a time, whisking well after each addition. (Note that in some recipes all the sugar is added at the beginning with the eggs, or all the sugar may need to be added once the eggs are frothy, so it is important to check the method.)

4 Continue to add the sugar a spoonful at a time and whisk. The more sugar you add and the more you whisk the mixture, the paler in colour and thicker in texture it will become.

5 Continue to whisk until the mixture has increased in volume considerably (often three times the original volume, depending on the eggs to sugar ratio) and has become very pale and thick.

6 Recipes often state that when the mixture has been whisked enough it should 'form a ribbon trail when the whisk is lifted'. To check if you have

Keep in mind ...

- Use eggs to be whisked at room temperature, as they will hold more air than chilled ones when whisked.
- Caster (superfine) sugar is best used for this method, as it will dissolve more readily than regular granulated sugar.
- Use the whisk attachment if using a stand mixer or hand-held electric beaters. If your hand-held beaters don't have a whisk attachment, the standard beaters will suffice.
- Whisk on high speed to reach the desired consistency in the least amount of time. Whisking on a lower speed is fine but, like using a balloon whisk, it will take longer.

Now get baking!

All sounds pretty simple? Well it is, and now is the time to get into the kitchen and really see how easy it is to master this method with recipes for sponge cakes, biscotti, puddings and more.

reached this point, stop whisking, lift the whisk out of the mixture and wave it across the surface of the mixture. If it leaves a ribbon trail that lasts on the surface for at least 3 seconds, it is ready. Alternatively, draw a figure eight on the surface and if the start of the figure is still visible when you finish it, it is ready. If not, whisk until this happens.

7 Sift over any dry ingredients and add any liquids.

8 Immediately whisk briefly on low speed until just combined. Alternatively, the recipe may say to fold in these ingredients with a spatula or large metal spoon. Your mixture is now ready for baking.

Classic Sponge

A sponge is the quintessential afternoon tea treat. A well-made one is totally sublime and unforgettable. There are two main tricks when making a sponge: don't overwhisk the mixture once you have added the flour, and keep a close eye on your sponge in the oven, as it won't take long to bake and will be dry if overcooked.

SERVES: 8

Preparation time: 25 minutes   Baking time: 18–20 minutes

Melted butter, to grease
4 eggs, at room temperature
165 g (5¾ oz/¾ cup) caster (superfine) sugar
60 ml (2 fl oz/¼ cup) milk
20 g (¾ oz) butter
110 g (3¾ oz/¾ cup) self-raising flour, plus extra, to dust
30 g (1 oz/¼ cup) cornflour (cornstarch)
185 ml (6 fl oz/¾ cup) thickened (whipping) cream
225 g (8 oz/⅔ cup) strawberry jam
Icing (confectioners') sugar, to dust

1 Place the oven rack in the lower third of the oven and preheat to 180°C (350°F) or 160°C (315°F) fan-forced. Brush two 20 cm (8 in) shallow (sandwich) cake tins with melted butter to lightly grease. Line the bases with circles of baking paper. Lightly brush the paper again with melted butter, then dust the bases and sides of the tins with a little flour to lightly coat, tapping out any excess.

2 Use an electric mixer with a whisk attachment on medium–high speed to whisk the eggs in a large bowl until frothy. Add the sugar a spoonful at a time, whisking well after each addition, until the mixture is very thick and pale (about 8 minutes). The mixture is ready when it forms a ribbon trail when the whisk is lifted.

3 Heat the milk and butter in a small saucepan over medium heat just until the butter melts. Remove from the heat.

4 Sift the flour and cornflour together over the egg mixture. Quickly pour the warm milk mixture down the side of the bowl and then immediately whisk again with the electric mixer on low speed briefly, until the flour mixture is just incorporated (be careful not to overmix).

5 Divide the mixture evenly between the tins (see Baker's tips) and gently tap them on the bench top 3 times to settle the mixture. Bake in the preheated oven for 18–20 minutes, or until the cakes are pale golden, spring back when lightly touched in the centre and start pulling away from the sides of the tins. Remove the cakes from the oven and leave to stand for 2 minutes before turning out onto a wire rack, top side up (see Baker's tips), to cool completely.

6 When ready to fill, use an electric mixer with a whisk attachment or a balloon whisk to whisk the cream in a medium bowl until firm peaks form. Spread one cake with the jam and then the whipped cream. Top with the remaining cake and dust with icing sugar.

Baker's tips

● Weigh the tins to ensure you have divided the cake mixture evenly.

● When removing the cakes from the tins, turn them onto a wire rack covered with a tea towel (dish towel) before inverting onto another rack. This will prevent the rack marking the tops of the cakes.

● Sponge cakes are best eaten on the day they are baked.

Gluten-free Mandarin, Polenta & Coconut Cakes

These cakes are a play on the original (and wonderful) Middle Eastern Orange Cake from the one and only Elizabeth David. Making use of seasonal mandarins and with the addition of coconut and polenta, this version is also flourless and gluten-free.

MAKES: 12

Preparation time: 20 minutes (+ 30–60 minutes simmering, cooling time and 20 minutes standing)   Baking time: 15–18 minutes

2 large mandarins (about 110 g/3¾ oz each)
Melted butter, to grease
100 g (3½ oz/1 cup) almond meal
95 g (3¼ oz/½ cup) instant polenta
45 g (1½ oz/½ cup) desiccated coconut
½ teaspoon baking powder
3 eggs, at room temperature
165 g (5¾ oz/¾ cup) caster (superfine) sugar
1½ teaspoons natural vanilla extract
    or essence

Mandarin icing
250 g (9 oz/2 cups) pure icing
    (confectioners') sugar
1½–2 tablespoons mandarin juice

1 Put the whole mandarins in a small saucepan, cover with water and set over high heat. Bring to the boil, reduce the heat and simmer for 30–60 minutes, or until very soft when tested with a skewer. (You may need to place a small saucer over the mandarins to keep them submerged.) Remove the mandarins from the water and set aside to cool slightly.

2 Meanwhile, preheat the oven to 180°C (350°F) or 160°C (315°F) fan-forced. Brush a 12-hole 80 ml (2½ fl oz/⅓ cup) capacity silicone or metal muffin tin with melted butter to grease. Quarter the mandarins and remove and discard the centre core and any seeds. Purée the skin and flesh in a small food processor or blender until smooth.

3 Put the almond meal, polenta, coconut and baking powder in a medium bowl and mix well to combine.

4 Put the eggs, sugar and vanilla in a medium bowl and use an electric mixer with a whisk attachment to whisk on high speed until very thick and pale and a ribbon trail forms when the whisk is lifted (about 3–4 minutes).

5 Add the mandarin purée to the egg mixture and use a spatula or large metal spoon to fold in until just combined. Add the polenta mixture and fold together until combined. Divide the mixture evenly among the muffin holes (you can pour it from a jug or use a ladle).

6 Bake in the preheated oven for 15–18 minutes, or until a skewer inserted in the cakes comes out clean. Cool the cakes in the tin for 5 minutes. Use a palette knife to ease the cakes out and transfer to a wire rack to cool.

7 To make the Mandarin icing, sift the icing sugar into a medium bowl. Gradually stir in the juice until the mixture is smooth and has a thick coating consistency, adding a little more juice if too thick. Cover with plastic wrap and set aside at room temperature until ready to use.

8 Spread the tops of the cooled cakes with the icing. Set aside for 20 minutes or until set.

Baker's tip

● These cakes will keep in an airtight container in a cool place (but not in the fridge) for up to 2 days.

Chocolate Fondant Puddings

The trick to chocolate fondants is not to let them sit around for too long after they are taken from the oven as the gorgeous gooey centre will disappear. Also, the dimensions of your ramekins will affect the final baking time – short and squat ones will require longer cooking than tall and skinny ones. Like anything, practice makes perfect and after a couple of goes you will discover how long it takes to bake your fondants perfectly.

SERVES: 10

Preparation time: 25 minutes   Cooking time: 11–13 minutes

Melted butter, to grease

Unsweetened cocoa powder, sifted, extra, to dust

250 g (9 oz/1⅔ cups) chopped good-quality dark chocolate

180 g (6 oz) unsalted butter, cubed

4 eggs, at room temperature

2 egg yolks, at room temperature

110 g (3¾ oz/½ cup) caster (superfine) sugar

2 tablespoons Frangelico, brandy or whisky

110 g (3¾ oz/¾ cup) plain (all-purpose) flour

2 tablespoons unsweetened cocoa powder, sifted

Icing (confectioners') sugar, to dust (optional)

Cream or vanilla ice cream, to serve

1 Preheat the oven to 200°C (400°F) or 180°C (350°F) fan-forced. Brush ten 125 ml (4 fl oz/½ cup) capacity metal dariole moulds (see Baker's tips) well with melted butter and then dust with the extra cocoa to lightly coat.

2 Put the chocolate and butter in a heatproof bowl over a saucepan of simmering water, making sure the base of the bowl doesn't touch the water. Stir occasionally until melted and smooth. Remove from the heat and set aside.

3 Use an electric mixer to whisk the whole eggs, egg yolks and caster sugar on medium–high for 4–5 minutes, or until very thick and pale and a ribbon trail forms. Whisk in the chocolate mixture and the Frangelico. Sift together the flour and cocoa powder, add to the chocolate mixture and use a large metal spoon or spatula to fold in until evenly combined.

4 Divide the mixture evenly among the prepared moulds and place on a baking tray. Bake in the preheated oven for 11–13 minutes, or until the puddings are set on top but still feel a little soft when you press in the centre with your finger. Remove them from the oven and turn out onto serving plates (see Baker's tips). Dust with icing sugar and serve immediately with cream or ice cream.

Baker's tips

● You can use ceramic ramekins or dishes instead of metal ones but you will need to increase the baking time by 2–3 minutes.

● These puddings are best served straight from the oven when the centres are still liquid.

Sour Cherry, Chocolate & Almond Biscotti

A twist on the traditional twice-baked Italian biscuit, these biscotti are studded with sour dried cherries, dark chocolate and almonds. And they are deliciously moreish. One batch makes quite a quantity so it's a good one for filling the biscuit jar. They also make the perfect gift.

MAKES: ABOUT 60

Preparation time: 20 minutes (+ 45 minutes cooling time) Baking time: 55 minutes

3 eggs, at room temperature

330 g (11½ oz/1½ cups) caster
   (superfine) sugar

2 teaspoons natural vanilla extract
   or essence

410 g (14½ oz/2¾ cups) plain
   (all-purpose) flour

½ teaspoon bicarbonate of soda
   (baking soda)

100 g (3½ oz/⅔ cup) dried sour cherries

100 g (3½ oz/⅔ cup) coarsely chopped
   good-quality dark chocolate

100 g (3½ oz/⅔ cup) whole
   blanched almonds

1 Preheat the oven to 180°C (350°F) or 160°C (315°F) fan-forced. Line two large baking trays with baking paper.

2 Use an electric mixer with a whisk attachment to whisk the eggs, sugar and vanilla on medium speed in a large bowl until thick and pale (this will take about 3 minutes). Sift the flour and bicarbonate of soda together. Add to the egg mixture with the whole cherries, chocolate and almonds, and use a wooden spoon to mix until evenly combined.

3 Turn the dough out onto a well-floured bench top and divide into 3 equal portions. Use well-floured hands to shape each portion into a log about 25 cm (10 in) long. Transfer the logs to the lined baking trays, making sure the ones that share a tray are at least 10 cm (4 in) apart. Use your hands to flatten each log slightly so they are about 7 cm (2¾ in) wide.

4 Bake for 30 minutes, swapping the trays after 15 minutes, or until light golden, firm to touch and cooked through. Remove from the oven and cool on the trays (this will take about 45 minutes).

5 Reduce the oven temperature to 130°C (250°F) or 110°C (225°F) fan-forced. Use a sharp knife to cut the logs diagonally into 1 cm (½ in) thick slices. Return the biscuits to the trays lined with baking paper (baking in two batches if necessary). Bake for 25 minutes, swapping the trays after 10 minutes, or until the biscuits are dry and lightly coloured. Cool the biscotti on the trays.

Variations

White Chocolate, Lemon & Macadamia Biscotti
Omit the dried sour cherries. Replace the dark chocolate with 150 g (5½ oz) good-quality white chocolate. Replace the almonds with 150 g (5½ oz) unsalted raw macadamias. Add the finely grated zest of 2 lemons with the white chocolate and macadamias.

Sour Cherry, Chocolate & Hazelnut Biscotti
Replace 35 g (1¼ oz/¼ cup) of the plain flour with 40 g (1½ oz/⅓ cup) sifted unsweetened cocoa powder. Replace the almonds with 150 g (5½ oz) hazelnuts.

Almond & Vanilla Biscotti – Omit the dried sour cherries and chocolate. Increase the almonds to 300 g (10½ oz). Replace the natural vanilla extract or essence with 3 teaspoons vanilla bean paste.

Baker's tip

● These biscotti will keep in an airtight container at room temperature for up to 3 weeks.

Raspberry Swiss Roll

A homemade jam roll is simple to make and blissful to eat. Once you have baked your own I promise you will never contemplate buying another again. Be firm when rolling it up – the sponge is not as fragile as you might think – and make sure the end is tucked in tightly at the start. Rolling it while still warm ensures that it won't crack.

SERVES: 10–12

IIIIIIIIIIIIIIIIIIIIIIIIIIIIIIIIIIIIIIIIIIIIIIIIIIIIIIIIIIIIIIIIIIIIIIIIIIIIIIIIIIIIIIIIIIIIIIIIIIIIIIIIIIIIIIIIIIIIIIIIIIIIIIIIIIIIIIIIIIIIIIIIIIIIIIIIIIIIIIIIIIIIIIIIII

Preparation time: 20 minutes (+ 30 minutes cooling time) **Baking time:** 12–15 minutes

Melted butter, to grease
3 eggs, at room temperature
1 teaspoon natural vanilla essence or extract
110 g (3¾ oz/½ cup) caster (superfine) sugar,
    plus 2 tablespoons extra, to sprinkle
110 g (3¾ oz/¾ cup) self-raising flour
2 tablespoons milk, warmed
165 g (5¾ oz/½ cup) raspberry jam
    (see Baker's tips)

1 Preheat the oven to 180°C (350°F) or 160°C (315°F) fan-forced. Brush a 20 cm x 30 cm (8 in x 12 in, base measurement) Swiss roll tin (jelly roll tin) or shallow slice tin with melted butter to grease, and line the base and sides with one piece of baking paper, cutting into the corners to fit.

2 Use an electric mixer with a whisk attachment to whisk the eggs and vanilla in a large bowl on medium–high speed until frothy. Add the sugar a spoonful at a time, whisking well after each addition, until the mixture is very thick and pale (about 5 minutes). Lift the whisk out of the mixture and draw a figure eight; if the trail stays on the surface long enough for you to finish drawing, the mixture is ready. If not, continue to whisk for a further minute and test again.

3 Sift the flour over the egg mixture. Immediately pour the warm milk down the side of the bowl and whisk again with the electric mixer briefly on low speed, until the flour mixture is just incorporated (be careful not to overmix).

4 Pour into the prepared tin and spread gently and evenly with a spatula or palette knife (it will be quite a thin layer). Bake in the preheated oven for 12–15 minutes or until pale golden and the sponge springs back when lightly touched.

5 Meanwhile, sprinkle a clean, dry tea towel (dish towel) with 1½ tablespoons of the extra caster sugar. Remove the sponge from the oven and turn immediately onto the tea towel. Peel away the baking paper and, starting from one short end, roll up the hot sponge with the tea towel to form a roll. Set aside for 3 minutes.

6 Unroll the warm sponge and spread evenly with the jam. Re-roll immediately with the tea towel around the outside to hold its shape. Set aside, seam side down, for 30 minutes.

7 Remove the tea towel, sprinkle with the remaining extra caster sugar and cut into slices to serve.

Baker's tips

● You can use any berry jam you wish – try strawberry, boysenberry, blackberry or mixed berry.

● This Swiss roll will keep in an airtight container at room temperature for up to 2 days.

The Kneading Method

This method is used when making yeast-containing breads and the like. Kneading develops the gluten that gives bread its ability to hold the air the yeast produces and retain its structure.

This is not a technique that involves being gentle. In fact, it's a great one to release any pent-up frustrations. It requires gusto and strong arm muscles, and it can prove to be quite therapeutic.

You may have heard of 'strong' or 'bread' flour, which contains the highest amount of gluten and which will give your bread dough the ability to stretch and expand with the gas produced by the yeast. Together with the combination and ratio of ingredients, kneading will also determine the texture of the final bread produced.

But before you can start kneading, you'll need to check the specifics of the recipe you have chosen – the ingredients and the preparation they'll need, as well as the sequence, timing and intensity of the kneading and, if it applies, the time needed for proving or resting the dough.

When you're ready to begin, this is what you need to know to become a hands-on kneading pro ...

Step by step

1 Turn the dough out onto a lightly floured bench top and bring it together into a ball.

2 Use the heel of your hand to push the dough down firmly in the middle and start to push it away from you.

3 Continue to push and stretch the dough away from you. Use your other hand to pull the other half of the dough towards you.

4 Use the fingertips of your kneading hand to fold the dough back on itself. Give the dough a quarter turn.

5 Repeat this pushing, stretching and turning process for 5–10 minutes. As you knead, the gluten in the flour is being developed and strengthened, and the dough will become smoother and more regular in texture, easier to handle and more elastic. How long you need to keep kneading will depend on the recipe and how efficiently (energetically and enthusiastically!) you do it.

6 The dough is ready when you can press your finger into it and it springs back. This is a sign that the gluten is well developed.

7 Put the dough into a bowl brushed with oil or melted butter, depending on the recipe. Turn the dough to coat it well.

8 Cover the bowl with plastic wrap and set aside in a warm, draught-free place.

9 Once the dough is well risen (often doubled in size) punch it down with your fist to deflate it. This will make it easier to handle and reinvigorate the yeast, giving the baked dough better texture and flavour.

10 Briefly knead the dough again, just until it is smooth and back to its original size, to get rid of any large air bubbles so the baked dough is evenly textured.

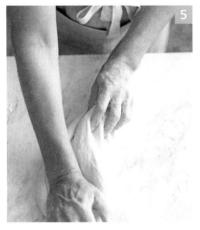

Keep in mind ...

- Once you get used to kneading in this way it will become one natural fluid, rhythmic motion.
- Refined flours (such as white flour) have more gluten than less-refined flours (such as wholemeal). When kneaded, breads based on 'strong' or high-gluten flour will become more elastic (almost silky smooth) than those based on wholemeal flour or flour with a lower gluten content.
- If dough isn't kneaded enough (until the dough springs back when you press your finger into it), the resulting bread or pizza base will have a holey, crumbly texture and a weak structure.
- Kneading can be done using a good-quality stand mixer with a dough hook attachment, usually on low speed (follow the mixer's instruction book), but it is always good to learn how to do it by hand so you get a feel for the texture of the dough and how it changes subtly during the kneading process. The exception is dough that is too wet to knead on a bench top, such as brioche dough.

Now get kneading!

Now is the time to flex those muscles and put some elbow grease into your kneading. Many people think making your own bread and pizza dough is tricky but that couldn't be further from the truth. The following recipes will help you master the technique.

Salsa Verde Pizza

This is a terrific pizza recipe that's particularly fun to make with children. When my kids were younger, pizza became a regular Friday night dinner they could help make with their friends who had come over to play. Using this recipe, together we would knead and roll the dough, then top it, bake it and eat it. They loved it, and I'm sure the kids –and adults –in your life will as well.

SERVES: 4

Preparation time: 30 minutes (+ 1 hour proving time)   Baking time: 15–18 minutes

450 g (1 lb/3 cups) strong bread or
   pizza flour, plus extra, to dust
7 g (¼ oz/1 sachet) dried yeast
1½ teaspoons salt
310 ml (10¾ fl oz/1¼ cups) lukewarm water
1 tablespoon olive oil, plus extra, to grease

Pizza sauce
1 tablespoon olive oil
½ brown onion, finely diced
1 garlic clove, crushed
½ teaspoon dried oregano
400 g (14 oz) tin diced tomatoes
½ teaspoon sugar, or to taste

Topping
2 tablespoons fresh oregano leaves
⅔ cup finely chopped flat-leaf (Italian) parsley
2 tablespoons rinsed baby capers
2 large garlic cloves, crushed or finely grated
270 g (9½ oz) bocconcini, cut into
   1 cm (½ in) thick slices
30 g (1 oz/¾ cup, tightly packed) rocket
   (arugula) leaves
Extra virgin olive oil, to drizzle

1 To make the dough, combine the flour, yeast and salt in a large bowl and make a well in the centre. Combine the water and olive oil, then add to the flour mixture. Use a wooden spoon and then your hands to mix to a soft dough.

2 Turn the dough onto a lightly floured bench top and knead for 5–8 minutes, or until it is smooth and elastic and springs back when you push your finger into it.

3 Place the dough in an oiled bowl, turning it to coat lightly with the oil. Cover with plastic wrap and place in a warm, draught-free place for 1 hour, or until doubled in size.

4 Meanwhile, to make the Pizza sauce, put the olive oil and onion in a medium saucepan over medium heat and cook, stirring occasionally, for 8 minutes or until the onion is tender. Add the garlic and oregano and cook for 1 minute or until aromatic. Add the tomatoes and bring to the boil. Reduce the heat to low and simmer for 15–20 minutes, stirring occasionally, or until it reaches a thick sauce consistency. Remove from the heat and season with sugar, salt and freshly ground black pepper to taste. Set aside to cool.

Recipe continued overleaf →

Variations

Three-cheeses Pizza – Omit the parsley, capers, garlic, rocket and extra virgin olive oil. Top the pizza base with the oregano, bocconcini, 200 g (7 oz) coarsely crumbled firm fresh ricotta and 80 g (2¾ oz/¾ cup) finely grated parmesan cheese and bake. Sprinkle with freshly ground black pepper and serve.

Chicken, Tomato & Spinach Pizza – Omit the parsley, capers, garlic and rocket. Top the pizza sauce with the bocconcini, 300 g (10½ oz) shredded cooked chicken and 200 g (7 oz) large grape or small heirloom tomatoes, halved (or quartered if large), and bake. Scatter over 2 tablespoons torn basil leaves and 50 g (1¾ oz) baby spinach leaves. Sprinkle with freshly ground black pepper and drizzle with olive oil.

Zucchini, Ricotta & Basil Pizza – Omit the parsley, capers, garlic, bocconcini and rocket. Top the pizza sauce with a handful of small or torn large basil leaves, 2 zucchini (courgettes) cut lengthways into thin slices using a vegetable peeler and 250 g (9 oz) coarsely crumbled fresh ricotta. Bake and scatter over extra fresh basil leaves. Sprinkle over freshly ground black pepper, drizzle with olive oil and serve.

Tomato, Bocconcini & Prosciutto Pizza – Omit the parsley, capers and garlic. Top the pizza sauce with the bocconcini and bake. Serve topped with 200 g (7 oz) large grape or small heirloom tomatoes, halved (or quartered if large), 8 thin slices prosciutto and the rocket leaves. Sprinkle with freshly ground black pepper and drizzle with olive oil.

5 Preheat the oven to 230°C (450°F) or 210°C (410°F) fan-forced.

6 Knock back the dough by punching it in the centre with your fist. Turn onto a lightly floured bench top and knead for 2–3 minutes, or until smooth and elastic. Divide the dough into 2 equal portions. Roll out 1 portion on a piece of baking paper large enough to line a large baking tray, to a rectangle about 3 mm (⅛ in) thick. Transfer the dough to the tray on the baking paper and prick all over with a fork. Repeat with the remaining dough and another piece of baking paper and large baking tray.

7 Spread the pizza bases with the pizza sauce. Scatter over the fresh oregano, parsley, capers and garlic. Top with the bocconcini slices, dividing them evenly. Bake in the preheated oven for 15–18 minutes, swapping the trays after 8 minutes, until the pizza bases are crisp, golden and cooked through.

8 Remove the pizza from the oven, cut into portions and serve topped with the rocket, sprinkled with freshly ground black pepper and drizzled with a little olive oil.

Four Seed Spelt Loaf

This is a wholesome loaf made with spelt flour, oats and lots of good-for-you seeds. It is delicious spread with soft goat's cheese or a creamy blue vein cheese, toasted for breakfast or used to make sandwiches.

MAKES: 1 LOAF (ABOUT 12 SLICES)

Preparation time: 30 minutes (+ 1¾–2¼ hours proving time)   **Baking time:** 25 minutes

480 g (1 lb 1 oz) whole spelt flour,
   plus extra, to dust
7 g (¼ oz/1 sachet) dried yeast
2 teaspoons salt
50 g (1¾ oz/½ cup) rolled (porridge) oats
40 g (1½ oz/¼ cup) sunflower seeds
2 tablespoons sesame seeds
1½ tablespoons linseeds (flax seeds)
1 tablespoon poppy seeds
350 ml (12 fl oz) lukewarm water
2 tablespoons honey
1 tablespoon olive oil, plus extra, to grease

Baker's tip

● This bread is best eaten the day it is baked. It will keep in an airtight container or plastic bag for up to 3 days for toasting. It can also be frozen, either whole or sliced, in a sealed freezer bag for up to 2 months.

1 Combine the flour, yeast, salt, rolled oats, sunflower seeds, sesame seeds, linseeds and poppy seeds in a large bowl, and make a well in the centre. Combine the lukewarm water, honey and oil, then add to the flour mixture. Use a wooden spoon and then your hands to mix to a soft dough.

2 Turn the dough onto a lightly floured bench top and knead for 5–8 minutes, or until it is smooth and elastic and springs back when you push your finger into it.

3 Place the dough in an oiled bowl, turning it to coat lightly with the oil. Cover with plastic wrap and place in a warm, draught-free place for 1–1½ hours or until doubled in size.

4 Grease a baking tray with the extra olive oil and dust lightly with the extra flour.

5 Knock back the dough by punching it in the centre with your fist. Turn onto a lightly floured bench top and knead for 2–3 minutes or until smooth and elastic. Shape the dough into a large oval about 20 cm (8 in) long. Transfer to the prepared tray. Cover the dough with a slightly damp tea towel (dish towel) and set aside in a warm, draught-free place for 45 minutes, or until almost doubled in size.

6 Preheat the oven to 220°C (425°F) or 200°C (400°F) fan-forced.

7 Dust the top of the loaf with a little extra flour. Use a very sharp knife to make 4–5 slits in the top, each about 1 cm (½ in) deep. Bake in the preheated oven for 25 minutes, turning the bread around after 15 minutes, or until the loaf is cooked through and sounds hollow when tapped on the base.

8 Leave the bread to stand on the tray for 5 minutes before transferring to a wire rack to cool.

Dried Cherry & Chocolate Hot Cross Buns

In this updated version of the traditional Easter hot cross bun, chunks of dark chocolate and tart dried cherries make these even more irresistible!

MAKES: 12

Preparation time: 25 minutes (+ 1½ hours proving time)   Baking time: 25 minutes

750 g (1 lb 10 oz/5 cups) bread or pizza flour
55 g (2 oz/¼ cup) caster (superfine) sugar
14 g (½ oz/2 sachets) dried yeast
1½ teaspoons mixed spice
1½ teaspoons ground cinnamon
1 teaspoon salt
150 g (5½ oz/1 cup) dried cherries
   (*see Baker's tips*)
75 g (2½ oz/½ cup) currants
435 ml (15¼ fl oz/1¾ cups) milk
60 g (2¼ oz) butter, cubed, plus extra,
   to grease and serve
2 eggs, at room temperature
1 teaspoon natural vanilla extract or essence
100 g (3½ oz/⅔ cup) chopped good-quality
   dark chocolate

Flour paste
75 g (2½ oz/½ cup) plain (all-purpose) flour
75 ml (2¼ fl oz) water

Glaze
55 g (2 oz/¼ cup) caster (superfine) sugar
2 tablespoons water

1 Put the bread flour, sugar, yeast, mixed spice, cinnamon and salt in a large bowl and mix to combine. Stir through the dried cherries and currants.

2 Heat the milk and butter in a small saucepan over medium heat until the butter has just melted and the milk is lukewarm. Whisk one of the eggs with the vanilla and add to the milk mixture. Whisk to combine. Add to the dry ingredients and use a wooden spoon and then your hands to mix to a soft dough.

3 Turn onto a lightly floured bench top. Knead for 8–10 minutes or until smooth and elastic. Lightly grease a clean large bowl with a little butter, add the dough and turn to coat the dough. Cover with plastic wrap and set aside in a warm, draught-free place for 1 hour or until doubled in size.

4 Line a large baking tray with baking paper. Punch the centre of the dough down with your fist. Turn onto a lightly floured bench top. Knead for 2–3 minutes or until smooth. Knead in the chocolate. Divide the dough into 12 equal portions. Roll each portion into a ball and place on the tray, allowing room for spreading. Cover with a damp tea towel (dish towel) and set aside in a warm, draught-free place for 30 minutes or until almost doubled in size.

5 Preheat the oven to 180°C (350°F) or 160°C (315°F) fan-forced. Meanwhile, make the Flour paste. Combine the flour and water in a bowl and beat with a wooden spoon until smooth. Spoon into a small plastic bag.

6 Whisk the remaining egg and brush the tops of the buns with it. Snip a small hole in the corner of the plastic bag containing the Flour paste and pipe crosses on the buns.

7 Bake in the preheated oven for 25 minutes or until the buns are cooked and sound hollow when tapped on the base.

8 Meanwhile, make the Glaze. Combine the sugar and water in a small saucepan over medium heat. Stir until the sugar has dissolved and simmer for 1 minute. Transfer the hot cross buns to a wire rack and brush the tops with the glaze. Serve warm, spread with butter.

Baker's tips

● Dried cherries are available at selected supermarkets, delicatessens, grocery shops and specialty food stores. You can replace them with good-quality dried cranberries.

● These hot cross buns are best eaten the day they are made. To freeze for up to 3 months, wrap in plastic wrap and seal in an airtight container. Thaw at room temperature.

Finger Buns

Just milk bread studded with sultanas, topped with pink icing and finished
with coconut – it's the simplicity that gives the finger bun its appeal!

MAKES: 12

Preparation time: 40 minutes (+ 1½ hours proving and 20 minutes standing)   Baking time: 30 minutes

375 g (13 oz/2½ cups) strong bread or
   pizza flour, plus extra, to dust
2 tablespoons caster (superfine) sugar
60 g (2¼ oz/⅓ cup) sultanas (golden raisins)
7 g (¼ oz/1 sachet) dried yeast
½ teaspoon salt
200 ml (7 fl oz) milk
40 g (1½ oz) butter, cubed
2 eggs, at room temperature
1 teaspoon natural vanilla extract or essence
Melted butter, to grease

Topping
185 g (6½ oz/1½ cups) pure icing
   (confectioners') sugar
5 teaspoons water
Pink food colouring (about 3 drops)
2 tablespoons desiccated coconut,
   to sprinkle

1   To make the dough, combine the flour, sugar, sultanas, yeast
and salt in a large bowl and make a well in the centre. Combine
the milk and butter in a small saucepan and heat over low heat
for 2–3 minutes, or until the butter has melted and the milk is
lukewarm. Remove from the heat. Whisk one of the eggs with
the vanilla and add to the butter and milk mixture. Whisk to
combine. Add to the flour mixture. Use a wooden spoon and
then your hands to mix to a soft dough.

2   Turn the dough onto a lightly floured bench top and knead
for 8–10 minutes or until it is smooth and elastic and springs
back when you push your finger into it.

3   Brush a large bowl with extra melted butter, to grease.
Add the dough, turning it to coat lightly with the butter.
Cover with plastic wrap and place in a warm, draught-
free place for 1 hour or until doubled in size.

4   Preheat the oven to 180°C (350°F) or 160°C (315°F)
fan-forced. Line two baking trays with baking paper.

5   When the dough has doubled in size, knock it back by
punching it in the centre with your fist. Turn onto a
lightly floured bench top and knead for 2–3 minutes or
until smooth and elastic. Divide the dough into 12 equal
portions. Shape each portion into a long oval shape
about 12 cm (4½ in) long and 3 cm (1¼ in) wide in the
centre, and place on the lined trays, leaving about 5 cm
(2 in) between them. Cover with a slightly damp tea
towel (dish towel) and set aside in a warm, draught-free
place for 30 minutes or until well risen.

6   Whisk the second egg and brush the rolls with it to glaze.
Bake in the preheated oven for 30 minutes, swapping
the trays halfway through baking, or until the buns
are golden and sound hollow when tapped on the base.
Transfer to a wire rack to cool.

7   To make the Topping, sift the icing sugar into a medium
bowl. Use a wooden spoon to stir in the water and mix to
a very thick pouring consistency. Add 2–3 drops of pink
food colouring to tint the icing. Spread the cooled finger
buns with the icing, allowing it to drizzle down the sides.
Sprinkle with the coconut and set aside for 20 minutes
for the icing to set before serving. These finger buns are
best eaten on the day they are made.

Sticky Cinnamon Pecan Scrolls

Serve these deliciously sticky, spicy and nutty scrolls straight from the oven.
They are best eaten the day they are made – but leftovers aren't generally an issue.

MAKES: 8

Preparation time: 40 minutes (+ 2½ hours proving time and 5 minutes standing)   Baking time: 35–40 minutes

350 g (12 oz/2⅓ cups) strong bread or
　　pizza flour, plus extra, to dust
55 g (2 oz/¼ cup) caster (superfine) sugar
7 g (¼ oz/1 sachet) dried yeast
½ teaspoon salt
185 ml (6 fl oz/¾ cup) milk
30 g (1 oz) butter, cubed
1 egg yolk, at room temperature
1 teaspoon natural vanilla extract or essence
Melted butter, to grease

Topping
80 ml (2½ fl oz/⅓ cup) pure maple syrup
50 g (1¾ oz) butter, melted
55 g (2 oz/¼ cup, firmly packed) brown sugar
60 g (2¼ oz/½ cup) pecans, toasted and
　　coarsely chopped

Filling
55 g (2 oz/¼ cup, firmly packed) brown sugar
2 teaspoons ground cinnamon
20 g (¾ oz) butter, melted
100 g (3½ oz/1 cup) pecans, toasted and
　　coarsely chopped

1 To make the dough, combine the flour, sugar, yeast and salt in a large bowl and make a well in the centre. Combine the milk and butter in a small saucepan and heat over low heat for 2–3 minutes, or until the butter has melted and the milk is lukewarm. Remove from the heat. Use a fork to whisk in the egg yolk and vanilla. Add to the flour mixture. Use a wooden spoon and then your hands to mix to a soft dough.

2 Turn the dough onto a lightly floured bench top and knead for 8–10 minutes or until it is smooth and elastic and springs back when you push your finger into it.

3 Brush a large bowl with the melted butter to grease. Add the dough, turning it to coat lightly with the butter. Cover with plastic wrap and place in a warm, draught-free place for 1 hour or until doubled in size.

4 Brush a 22 cm (8½ in) round cake tin with melted butter. To make the Topping, combine the maple syrup, butter, brown sugar and pecans in a bowl. Pour into the tin to cover the base, spreading the pecans evenly. Set aside.

5 When the dough has doubled in size, knock it back by punching it in the centre with your fist. Turn onto a lightly floured bench top and knead for 2–3 minutes or until smooth and elastic. Divide into 2 portions. Use a lightly floured rolling pin to roll out each portion to a 20 cm x 30 cm (8 in x 12 in) rectangle about 1 cm (½ in) thick.

6 To make the Filling, combine the brown sugar and cinnamon, breaking up any lumps. Brush both dough rectangles with the melted butter and sprinkle evenly with the pecans and the brown sugar mixture, leaving a 1 cm (½ in) border. Use the rolling pin to gently roll the filling into the dough, pressing the pecans into the dough slightly. Starting from the short end of one dough portion, roll up to enclose the filling. Repeat with the remaining dough portion. Cut each roll into 4 portions and place in the prepared tin (one in the centre and the remaining seven around the outside). Cover with a damp tea towel (dish towel) and set aside in a warm, draught-free place for 1½ hours or until doubled in size.

7 Preheat the oven to 180°C (350°F) or 160°C (315°F) fan-forced.

8 Bake for 35–40 minutes or until golden and the scrolls sound hollow when tapped. Leave to stand for 5 minutes before turning out. Serve warm or at room temperature. They are best eaten on the day they're made.

Fennel Grissini Sticks

The ultimate accompaniment to an antipasto or cheese plate, these grissini are simply seasoned with fennel and sea salt – but go ahead and experiment with other flavour combinations.

MAKES: ABOUT 24

Preparation time: 30 minutes (+ 1 hour proving time)   Baking time: 35–40 minutes

300 g (10½ oz/2 cups) strong bread or pizza flour, plus extra, to dust
1 teaspoon dried yeast
1½ teaspoons salt
200 ml (7 fl oz) lukewarm water
2 tablespoons extra virgin olive oil, plus extra, to grease and brush
1 tablespoon fennel seeds, coarsely crushed
1 teaspoon sea salt flakes

Baker's tips

● These grissini will keep in an airtight container at room temperature for up to 1 week.

● If the grissini lose a little of their crispiness on storing, refresh them by placing on a lined oven tray and bake at 180°C (350°F) or 160°C (315°F) fan-forced for 10 minutes or until crisp and aromatic.

1 Combine the flour, yeast and salt in a large bowl and make a well in the centre. Combine the water and olive oil, then add to the flour mixture. Use a wooden spoon and then your hands to mix to a soft dough. Turn the dough onto a lightly floured bench top and knead for 5–8 minutes or until it is smooth and elastic and springs back when you push your finger into it.

2 Place the dough in an oiled bowl, turning to coat lightly with the oil. Cover with plastic wrap and place in a warm, draught-free place for 1 hour or until doubled in size.

3 Preheat the oven to 180°C (350°F) or 160°C (315°F) fan-forced. Line two large baking trays with baking paper.

4 Knock back the dough by punching it in the centre with your fist. Turn onto a lightly floured bench top and knead for 2–3 minutes or until smooth and elastic. Divide the dough in half and use a lightly floured rolling pin to roll out each portion of dough to a 20 cm x 25 cm (8 in x 10 in) rectangle about 7–8 mm (¼–⅜ in) thick. Sprinkle the combined fennel seeds and salt over the dough. Lightly roll over it with the rolling pin so the seasoning sticks.

5 Use a large sharp knife to cut the dough lengthways into 1.5 cm (⅝ in) wide strips. Use your hands to roll each strip into a thin log about 32 cm (12¾ in) long. Place the grissini on the lined trays as you roll them, about 1 cm (½ in) apart.

6 Brush the grissini lightly with a little extra oil. Bake in the preheated oven for 35–40 minutes, swapping the trays halfway through baking time, or until deep golden and crisp. Leave the grissini to cool on the trays.

Dinner Rolls

There is nothing quite like a really good, simple white bread roll. These ones have a lovely soft crumb and a thin crust – perfect to have for dinner or, as the Italians do, for breakfast with lots of butter and jam or cheese.

MAKES: 16

Preparation time: 30 minutes (+ 1½ hours proving)   Baking time: 25–30 minutes

500 g (1 lb 2 oz/3⅓ cups) strong bread or pizza flour, plus extra, to dust

1 tablespoon caster (superfine) sugar

7 g (¼ oz/1 sachet) dried yeast

1 teaspoon salt

375 ml (13 fl oz/1½ cups) lukewarm water

40 g (1½ oz) butter, melted and cooled, plus extra, to grease

1 egg yolk, at room temperature, whisked

1 tablespoon milk

Poppy or sesame seeds, to sprinkle

1 Combine the flour, sugar, yeast and salt in a large bowl and make a well in the centre. Combine the lukewarm water and butter, then add to the flour mixture. Use a wooden spoon and then your hands to mix to a soft dough.

2 Turn the dough onto a lightly floured bench top and knead for 5–8 minutes or until it is smooth and elastic and springs back when you push your finger into it.

3 Brush a large bowl with melted butter. Add the dough, turning it to coat lightly with the butter. Cover with plastic wrap and place in a warm, draught-free place for 1 hour or until doubled in size.

4 Preheat the oven to 200°C (400°F) or 180°C (350°F) fan-forced. Line two baking trays with baking paper.

5 Knock back the dough by punching it in the centre with your fist. Turn onto a lightly floured bench top and knead for 2–3 minutes or until smooth and elastic. Divide the dough into 16 equal portions. Shape each portion into a ball by rolling it on the bench top and place on the lined trays, leaving about 5 cm (2 in) between them. Cover with a slightly damp tea towel (dish towel) and set aside in a warm, draught-free place for 30 minutes or until well risen.

6 Whisk together the egg yolk and milk and brush over the rolls. Sprinkle with poppy or sesame seeds and bake in the preheated oven for 25–30 minutes, swapping the trays halfway through baking, or until the rolls are golden and sound hollow when tapped on the base. Transfer to a wire rack to cool.

Variations

Oval Rolls – In Step 5, roll each portion of dough into an oval shape about 7 cm (2¾ in) long. Use a small sharp knife to cut a slit, about 1 cm (½ in) deep, along the length of the roll, starting and finishing about 1 cm (½ in) from each end, then continue with the recipe.

Knot Rolls – In Step 5, roll each portion of dough into a sausage shape about 30 cm (12 in) long. Tie into a loose knot and continue with the recipe.

Baker's tip

● These rolls are best eaten the day they are made, however they do freeze well – seal in a freezer bag and freeze for up to 1 month.

Caramelised Onion & Blue Cheese Flatbread

The wonderful combination of the sharp gorgonzola and lightly caramelised
onion makes a rich but irresistible topping for this focaccia-like bread.

SERVES: 10 AS AN APPETISER

Preparation time: 40 minutes (+ 1 hour proving time)   Baking time: 18–20 minutes

150 g (5½ oz) gorgonzola cheese,
crumbled (*see Baker's tips*)

50 g (1¾ oz/⅓ cup) pine nuts

40 g (1½ oz) rocket (arugula) leaves, to serve

Caramelised onions

20 g (¾ oz) butter

3 red onions, halved and sliced

2 tablespoons brown sugar

Flatbread dough

450 g (1 lb/3 cups) bread or pizza flour,
plus extra, to dust

7 g (¼ oz/1 sachet) dried yeast

1 teaspoon salt

250 ml (9 fl oz/1 cup) lukewarm water

60 ml (2 fl oz/¼ cup) olive oil, plus extra,
to grease

Baker's tips

● Use either picante or dolce gorgonzola.

● The dough can be made the day before cooking
and serving. After kneading, place it in the oiled
bowl, cover and place in the fridge overnight
instead of proving in a warm place. When ready to
bake, remove from the fridge and leave standing in
a warm, draught-free place for 2 hours or until at
room temperature and then continue from Step 4.

● The caramelised onion can be made up to 4 days
ahead. Keep in an airtight container in the fridge.

1   To make the Flatbread dough, combine the flour, yeast
and salt in a large bowl and make a well in the centre.
Combine the lukewarm water and olive oil then add to
the flour mixture. Use a wooden spoon and then your
hands to mix to a soft dough. Turn the dough onto a
lightly floured bench top and knead for 5–8 minutes
or until it is smooth and elastic and springs back when
you push your finger into it.

2   Place the dough in an oiled bowl, turning it to coat lightly
with the oil. Cover with plastic wrap and place in a warm,
draught-free place for 1 hour or until doubled in size.

3   Meanwhile, to make the Caramelised onions, put the
butter and onions in a medium saucepan over medium
heat. Cook, stirring, for 12–15 minutes or until the
onions are soft. Sprinkle with the sugar and cook for a
further 5–8 minutes, stirring often, or until the onions
are glossy and slightly caramelised and any excess liquid
has evaporated. Remove from the heat and set aside.

4   Preheat the oven to 230°C (450°F) or 210°C (415°F)
fan-forced. Line a large baking tray with baking paper.

5   Knock back the dough by punching it in the centre
with your fist. Turn onto a lightly floured bench top
and knead for 2–3 minutes or until smooth and elastic.
Use a lightly floured rolling pin to roll out the dough
to a 25 cm x 40 cm (10 in x 16 in) rectangle about 1 cm
(½ in) thick. Transfer to the lined tray.

6   Top the dough with the caramelised onion, leaving a
border around the edge. Scatter the gorgonzola and pine
nuts over and season with freshly ground black pepper.

7   Bake in the preheated oven for 18–20 minutes or until
golden and cooked through. Scatter the rocket over the
flatbread and serve warm, cut into fingers or wedges.

Classic Focaccia

This traditional Italian bread is wonderful served alongside soups, with dips or as part of an antipasti plate. It is also great split, filled and toasted as a sandwich.

SERVES: 6–8

Preparation time: 25 minutes (+ 1½ hours proving time)   Baking time: 20 minutes

600 g (1 lb 5 oz/4 cups) strong bread or pizza flour, plus extra, to dust
3 teaspoons dried yeast
2 teaspoons salt
310 ml (10¾ fl oz/1¼ cups) lukewarm water
2 tablespoons olive oil, plus extra to grease, and another 2 tablespoons to drizzle and brush
1 tablespoon coarsely chopped rosemary leaves
1 tablespoon thyme leaves
Sea salt flakes, to sprinkle

Variation

Blue Cheese & Grape Focaccia – Omit the rosemary and extra oil. Scatter 125 g (4½ oz) crumbled blue cheese and 150 g (5½ oz) small red grapes, halved, over the focaccia with the thyme. Continue with the recipe.

1 To make the dough, combine the flour, yeast and salt in a large bowl and make a well in the centre. Combine the lukewarm water and olive oil, then add to the flour mixture. Use a wooden spoon and then your hands to mix to a soft dough.

2 Turn the dough onto a lightly floured bench top and knead for 5–8 minutes or until it is smooth and elastic and springs back when you push your finger into it. Place the dough in an oiled bowl, turning it to coat lightly with the oil. Cover with plastic wrap and place in a warm, draught-free place for 1 hour or until doubled in size.

3 Preheat the oven to 220°C (425°F) or 200°C (400°F) fan-forced. Line a large baking tray with baking paper.

4 Knock back the dough by punching it in the centre with your fist. Turn the dough onto the lined tray and use your hands to press down on it, and to pull and stretch it to form a rough rectangle about 20 cm x 30 cm (8 in x 12 in) and 1.5 cm (⅝ in) thick. Use your fingertips to press into the surface of the dough to form dimples.

5 Drizzle lightly with oil then sprinkle with the herbs and sea salt. Set aside in a warm, draught-free place for 30 minutes or until risen slightly.

6 Bake in the centre of the preheated oven for 20 minutes or until golden and cooked through. Remove from the oven and brush lightly with olive oil. Serve the focaccia warm or at room temperature – it is best eaten on the day it is baked.

Fig & Walnut Bread

I love bread like this – dense with dried fruits, lightly spiced and suitable with either sweet or savoury toppings. Perfect toasted and spread with butter or served with soft cheese.

MAKES: 1 LOAF (ABOUT 12 SLICES)

Preparation time: 40 minutes (+ 2–2½ hours proving time)   Baking time: 30–35 minutes

300 g (10½ oz/2 cups) strong bread
  or pizza flour, plus extra, to dust
150 g (5½ oz/1 cup) wholemeal plain
  (all-purpose) flour
7 g (¼ oz/1 sachet) dried yeast
1 teaspoon salt
1½ teaspoons ground cinnamon
Finely grated zest of 1 orange
300 ml (10½ fl oz) water
90 g (3¼ oz/¼ cup) honey
1 teaspoon natural vanilla extract or essence
150 g (5½ oz) dried figs, coarsely chopped
125 g (4½ oz) seedless raisins
150 g (5½ oz) walnuts, toasted and
  coarsely chopped
Melted butter, to grease
1 egg, lightly whisked, to glaze
1 tablespoon poppy seeds

Baker's tips

● This bread will keep in an airtight container or plastic bag for up to 3 days. It is best toasted after 1 day.

● To freeze, either leave whole or slice, seal in a freezer bag and freeze for up to 1 month. Thaw at room temperature or toast straight from the freezer.

1 Combine the flours, yeast, salt, cinnamon and orange zest in a large bowl. Make a well in the centre. Heat the water and honey in a small saucepan over low heat, stirring occasionally, for 2–3 minutes or until lukewarm. Remove from the heat and add the vanilla. Add to the flour mixture and use a wooden spoon and then your hands to mix to a soft dough.

2 Turn the dough onto a lightly floured bench top and knead for 8–10 minutes or until it is smooth and elastic and springs back when you push your finger into it. Add the figs, raisins and walnuts and knead until evenly distributed through the dough.

3 Brush a large bowl with melted butter. Add the dough, turning it to coat lightly with the butter. Cover with plastic wrap and place in a warm, draught-free place for 1–1½ hours or until doubled in size.

4 Line a large baking tray with baking paper. When the dough has doubled in size, knock it back by punching it in the centre with your fist. Turn onto a lightly floured bench top and knead for 2–3 minutes or until reduced to its original size. Shape into a 30 cm (12 in) log, flatten slightly and place on the lined tray. Brush the top with the whisked egg and sprinkle with the poppy seeds. Cover with a slightly damp tea towel (dish towel) and place in a warm, draught-free place for 1 hour or until almost doubled in size.

5 Preheat the oven to 240°C (475°F) or 220°C (425°F) fan-forced.

6 Place the loaf in the oven and reduce the heat immediately to 190°C (375°F) or 170°C (325°F) fan-forced. Bake for 30–35 minutes or until cooked through and the loaf sounds hollow when tapped on the base. Transfer to a wire rack to cool. Serve in slices.

Why is homemade best?

I am passionate about the quality of the food I eat and the ingredients I use in my baking and cooking. And I believe quality is available to everyone – you just need to know what you're looking for and where to find it.

Baking provides a multisensory experience that allows you to connect with food on many levels, whether through the energetic kneading of dough, the heady aroma of a freshly baked loaf of bread, or the indulgent sweet bliss of a mouthful of rich chocolate cake. The act of baking can also give you a greater understanding of what is in your food, and of the importance of choosing quality ingredients. It's time for us all to start changing the way we look at food – to really think about what we are putting into our mouths, and to recognise the joy food can bring to our lives. Baking your own food is a fabulous way to begin this reconnection.

Due to the economic realities of modern life, quality is not always a priority for many companies who mass-produce goods – including baked products. For them, it is all about making their goods as cheaply as possible with as long a shelf life as they can manage, which means that most baked products you buy in supermarkets, and often in bakeries, contain many artificial and highly processed ingredients. Unfortunately, some of the most cost-effective ingredients you find in many commercially made cakes and biscuits, such as hydrogenated fats and high-fructose corn syrup, aren't necessarily good for you (see below).

Additives, such as artificial flavours and colourings, are then used to mask the flavour and appearance of these low-quality ingredients. Additives are also used to emulate a desired flavour, colour or texture that is absent, again due to the use of cheaper, highly processed ingredients. They then throw in a few preservatives as well, to make sure the product won't deteriorate while sitting on a shelf at room temperature for a couple of days, weeks and sometimes even longer, while waiting to be sold.

According to Australian nutritionist and author Chrissy Freer, a fellow passionate foodie, there are four main nasties that creep into commercially baked products that are best avoided – additives, hydrogenated fats, sodium and sweeteners.

BEWARE OF ADDITIVES

If you aren't yet convinced that homemade baked goods are preferable to store-bought, read on to discover what additives lurk within many a bought baked goodie.

Food colourings

Colours, which are generally added to make food appear more attractive, are derived from natural sources or artificial synthetic compounds. On food packaging, colouring agents appear as numbers in the 100s.

A small number of people will have a sensitivity or allergic reaction to some of the synthetic colourings, particularly red (E120) and yellow (E102). Sensitivity symptoms include skin rashes, nasal congestion, hives and even asthma, so they are worth keeping an eye out for. Artificial food colourings have also been linked in some studies to hyperactivity (especially in children) and cancer. Some potentially carcinogenic colourings are now banned in countries such as the US, but are yet to be banned in Australia.

The best way to avoid artificial food colourings in what you buy is to check product ingredient lists, look for products that use natural colours or avoid processed foods.

Flavours and flavour enhancers

Flavours impart taste to foods and can either be naturally occurring (such as with extracts from herbs and spices) or artificial. Manufacturers have developed synthetic or artificial flavours that taste similar to natural flavours to meet the ever-increasing demands of the food industry.

Flavour enhancers increase the flavours in food, without adding any flavour of their own. On packaging, they appear as numbers between 620 and 625 and include monosodium glutamate (MSG), which is often used in processed savoury biscuits. Be aware that flavours and flavour enhancers are classified as different categories on food labels, so a label can state 'no artificial flavours' but still contain MSG.

Health issues linked to consuming large quantities of artificial flavourings and enhancers include nausea, headaches, stomach cramps and sleep disturbances.

Preservatives

Most home-baked products are highly perishable and become stale quickly due to the type and combination of ingredients used to make them – they aren't meant to last for more than a couple of days, if that. However, commercially baked goods and the ingredients they are made from will often contain synthetic preservatives to extend their shelf life. The main ones include:

- sulphites – mainly used in dried fruits and jams but can also be found in some breads and biscuits
- benzoates – used in margarine and some baked goods
- butylated hydroxyanisole (BHA) – used in some fats, such as margarine, to prevent rancidity
- salt – used not only as a flavour enhancer, but also often in high quantities to extend the shelf life of baked goods (more on salt later).

A cocktail of these additives, along with others such as sugar and synthetic antioxidants (including vitamins A and D), are often used to extend the shelf life of baked goods.

The consumption of synthetic preservatives has been linked to health complaints such as skin irritations, stomach upsets, headaches, diarrhoea, kidney damage and fluid retention. They are thought to be especially dangerous for asthmatics, with a suggestion that some preservatives can cause or increase the severity of attacks.

Others

When eating mass-produced commercially baked goods, you may also be consuming stabilisers and thickeners, humectants that help preserve moisture, bleaching agents such as bromates and peroxides that hasten the ageing and whitening process of milled flour, and anticaking agents. Probably much more than you bargained for!

AVOID HYDROGENATED FATS

Trans fatty acids have received much attention – for good reason. They occur both naturally and artificially. Natural trans fatty acids occur in small amounts in dairy products and animal meat. However, the greatest contributors of trans fats to our diets are those artificially produced through a process called partial hydrogenation, where liquid vegetable oils are converted into solid fats. This process is widely used throughout the food industry to thicken and preserve food products, extending their shelf life significantly.

Trans fatty acids are of particular concern nutritionally, as they are structurally similar to saturated fats. Both trans fats and saturated fats increase the level of bad cholesterol; in addition, trans fats also decrease the amount of good cholesterol. Therefore there is evidence that trans fats increase our risk for coronary heart disease. Commercially baked products that often contain artificial trans fats include muesli bars, packet cake mixes, muffins and cakes.

The issue of identifying trans fats on food labels is a hot topic right now, with increased pressure for more stringent labelling. Currently in Australia compulsory labelling of trans fats only has to occur if the packaging contains a nutrition claim about cholesterol, poly or monounsaturated fats, or omega 3, omega 6 or 9 fatty acids, so often they aren't even mentioned. The best way to avoid trans fats is to avoid any product that contains 'partially hydrogenated vegetable oil' or vegetable shortening in its ingredients list, and to use butter or pure oils in your baking.

LIMIT SODIUM

Generally, table salt is made up of 40 per cent sodium and 60 per cent chloride, and it is the sodium content that can be detrimental to our health. Sodium occurs naturally in low levels in almost all foods. However many commercially baked items have large quantities of salt added to enhance flavour and extend shelf life. In baked goods (both commercially made and home baked), raising agents such as sodium bicarbonate and baking powder are a major source of sodium. Be aware that items such as cakes, biscuits and quick breads that contain these raising agents will have a higher sodium content than those that don't contain them. High sodium intake is a contributing factor in high blood pressure, which is one of the most common health issues in society and increases the risk of both stroke and heart disease.

TAKE CARE WITH SWEETENERS

The term 'sugars' refers to all forms of carbohydrate and includes glucose (from grains and vegetables), lactose (from dairy products), fructose (from fruits and honey), sucrose (regular cane sugar), and high fructose corn syrup (HFCS), which is the product of processing corn into starch, processing the starch to form glucose syrup, and adding enzymes that convert some of the glucose into fructose.

Refined sugars such as HFCS, crystalline fructose and sucrose are highly processed and are generally found in processed breakfast cereals, jams, flavoured yoghurts and, in frighteningly high amounts, in packaged baked products. These sugars are linked to many detrimental health effects, including excess fat in the liver. Fructose is converted into glucose in the body, and the glucose is then stored in the liver or muscles to be used as an on-demand energy source.

Compare if you dare

So let's see how a mass-produced coconut chocolate-chip muffin you'd find in a large supermarket chain stacks up against a homemade one, in particular looking out for the four nasties – additives, hydrogenated fats, sodium and sweeteners. If you were to make a similar muffin at home, it would typically contain: **wheat flour, butter (or oil), sugar, eggs, milk, chocolate, coconut and vanilla.**

In comparison, the ingredients list for the bought muffin reads like this: **wheat flour, sugar, vegetable oil, egg, Bounty [sugar, desiccated coconut, wheat glucose syrup, milk solids, cocoa butter, cocoa mass, invert sugar, vegetable fat, vegetable emulsifiers (471, 322 from soy), humectant (422), salt, flavourings, water, dark compound chocolate {sugar, hydrogenated vegetable oil, cocoa powder, dextrose, vegetable emulsifier (322 from soy), flavouring}, desiccated coconut, preservative (223)], dextrose (wheat derived), milk solids, thickener (1422), raising agent (450, 500), salt, preservative (202), flavouring.**

That's over 30 ingredients, with all but two falling into the 'nasties to be avoided' category, and many of which you probably would never have heard before. This is not real baking.

If the body is already overloaded with glucose, it converts the fructose to triglycerides (fat). Another frightening health implication of HFCS is the growing evidence showing it does not suppress our hunger hormone (leptin). This is one of the theories behind the increasing consumption of refined fructose and the rising rate of obesity. Other sweeteners to avoid if possible are corn syrup, levulose, fruit sugar and corn maize starch.

The best sugars to use in baking, from a nutritional perspective, are the unrefined sugars that are still in their most natural form, such as raw and brown sugars, or natural sources of fructose such as honey or fresh fruit. The main benefit of home baking when it comes to sugar is that you are in control of the types and amounts you use.

LESS IS BETTER

I always say that if a product has more than six to eight ingredients, some or all of which your grandmother wouldn't recognise, then alarm bells should start ringing. All of these 'bonus' artificial and highly processed ingredients can't be good for our bodies. Unfortunately, even though we now know the negative short-term effects these ingredients have on our health, they haven't been used for long enough in our food for a full understanding to emerge of the long-term effects they may cause. It will be at least another 50 years before we know this. In the meantime, do you really want to risk your or your children's health?

QUALITY CONTROL

It's no wonder, with ingredient and additive lists like the one opposite, that strong links between today's obesity crisis and the huge amounts of processed foods being eaten have been made (especially considering the evidence that some ingredients, such as HFCS, are actually giving your body the message that you need to eat more!) so it's important to recognise that you have little control over what goes into your food when buying mass-produced baked products – and that home baking gives you back this control. You also have control of the quality of ingredients you use. Not only can you make sure you aren't consuming unnecessary additives, you can also improve the quality of the food you eat.

'Baking has timeless benefits:
it nurtures conversations, inspires
creativity and encourages discovery.'

Glossary

‖‖

AIRTIGHT CONTAINER

A plastic container or a glass jar that is airtight when sealed. Store your baked goodies in either to keep them as fresh as possible.

AT ROOM TEMPERATURE

The same as 'softened', a description of butter that is soft enough to spread but still firm enough to give a little resistance, so it can be combined easily and evenly with other ingredients. Also can refer to eggs, where being at room temperature gives them a greater ability to hold air when whisked, and therefore to be more easily combined with other ingredients.

BEAT

To mix vigorously with a wooden spoon, or using the paddle or beater attachments of an electric mixer. It is often done to soften a mixture or combine ingredients quickly and efficiently. When a recipe states to 'cream' butter and sugar, you will need to 'beat' it until the combined ingredients are smooth, creamy and slightly paler in colour.

BLIND BAKE

To bake a pastry case before a filling is added. This prevents the pastry becoming soggy and ensures it is cooked through. It is done especially for pies and tart (flan) cases that are to be filled with wet mixtures and ingredients. A layer of baking paper or foil on top of the pastry holds baking weights (or uncooked rice or beans) to weigh down the pastry during cooking.

COMBINE

To mix together two or more ingredients or mixtures until they are blended.

COOKED WHEN TESTED WITH A SKEWER

Cakes, muffins and slices are often tested with a skewer or cake tester to see if they are cooked. Insert the skewer in the centre and if it comes out clean – if it's dry with no batter on – it is ready. This is unless the recipe specifies that 'moist crumbs cling to the skewer' when it is removed (see the Flourless Chocolate & Hazelnut Cake on page 186).

CREAM

A mixing method used at the start of recipes such as cakes, biscuits and slices, most often used to describe when butter and sugar are beaten together until the mixture is pale and creamy (see BEAT).

CUBED

A term used to describe butter that has been cut into cubes, generally about 1 cm (½ in) square. Butter that has been cubed will soften more quickly and is also easier to beat.

DUST

To sprinkle icing (confectioners') sugar or unsweetened cocoa powder over baked goods; to sprinkle flour over a bench top before kneading dough on it, to prevent sticking; to sprinkle flour over a tray or cake tin to prevent sticking; to sprinkle flour over scones or bread as a rustic decoration before baking. Also known as 'dredging'.

You can use a sieve to do this or, especially when dusting a bench top or bread dough with flour, you can shake it through your fingertips with your palms facing upwards.

FIRM PEAKS

A term used to describe the texture of whisked egg whites, whisked egg whites and sugar, or cream. The peaks are called firm if the mixture stands up and stays up when the whisk or whisk attachment for an electric mixer is lifted out of the mixture.

The stage before this is known as soft peaks (see page 269), and it only takes a very short while for firm peaks to be reached after this stage.

Once firm peaks are formed, don't whisk any more as it is very easy to overwhisk, causing egg whites to become dry and grainy, and cream to separate.

FOAMY OR FROTHY

These terms are used interchangeably to describe egg whites or whole eggs when they have only been whisked for a very short time, and the air is only just beginning to be incorporated. The air pockets formed in the mixture are still quite large and, as a result, it will not yet hold its structure at this stage.

FOLD

A mixing technique used to fold flour into a base mixture, wet ingredients into dry ingredients, or whisked egg whites into a heavier mixture. A large metal spoon or spatula is best used for this method. (See page 84 for more details.)

GLAZE

To brush a liquid over the top of bread, quick bread or pastry, either before baking to help give colour and encourage browning (such as a mixture of egg and water or milk, or straight whisked egg or milk), or after baking to add a shiny coating (such as a sugar syrup or warmed sieved jam).

GLUTEN

A protein in flour that is developed when liquid is mixed with the flour and the resulting dough is kneaded. It is the gluten that makes it elastic (which is why the more you knead, the more elastic it becomes) and gives the final product its structure.

HEATPROOF BOWL

A bowl, usually made of glass, ceramic or metal, that won't be damaged if heated. You need to use a heatproof bowl when melting chocolate or whisking whole eggs and sugar over simmering water. Make sure the base of the bowl doesn't touch the water in the saucepan it is sitting over, as it is the gentle steam from the simmering water that you want to heat the mixture, not the water itself.

KNEAD

To work dough mixture by hand or with a stand mixer using the dough hook when making bread; this develops and strengthens the gluten in the flour to give the baked bread structure. (See page 238 for more details.)

KNEAD LIGHTLY

As above, to bring the mixture together, but very gently, for pastry, biscuit dough or quick bread dough (such as scones) that needs to be handled carefully so as not to develop the gluten in the flour. If kneaded too heavily or too much, the dough will produce tough and heavy pastry, biscuits or quick breads.

KNOCK BACK

To punch a risen yeast dough with your fist so the air produced by the yeast is released, the dough is deflated and the yeast reinvigorated. This is done in bread-making after the first rising of the dough, and before it is kneaded briefly for the second time and shaped ready for baking.

LIGHTLY FLOUR

To lightly dust with flour to prevent sticking. Usually refers to sprinkling flour over a bench top when kneading bread or pizza dough or when rolling pastry; or over your palms when rolling biscuit dough into balls. It is important that you use only enough flour to prevent sticking; too much will alter the consistency of the dough or the pastry.

LINE THE TIN

To place baking paper on the base, and sometimes the side, of a cake tin to prevent sticking and make it easier to turn out the cake. (See page 31 for more details.)

MIX

In baking, a frequently used direction meaning to combine or blend two or more ingredients or mixtures. Usually the recipe will indicate what utensil (such as a wooden spoon, metal spoon or whisk) you need to use.

MOIST CRUMBS CLING TO A SKEWER

A term that refers to the 'doneness' of moist and/or flourless chocolate cakes and brownies that have a dense, 'muddy' texture. It describes how moist (not wet) crumbs will cling to a skewer when inserted in the centre. The crumbs show the cake or brownie is still moist inside and will give you the correct texture when cooled. The more moist the crumbs, the more 'muddy' the final texture will be.

PALE AND CREAMY

A description of the colour and texture of a butter and sugar mixture when beaten adequately to combine the ingredients evenly and incorporate air into the butter.

PREHEAT THE OVEN

To heat the oven to the correct temperature before using it to bake. This will generally take at least 20 minutes. (See page 30 for more details.)

PROVE

Leaving a kneaded yeast bread dough to rise, often covered in a warm and draught-free place. A recipe can involve proving one or two times, after the dough is shaped and/or just before baking.

QUICK BREAD

Any bread-like baked products, such as muffins, soda breads and scones, that use bicarbonate of soda (baking soda) or baking powder instead of yeast as the leavening agent.

REST

In pastry-making, to wrap the pastry in plastic wrap and refrigerate it for a period of time before and/or after rolling. This allows any gluten that has formed to 'relax' and the butter to set, which makes the pastry easier to handle, less likely to shrink during cooking, and lighter, or 'shorter', in texture.

RISE

Yeast bread dough is left to rise in a warm, draught-free place to increase in volume after kneading and before shaping (see PROVE).

ROUND-ENDED KNIFE

A knife with a thin blade and round end that will cut cleanly through the mixture when making scones and other quick breads. Can also be referred to as a butter knife.

RUB IN

To combine flour and butter using your fingertips until it reaches a breadcrumb-like texture. (See page 148 for more details.)

SEPARATE (EGGS)

To separate the egg yolk from the egg white. (See page 18 for more details.)

SIFT

To shake dry ingredients such as flour, icing (confectioners') sugar, unsweetened cocoa powder or cornflour (cornstarch) through a sieve to remove any lumps and incorporate air.

SIMMER

When water in a saucepan over heat is gently bubbling. It is important to use simmering water, not boiling water, under a heatproof bowl when melting chocolate or whisking whole eggs and sugar so as not to overheat the mixture in the bowl sitting above it.

SOFTENED

See AT ROOM TEMPERATURE for its reference to preparing butter for easy incorporation when baking.

SOFT PEAKS

A description of whisked egg whites, combined egg whites and sugar, or cream when whisked until the mixture forms a peak that then falls over on itself when the whisk is lifted from the mixture (also see FIRM PEAKS).

SPRING-FORM TIN

A cake tin with a sprung latch that releases a removable base when opened. It's ideal for delicate cakes (such as the Flourless Chocolate & Hazelnut Cake on page 186) and cheesecakes that can't be 'turned out'. The base should fit snugly and the latch should be firm when closed to prevent any batter from leaking out.

If you turn the base upside down, it will create a base without a lip that will make removing the cake even easier.

STIR

To mix ingredients by hand using a circular motion with a utensil such as a wooden spoon.

WELL

To form a hole in the centre of dry ingredients in a bowl. One-bowl mixes such as muffins will often ask you to make a 'well' in the centre of the dry ingredients and then pour the wet ingredients into it. This allows for more efficient and even mixing.

WHISK

To use either a balloon or hand whisk, or a whisk attachment for an electric mixer, to mix ingredients (most often egg whites, egg whites and sugar, or whole eggs and sugar) and incorporate air to increase the volume of the mixture. (See pages 184, 198 and 224 for more details.)

ZEST

The very thin outer layer of a citrus fruit, such as orange, lemon and lime, that contains the intensely aromatic citrus oil. It can be finely or coarsely grated, or removed with a citrus zester or vegetable peeler, separating it from the bitter white pith underneath.

Weights & Measures Conversion Guide

OVEN TEMPERATURES

70°C	150°F
100°C	200°F
150°C	300°F
160°C	315°F
180°C	350°F
190°C	375°F
200°C	400°F
220°C	425°F
240°C	475°F

LENGTH MEASURES

2 mm	¹/₁₆ inch
3 mm	⅛ inch
5 mm	¼ inch
8 mm	⅜ inch
1 cm	½ inch
1.5 cm	⅝ inch
2 cm	¾ inch
2.5 cm	1 inch
5 cm	2 inch
7.5 cm	3 inch
10 cm	4 inch
15 cm	6 inch
20 cm	8 inch
23 cm	9 inch
25 cm	10 inch
30 cm	12 inch
50 cm	20 inch

LIQUID MEASURES

30 ml	1 fl oz	
60 ml	2 fl oz	¼ cup
80 ml	2 ½ fl oz	⅓ cup
100 ml	3 ½ fl oz	
125 ml	4 fl oz	½ cup
150 ml	5 fl oz	
160 ml	5 ¼ fl oz	
185 ml	6 fl oz	¾ cup
200 ml	7 fl oz	
250 ml	9 fl oz	1 cup
300 ml	10 ½ fl oz	
350 ml	12 fl oz	
375 ml	13 fl oz	1½ cups
500 ml	17 fl oz	2 cups
750 ml	26 fl oz	3 cups
1 litre	35 fl oz	4 cups

WEIGHT MEASURES

5 g	⅛ oz
10 g	¼ oz
15 g	½ oz
20 g	¾ oz
30 g	1 oz
60 g	2¼ oz
100 g	3½ oz
125 g	4½ oz
150 g	5½ oz
200 g	7 oz
250 g	9 oz
500 g	1 lb 2 oz
1 kg	2 lb 3 oz

All recipes in this book:

● Use level cup and spoon measures (see page 32 for more details on how to accurately measure dry ingredients)

● Use 20 ml (4 teaspoon) tablespoon measures. If you are using a 15 ml (3 teaspoon) tablespoon, add an extra teaspoon for each tablespoon specified.

● Use eggs with an average weight of 59–60 g.

● Include cooking times for both conventional and fan-forced ovens. Cooking times may vary slightly depending on your oven.

Measurement Abbreviation Guide

Quantities for ingredients, measurements and oven temperatures in recipes are often abbreviated, so here is a quick guide to what they stand for:

tsp = teaspoon	**lb** = pound	**cm** = centimetre	°**F** = degrees Fahrenheit
tbsp = tablespoon	**oz** = ounce	**mm** = millimetre	**sec** = second
g = gram	**ml** = millilitre	**in** = inch	**min** = minute
kg = kilogram	**L** = litre	°**C** = degrees Celsius (or centigrade)	**hr** = hour

Acknowledgements

This book is not only a reflection of my love of baking but also of the people around me – those who have inspired and shaped my passion and have taught me all that I am sharing in this book.

Thank you Paul, Brooke and Ben. You have always been my biggest fans and most valued taste-testers. Thank you for always keeping me grounded and forever providing me with an excuse to bake whenever I feel like it.

Thank you Mum and Dad (Jock and Jos Mitchell) for teaching me that you should do what you love, not what you (or others) think you should do – a lesson for all of us to live by. Thank you for your endless support and unwavering interest in everything I do – especially eating with enthusiasm those 'creations' I produced during my early baking days.

Thank you to the most brilliant and talented team at Murdoch Books, particularly my publisher, Diana Hill, for your calm and well-considered approach; my editorial manager, Virginia Birch, for always keeping me on track and making the whole editorial process seamless (for everyone around you at least!); and design manager, Madeleine Kane, for interpreting my vision for this book so accurately.

Thank you to my editor Lucy Tumanow-West, quite simply, you are the best! Thank you for being kind to my words, creating a painless editing process and making it look like I can spell!

Thank you to photographer Alan Benson (with your never-failing professionalism and puny humour), home economist Tina McLeish (with your incredible organisational ability and the warmth you bring to the kitchen) and food stylist Bhavani Konings (with your eye for all things beautiful while keeping it real) – you are the most awesome shoot team I could have asked for (and did!). Your creative collaboration and the visuals you produced are a true reflection of what this book is all about – real, but completely and irresistibly scrumptious.

Thank you to designer Alex Frampton for your creativity and attention to detail – you have managed to create a design that is not only approachable but also visually inspiring.

Thank you to nutritionist and good friend Chrissy Freer, for being part of this book, and adding important weight to my belief in home baking.

And finally, to all my readers, past, present and future. When you take my recipes into the kitchen, it's the ultimate compliment. Please continue to use them often and never regret a buttery smudge, a chocolatey mark or a dusting of flour on the pages – they are all signs that my words are being used and that you like having me in your kitchen!

Index

Published in 2016 by Murdoch Books, an imprint of Allen & Unwin

Murdoch Books Australia
83 Alexander Street
Crows Nest NSW 2065
Phone: +61 (0) 2 8425 0100
Fax: +61 (0) 2 9906 2218
murdochbooks.com.au
info@murdochbooks.com.au

Murdoch Books UK
Erico House, 6th Floor
93–99 Upper Richmond Road
Putney, London SW15 2TG
Phone: +44 (0) 20 8785 5995
murdochbooks.co.uk
info@murdochbooks.co.uk

For Corporate Orders & Custom Publishing contact Noel Hammond,
National Business Development Manager, Murdoch Books Australia

Publisher: Diana Hill
Editorial Manager: Virginia Birch
Design Manager: Madeleine Kane
Editor: Lucy Tumanow-West
Designer: Alex Frampton
Photographer: Alan Benson
Stylist: Bhavani Konings
Home Economist: Tina McLeish
Production Manager: Mary Bjelobrk/Alex Gonzalez

A cataloguing-in-publication entry is available from the catalogue of the National Library
of Australia at nla.gov.au.

ISBN 978 1 74336 571 7 Australia
ISBN 978 1 74336 572 4 UK

A catalogue record for this book is available from the British Library.

Colour reproduction by Splitting Image Colour Studio Pty Ltd, Clayton, Victoria

Printed by 1010 Printing International Limited, China

IMPORTANT: Those who might be at risk from the effects of salmonella poisoning (the elderly,
pregnant women, young children and those suffering from immune deficiency diseases) should
consult their doctor with any concerns about eating raw eggs.

OVEN GUIDE: You may find cooking times vary depending on the oven you are using.

MEASURES GUIDE: We have used 20 ml (4 teaspoon) tablespoon measures. If you are using a
15 ml (3 teaspoon) tablespoon add an extra teaspoon of the ingredient for each tablespoon specified.

The author and publishers would like to thank the following for providing props for the photoshoot:
Frockk, KitchenAid, MH Ceramics, Mud Australia, STONEetsy, Studio Enti and Wiltshire.